There is magic in the grand old tales that have survived through centuries of time. Even the names of the books have a ring that sets the blood pounding—THE VOLSUNGA SAGA, THE SHAH-NAMAH, THE MABINOGIAN.

From all over the world, from all periods of ancient time, the great myths and heroic tales thunder down through the ages. Each country, each region has its legends. Somewhere, sometime, somehow, some often unknown scribe has set the tales down in permanent form.

In this volume Lin Carter has gathered together samplings from this richest of all sources of adult fantasy and although their original names may sometimes be anonymous, there surely has never been such a pride of taletellers together at one time as we have in

DRAGONS, ELVES, AND HEROES

Other Lin Carter titles

**TOLKIEN: A LOOK BEHIND *THE LORD OF THE RINGS***

**THE YOUNG MAGICIANS** (Ed.)

*Also available from Ballantine Books.*

This is an original publication—not a reprint.

# Dragons, Elves, and Heroes

Edited,
with an Introduction
and Notes,
by
Lin Carter

BALLANTINE BOOKS • NEW YORK

Copyright © 1969 by Lin Carter.

*The Ogre* is from *The Medieval Myths*, copyright 1961 by Norma Lorre Goodrich, reprinted by arrangement with The New American Library; *Manawyddan Son of the Boundless* is from *The Book of Three Dragons* by Kenneth Morris, copyright 1930 by Longmans, Green and Company, reprinted by permission of David McKay Company, Inc., the present holders of the copyright; *Puck's Song* is from *Puck of Pook's Hill* by Rudyard Kipling, copyright 1905 and 1906 by Rudyard Kipling, published by Doubleday and Company, Inc.; *Wonderful Things Beyond Cathay* is from *The Marvellous Adventures of Sir John Maundevile, Kt.*, ed. by Arthur Layard and published by Archibald Constable and Co., Westminster, 1895; *The Lords of Faerie* is from Book II, Canto X of *The Faerie Queene* by Edmund Spenser, published by The Heritage Press, New York, 1953; *Barrow-Wight* is from *Grettir the Outlaw* by S. Baring-Gould, Scribner and Welford, New York, n.d.; *Tales of the Wisdom of the Ancients* is from *The Gesta Romanorum* (Tales LVII, CII, CIII, CLXII, and CLXXV), translated and edited by Charles Swan and Wynnard Hooper, published by Dover Publications, Inc., New York, 1959; *Rustum Against the City of Demons* is from the *Shah-Namah* of Firdausi, it was especially translated for appearance in this anthology and is copyright 1969 by Lin Carter; *The Princess of Babylon* is from *The Best Known Works of Voltaire*, published by Literary Classics, Inc., New York, n.d.

Cover Painting: Sheryl Slavitt.

First Printing: October, 1969

Printed in the United States of America

BALLANTINE BOOKS, INC.
101 Fifth Avenue, New York, New York 10003

DRAGONS, ELVES, AND HEROES
is dedicated to
the two writers of this century
who have worked in this ancient tradition
and who have exerted the most
powerful influence on living
fantasy:

LORD DUNSANY AND
J. R. R. TOLKIEN

# Contents

Introduction:
Over the Hills and Far Away by Lin Carter ..... 1

*The Ogre* ..... *Beowulf*
Norma Lorre Goodrich ..... 10

*The High History of the Sword Gram*
..... *The Volsunga Saga*
William Morris ..... 30

*Manawyddan Son of the Boundless* ..... *The Mabinogion*
Kenneth Morris ..... 54

*Puck's Song*
Rudyard Kipling ..... 64

*Barrow-Wight* ..... *The Grettir Saga*
S. Baring-Gould ..... 67

*Fingal at the Siege of Carric-Thura*
..... *The Poems of Ossian*
James Macpherson ..... 75

*The Sword of Avalon* ..... *Le Morte d'Arthur*
Sir Thomas Malory ..... 83

*Tom O'Bedlam's Song*
Anonymous ..... 98

*The Last Giant of the Elder Age* ..... *The Kiev Cycle*
Isabel Florence Hapgood ..... 102

*The Lost Words of Power* ..... *The Kalevala*
John Martin Crawford ..... 112

*Wonderful Things Beyond Cathay*  
                                   *Maundevile's Travels*  
  Arthur Layard                                       125

*Prospero Evokes the Air Spirits*  
  William Shakespeare                      135

*The Lords of Faerie*                 *The Faerie Queene*  
  Edmund Spenser                               138

*Tales of the Wisdom of the Ancients*  
                              *The Gesta Romanorum*  
  Charles Swan and Wynnard Hooper     144

*The Magical Palace of Darkness*   *Palmerin of England*  
  Francisco de Moraes                      160

*Rustum Against the City of Demons*  *The Shah-Namah*  
  Lin Carter                                        178

*Childe Roland to the Dark Tower Came*  
  Robert Browning                               197

*The Princess of Babylon*                  *The Romances*  
  Voltaire                                               203

*The Horns of Elfland*  
  Alfred Lord Tennyson                          275

# Introduction:

## Over the Hills And Far Away

MEN have always had a thirst for the Miraculous and an itch to find out what lies over the next horizon.

This simian trait called curiosity is one of our most precious possessions. It drove us to explore the most perilous and inaccessible portions of the globe, to peer through the microscope into the amazing world of the ultra-small and to dream of conquering the stars. It is what impelled us towards science, mathematics, philosophy, magic, religion, medicine and literature.

As a race, we have always been willing to listen to the man with a good story to tell—and the more dragons and wizards and enchanted princesses in the yarn, the better. And whenever man develops an itch, he also invents a class of men willing to scratch it for him, hence the tellers-of-tales.

We have always known the world was filled with marvellous things, and we have always been perfectly willing to believe in them. While it is regrettably true that the local countryside is noticeably barren of Basilisks, they are unquestionably as common as house-flies in Golden Ind and Far Cathay. After all, the occasional travellers who have come back from those glittering, splendid and far-off countries hardly talked of anything else. We have fondly preserved the memories of such men, for we are greatly in their debt: they helped to keep Wonder alive in all of us, and (as noted above), Wonder is a precious thing.

For example, we remember the Greek physician Ctesias—not because of his very excellent treatise on rivers, or his learned analysis of the Persian system of revenues —but for the happy fact that he was the first man to see the unicorn (or, at least, the first to *say* he had).

Yes, the world has always been filled with magic and mystery and monsters. The skulls of the giant one-eyed Cyclops were on display in the town-halls of Italy during the Middle Ages; the petrified bones of dragons were the proud possessions of the kings of Europe; and that sober old Roman, Pliny, recorded eye-witness descriptions of the dog-headed men who lived in the depths of Africa. Pliny was outdone in his marvel-mongering only by Herodotus, who came back from his trip to Egypt to tell us that the secret temple records kept by the Egyptian hierophants covered the past thirteen thousand, three hundred and forty years, and that every five centuries the gold and crimson Phoenix comes flying out of Arabia to build a nest of myrrh on the high altar of the Temple of the Sun, whereon he burns himself to ashes and arises, recharged and ready for another five hundred. He also tells how every spring a tremendous fleet of flying serpents come, winging from Arabia into Egypt where, near the city of Buto, a flock of ibises devour them in mid-air. He saw this himself: at least he saw the valley filled with their bones . . . and who is so crass as to impute the veracity of the Father of History?

Or, for that matter, of the Church? For the *Lives of the Saints* is packed with plenty of marvels. The Saints, we are told by the church historians, were great hands at dragon-fighting. St. Clement slew one at Metz. St. Saturnin killed another at Bernay. St. Armond fought one near Maestricht. And there was even a dragon-slayer among the Twelve Apostles, for St. Andrew had a battle with a member of the scaly, bat-winged brood.

Then, of course, there is always the famous St.

George. He made a full-time career out of it, and left cadavers of the poor brutes scattered all over the landscape from Mansfield, Germany, to Cappadocia, Persia and Beirut, not to mention Egypt. It was there (at Selena in Libya, to be precise) that he tackled a ferocious specimen in the act of devouring the Princess Sabia, daughter of King Ptolemy; luckily, St. George had his celebrated magic sword, Ascalon, with him at the time. Of course, his most famous match was the dragon of Dunsmore Heath, near Coventry, England. This is the battle Spenser describes in the first book of *The Faerie Queene*.

But most other Saints who dabbled at all in dragons, much preferred overwhelming them by sheer force of chastity or something, rather than the crude physical expedient of hacking them up with enchanted swords. When St. Romain was Bishop of Roven, he tamed one by simply tossing his episcopal stole around its neck. And when St. Martha was busily converting the pagans at Arles, a dragon came roaring up, interrupting the sermon. She knocked it silly with sheer overwhelming virginity, doused it from stem to stern with a couple of bucketsful of holy water, and led it around the streets using her garters for a leash. (A convincing demonstration of the power of faith, to say the least; I don't doubt that every pagan for miles around signed up on the spot.)

There is lots more of this sort of thing. Lack of space does not permit me to regale you with the various dragon-busting exploits of Sts. Margaret, Veneranda, Radegund, Bernard, Samson, Marcel or Germanus.

Dragons aside, the Saints of the Middle Ages quite frequently mingled with mythological creatures. Such as that great anchorite, the most famous of the Desert Fathers, St. Anthony himself, who had a very interesting conversation with a genuine Satyr. (We have the solemn word of St. Jerome on this.)

Then there was the celebrated goldsmith Benvenuto Cellini, who once saw a Salamandre (a fire-elemental; a kind of nature spirit). We know he did because he tells us so in his famous *Autobiography* (I, iv).

*

So much for the earlier writers, who wrote from a naïve and wide-eyed *Weltanschauung*. Other more sophisticated authors who dealt with fantasy generally did so from a didactic or satiric motive. They deliberately concocted non-existent realms and mythic beings to ram home a sober moral: making the bitter pill palatable, so to speak, by giving it a sugary coating of romantic fiction. As did Dean Swift with his accounts of Liliput, Brobdingnag, and the Flying Island of Laputa.

Or they liked to deflate the local politicians through a sort of verbal caricature, but to avoid the contemporary version of a libel suit (i.e., the old cup of hemlock) they would shift the scene to Cockaigne or Never-Never-Land. As did Aristophanes with his invented Nephelococcygia ("Cloud-Cuckoo-Land"), which is really just 4th Century B.C. Athens in feathers. Such writers were gambling on the fact that the local yokels always had an appetite for the fantastical, and were willing to swallow a little social criticism to get it.

But whatever the purpose for which it was written, this sort of thing can be marvellous fun. The untrammelled imagination can paint a far more lovely and interesting landscape than the one you can find in Central Park after an hour on the subway. The history of Oz is very much more interesting to me than that of Uruguay. In fact, to be honest, I can hardly imagine the person who would prefer reading about Uruguay: doubtless there are many such, but if so, I feel sorry for them. They don't know what they're missing.

Sad to say, a surprisingly large number of otherwise sound and good people find fantasy difficult and distasteful to read. I frequently encounter them, although I do not seek them out. When I happen to confess, for example, that I would rather hear how the hero Astolpho flew to the moon astride the Winged Horse of the Pyre-

INTRODUCTION 5

nees to bring back the lost wits of his knightly comrade Roland (in *Orlando Furioso*) than read any number of cowboy stories, no matter how "realistic" they may be and true to history, such persons react either with scorn, derision or utter bafflement. And should I chance to admit it that Blunderbore (in *Jack the Giant-Killer*) interests me more than Benito Mussolini, or that there is, for me, more of the genuine essence of poetry in the single line, "East o' the Sun and West o' the Moon" than in any ten pages of T. S. Eliot, they usually leave the room in a hurry.

The standard reaction of such people, people who genuinely do not understand why you and I enjoy reading fantasy, or even exactly how our enjoyment in our favorite reading matter differs from theirs, is one of bafflement. Winged horses do not exist, never have existed. Giants are a biological impossibility, at least giants as big as Blunderbore. And "East o' the Sun and West o' the Moon" is a fairy-tale, and, being such, is fit reading only for children.

There is just no arguing with such people. They are perfectly serious and sincere. They simply do not understand that, to you and I, it does not at all matter if there are no real giants. It is the *idea* of giants we are after: the essence of the thing—the very *giantness* of them. The shuddersome awe we lesser beings feel before the vision of such ponderous, dull-eyed, slow, immeasurably huge creatures. Like walking hills brought to terrible and thrilling life: bristling with shaggy, matted beards and manes, shaking the earth with every shuffling step. In vain the anti-fantasts push before us pictures of brontosauri as reconstructed by paleontologists. But that's not what we want. As C. S. Lewis puts it in his excellent essay "On Stories": "Nature has that in her which compels us to invent giants: and only giants will do."

And it is the same with winged horses. A bird can be beautiful and graceful in flight; a horse can be noble and majestic: but Pegasus is more to us than just a white horse with wings stuck onto its sides somehow. It is a symbol, a hieroglyph, which stands for the awe and wonder and heart-rending ecstasy and wild, romantic freedom *of the very concept of flight itself.* But we can no more explain to the fantasy-haters why our hearts lift at the thought of Pegasus than we can explain to a deaf person what Beethoven's Ninth means to us.

And there is something terribly wrong with the whole idea that fairy-tales are for children only. It simply is not true, in point of historical fact. Fairy-tales—*real* fairy-tales, as differentiated from *Märchen* and folk-tales—were originally written for the pleasure of adults alone. The fairy-tale was a literary fad at the French Court during the early 17th Century. Under the Bourbons, polished and witty *contes des fées* flourished, and writers of charm and elegance like Charles Perrault and Madame d'Aulnoy brought the art-form to its height. They were writing for a sophisticated audience of languid aristocrats: certainly *not* for the kiddies.*

Professor Tolkien deals with this in his great essay "On Fairy-Stories." He points out that when adults outgrew or got tired of the fad, they relegated these tales to the nursery, much as they did with the furniture they grew weary of seeing around. Of course, it is perfectly true that children enjoy reading fairy-tales (or some children, at any rate), but this does not mean the art-form was invented for their pleasure, any more than it means that other "children's favorites" like *Gulliver* or *The Arabian Nights* were written for children. It is true that bowdlerized and brutally edited *versions* of these two books are printed for the juvenile market, but take a look at the original texts sometime. *Gulliver* is a savage and merciless satire on man's own inhumanity, and strong stuff for youthful stomachs (such as the scene in which Gulliver extinguishes the fire in the city of the Lilliputians by urinating upon it, which of course is omitted from the children's editions, as is the scene in

---

* Perrault wrote *La Belle au Bois Dormant* ("the Sleeping Beauty of the Wood"), as well as *Cinderella, Bluebeard* and *Puss-in-Boots.* He was a poet and architect in the reign of the Sun King, Louis XIV. The Comtesse d'Aulnoy wrote *The White Cat* and *The Blue Beard,* and my personal favorite, *The Yellow Dwarf.* They were exact contemporaries.

giant-land where Gulliver is crawling about on the monstrous breasts of his Brobdingnagian nurse). And, as for *The Arabian Nights*—more properly, *Alf Laylah wa Laylah*, The Thousand Nights and One Night—it was composed very much as were the French fairy-tales, for the amusement of a jaded and decadent Court, although an Islamic one and not French. In the original, the tales are deliciously erotic and bawdy.

*

In this book I have collected the finest examples of the heroic fantasy laid against imaginary lands I have been able to find among these ancient writers. This book, then, forms a perfect counterpart to its companion volume, *The Young Magicians*, which consists entirely of tales drawn from recent or modern writers. The dividing line is the *floruit* of William Morris. Morris (1834–96) was the first modern writer of any importance to devote himself to tales of war, quest and adventure laid in purely imaginary worlds where magic works. I make Morris' life the point of division between the ancient fantasy writers and the modern, not necessarily through any sense of balance, but because he founded the tradition of the imaginary-world heroic fantasy which was followed after him by such writers as Lord Dunsany, E. R. Eddison, James Branch Cabell, Clark Ashton Smith, Robert E. Howard, C. S. Lewis and J. R. R. Tolkien (among others)—most of whom are represented in the companion volume to this anthology. Morris' first real venture into these fictional half-worlds was a novel called *The Wood Beyond the World* which he published on the 11th of May, 1895.

I call this the first important imaginary-world fantasy, and the direct literary progenitor of the tradition which includes *The Worm Ouroboros* and *The Silver Stallion* and *The Lord of the Rings* and the Narnia books and all the other things on our bookshelves we love best. You can quibble about the primacy of Morris if you feel so inclined: you could make a case for George Macdonald's

*Lilith* or Beckford's *Vathek* or even *Amadis of Gaul*, the great 13th Century Portuguese prose romance—all of which came earlier than Morris. But this is splitting hairs: there were white-boy-raised-in-the-jungle yarns before *Tarzan of the Apes*, and historical romances before Sir Walter Scott, and Fausts before *Faust*. Literary history is a knotty tangle: we usually simplify the question by assuming that the writer who made the biggest impact with a new idea—the man who started the trend —was the milestone, even if he borrowed the idea from somebody earlier.

The selections herein are drawn from among an enormous number of sources. Those of you who may have seen my recent book, *Tolkien: A Look Behind "The Lord of the Rings"*—and who remember my very detailed exposition of the evolution of the major themes and plot-elements that make up the so-called "Tolkienian" school of fantasy (in chapters 10 through 13 of that book) may expect this anthology to be filled with selections from the major sources Tolkien used. Such, however, is most definitely *not* the case.

I did not assemble this collection to prove my theory of the evolutionary history of the imaginary-world fantasy. My only criterion for each of the selections included here was—is it a really good fantasy story? Is it exciting, imaginative, colorful, thrilling?

I have drawn from epic and saga, from Sir John de Mandeville and *The Mabinogion*, from the mythological and heroic fantasy literature of Persia, Finland, Wales, the Teutonic or Anglo-Saxon peoples, from Malory and the English ballad. My only interest was in finding the very best stories I could possibly locate. I looked at nine different versions of the Russian heroic mythos of Ilya of Murom before picking the precise tale I wanted, in just the right redaction, and in the most savory and rich translation. For the scene I wanted to use from *Beowulf*, I passed over a dozen more famous and "approved" translations, to pick one by a scholar you have probably never even heard of (Norma Lorre Goodrich)—I wanted it because it had the tension, the heightened intensity and richness of color the others lacked. For my selection from the history of Zal and Rustum in the Persian national epic, *The Shah Namah*, I inspected a half-dozen translations made over a full century: dissatisfied with them all, I made my own version.

So, for those of you who have a thirst for marvels and an itch to see what lies "over the hills and far away," here is a bookful of some of the most spectacular, magical, haunting, exciting, evocative and entertaining fantasy ever written.

I wish you a happy voyage.

> LIN CARTER
> Editorial Consultant:
> The Ballantine Adult Fantasy Series

*Hollis, Long Island, New York*

# The Ogre

## *from* Beowulf

## *Norma Lorre Goodrich*

OUT OF THE DARKNESS of the prehistory of our race, a superb and splendid hero emerged to do battle with the monstrous forces of evil.

His magnificent deeds were set down by a poet of great genius, in an epic so marvellous and so beautiful that to this day students master a dead language so that they may taste the pleasures of reading it in the tongue in which it was written.

This mighty poem stands at the very beginning of English literature, as if setting an example of glorious storytelling which all those to come after must strive to equal.

But, not only was this masterpiece lost and forgotten for nearly a thousand years—thus exerting no influence at all on the first great writers of our literature—but it also came within a hair's breadth of being destroyed before it had even been discovered.

*Beowulf* was written shortly before the year 750 A.D., and most likely in Northumbria. It is the greatest literary masterwork of the Anglo-Saxon peoples. At least, it is the first great poem of that literature which is known—the earliest work of that people's genius which still survives.

Only one manuscript of *Beowulf* exists. Sir Robert Cotton discovered it back in the 17th century, among a collection of nine other ancient parchments, a collection known to scholars as the Codex Vitellius. All other copies are presumed to have been destroyed in ancient times, when the monasteries were ravished and burned in the waves of warfare and invasion which swept the land of our forefathers in the Dark Ages. It is frightening to think how easily this last, lone manuscript of *Beowulf* might also have met destruction at the hands of ignorant savages who knew no better than to despise art and learning. One wonders what other works of genius were produced by the Anglo-Saxons . . . works which, sadly, were not so lucky as *Beowulf*. But this we shall probably never know.

A thousand years after it was written, and having already survived the invasion of England and the rape of the monastic libraries, the last precious manuscript of *Beowulf* barely was rescued from a second brush with the flames. For it was by then among the other rare documents Sir Robert Cotton had collected and carefully preserved; but when Sir Robert died, his collection was sold in the year 1700 and was borne off to a new home in Ashburnham House, a name curiously apt, for the house caught fire in 1731 and the *Beowulf* manuscript was slightly damaged in the flames, although rescued from destruction before it was anything more than merely singed. In 1753 the priceless Anglo-Saxon manuscript was housed in the British Museum, where, let us hope, it is at last safe.

There are many different translations of *Beowulf*, and some of them are, in their own right, brilliant works of art—such as those of Francis B. Gummere, Charles W. Kennedy, Edwin Morgan and William Ellery Leonard. I have, however, passed over these famous translations in favor of a more recent, if less well-known, version—that of Norma Lorre Goodrich.

Miss Goodrich made this version for her book *The Medieval Myths* in 1961. I have chosen her translation over all the rest, because, despite certain infelicities of phrasing and word-choice, the Goodrich version tells the *story* of the poem with a vigor and pace and color and excitement that I have not seen equalled elsewhere. It was Professor Tolkien who was responsible for turning the tide of *Beowulf* studies from the sterile byways of scholarly research to a fresh new consideration of the poem as a thrilling and exciting story and as a work of poetry. He affected this scholarly revolution with a paper called *"Beowulf: The Monsters and the Critics,"* first read in 1936. The influence of his thought can, I think, be clearly seen in the following English version which concentrates on the excitement and the heroic impetus of what is, after all, one of the world's most splendid stories.

One final note. The *Beowulf* epic breaks apart in two halves quite neatly. The first half, that of the battle against the ogre Grendel and his fearsome dam, shows Beowulf in the full lusty vigor of his youth, and forms a complete episode. The second half of the poem, the struggle against the fire-breathing dragon, shows him in old age. Since I have included elsewhere in this anthology the story of Sigurd the Dragon-Slayer from the famous William Morris translation of *The Volsunga Saga,* and since one dragon-fight reads very much like another, I have settled on the first part of *Beowulf,* and I give you here the ancient tale of Beowulf and the Ogre . . .

---

I SHALL unlock my hoard of words at your will. I shall unfold before you, O King, the story of my wanderings, for truly I have roamed long years over this wonderful world."

The fire burned brightly in the castle hearth. On his high seat the king of Anglia, well wrapped in furs, lounged carelessly while his earls took places below him preparing to hear a renowned bard who was raising his harp and clearing his throat. Gusts of wind blew fragrant smoke out the open doors or curled it about the heavy oak rafters. The night had fallen early, but the hall door stood wide open at either end of the rectangular room . . . No enemies would enter, for the land was at peace. The Angles had long before stopped their restless wanderings over the North Sea. They had cut Northumbria into marches, and the marches into shires. The once fierce Vikings had long since become peaceful farmers; their leaders were called earls. Over them all ruled a fair king, noteworthy because he upheld the freedom of his people, earls and carls alike.

These Angles, lovers of poetry, had ages before skimmed over the North Sea, westward from Sweden and Denmark, until they founded their new kingdoms in Britain: Mercia, Northumberland, and East Anglia. In the south of their new homeland their brothers, the Saxon kings, ruled Sussex, Wessex, and Essex. The Roman legions, who for four hundred years had kept order in Britain, were only a distant memory. Their missionaries had returned, however, to convince these settlers from over the seas to put away their worship of their pagan gods—Freya, Woden, Thor, Eostre, and the awesome Wyrd, goddess of death.

"O King," sang the bard, "I have tramped the whole world over in the course of a lifetime. Every mighty king have I seen with my own these eyes. Every land have I understood, each with its own customs and habits, each with its own law. One truth have I learned above all others! A king who seeks to rule his people and his lands without warfare must take this as his plan: he must work first and foremost for his people's good!

"Therefore since the world began, this wandering star upon whose breast we live, one king has shone more brightly than all others. He was Alexander of Macedon.

"In the far-flung realms of Rome have I wandered, as a guest made welcome for his songs. In imperial Rome have I seen great Caesar ruling in all pomp and majesty. Through the lands of Greece have I also roamed, and farther eastward even than that. I have seen the splendor of Persian kings. I have glimpsed the sands of Africa and watched the foreign folk who dwell in Egypt's land. I have looked eagerly upon the wealthy men of the East and gaped at their trading vessels proudly riding the waves of Italy's harbors. Men have I seen who dwell by the Ganges' waters, whose flood waves ride down into an unknown sea near Eostre's far home. Lombardy have I seen also, and Franconia.

"In the halls of great kings the mead has always flowed freely; there gold armlets were the reward of my songs . . . I have sung before the chiefs of the Angles here in Britain, and before the Jutes on the Island of Wight, and in the cold lands of the northernmost Picts and Scots. I have sung before the Saxons and the Swedes and the Danes, and wayworn fared to where the Elbe River joins our northern sea. I have willingly sought the hordes of fierce Huns over whom Attila holds sway, and stopped on my way home at the mead halls of the Franks across the sea. Pirates of the northern coasts have I recalled in my songs, and fought my way into the eastern land of the Finns. Six hundred shillings of pure gold has been my fee, and acres of land as a gift from the Queen of Mercia. Born was I in the Anglian land of Britain, and there shall I die, a faithful son of song.

"One truth would I set high above all others," repeated the gleeman. "Only the king who loves his people is beloved in turn of them. That king alone shall never be forgotten. Bards even now unborn shall sing of his feats, his strength, his faithfulness, and his openhandedness. Let the bards be ever entrusted to write the songs of a hero, and his people will have them to sing always."

The last sound of the harp drifted across the hall. Slowly the king roused himself. Pulling one of the massive gold armlets from his own arm, he sent it to the bard. The world was, indeed, very wide; and he for one had too much to do at home in Anglia ever to fare so far. What was the life of a man? What, indeed, was the life of a king unless he worked hard for his people who had raised him to the throne? What more than the flight of a gull through the mead hall, a sudden bright sweep of white wings against the smoke-blackened rafters? Only the unselfish, only the great in heart were worthy of being sung by the bards.

"Sing us a song of the Angles," ordered the king. "Tell

us again our own story that we may steep ourselves in kingship. Sing of *The Hero*."

Like a distant foreword to the swelling song the heavy rumble of the waves, driven by the evening tide, moaned and tore at the strand. They were the same waters that washed the headlands of Denmark, the olden home of the Angles . . . The great hall was still. The song they would hear was such an old one, sung down the ages, recalling a time so long ago that only the great in heart had been remembered from it . . . Gently the gleeman stroked his harp, in long lonesome chords like the mournful sound of a wild wind shrieking through darkness. Shivers pierced the bones of the listeners as the old, homely words rang again in their ears:

*

Sing of the Danes in the days gone by, deeds of our kings who were scatheless in war! Tell about Scyld, the son of Scef, how he stole the mead from the foemen's halls, how he ripped their thrones from under their feet, how he drove his prow through the ways of the whale, how he gulped down tribute from all of the tribes that clung to their cliffs by the chilly sea.

Shout about Scyld with his strength and his might, building wide mead halls ribbed with gold. That was an earl—that Scyld, son of Scef! Ah, what a king we had! In the distant days of the Danes!

The great king called Scyld ruled for many years over the seafaring peoples of the north, and God gave him a fair, strong son to rule after him. According to the old king's will, his body was borne down the sea cliffs and placed on the earlmen's ship. Bronze shields bright with gold flashed along her gunwales, and from her masthead flew the shining flag of Scyld. The dead king, dressed in full mail and wearing his gem-studded crown, was laid on the open deck. On his chest lay heaped the wealth he had gathered during his long rule over the sea realms. Battle-axes and swords lay flashing in the winter sunlight about his body. Sadly the earls pushed the shining ship away from the jetty and watched the first deep swells of the sea catch her and sweep her along over the deep. To this day no man can say what became of King Scyld or his seaworthy ship! The waves hold him in trust —the wild, western sea.

The Scylding kings, descended from Scyld, reigned in Denmark for countless ages until the people became a whole, one in heart and mind. Then ruled an unselfish king named Hrothgar, who dreamed of a deed that would awe the bards so deeply that his name would be recalled among the Vikings forever more. Hrothgar unfolded his plan. He would have built in Denmark a great hall, so lofty, so heavy with gold, so braced with iron bands, that its like the northern folks had never thought to witness! There on a lofty seat Hrothgar would sit in state, night after night, giving rings to his earls, granting wealth to young and old alike, sharing even before his death all the gold of Denmark.

In this way and to this end was built Heorot Hall, the house of the deer, a wonder so famous that gleemen from all over the sea-swept lands came to gasp at its rows of stag's antlers, its bronze-bound doors, its lofty ceiling, and the lavishness of King Hrothgar. There every evening sat the Danish earl with his Queen Wealhtheow beside him, the handsome two, givers of gifts. From the lands around earls came to swear fealty to Hrothgar.

Night after night, however, the fiends of evil, those who live in the underworld, writhed and curled with hatred as the sweet sound of the harp rose from the hearthside. Jealous and full of anger, they leered as the soft song of the scop praised the All-Powerful. He who had fashioned the earth, with its level fields and shimmering pools, with its girdle of sparkling green sea. He it was who had thrust the sun and moon up into the blue skies where they could stand as torches, as beacons for all homecomers over the seas. He it was who had bespangled the earth with russet leaves and reeds, and who had breathed the breath of life into beings.

Hrothgar and his eldermen lived happily in Heorot

Hall until the day that Grendel, a living fiend out of hell, a Satan who ruled over the swamps and marshes, came stalking toward them. Grendel and his folk had been banished to the fens eras before because of their slaying of Cain. To Grendel's accursed folk belonged the ghouls, the dragons, the lemurs, the elves, and all evil curs. The giants also had been outlawed along with Satan because they had fought against God. Therefore God was giving them a fitting reward through everlasting ages.

So in the dark night, gliding among the shadows, Grendel crept stealthily toward Heorot. Drooling with spit, stinking and hairy, he leaped the outside walls, and stopped to listen . . . No one had heard him. Only the leaves rustled overhead . . . Then with a bloodcurdling scream he rushed headlong into the hall where the Danish warriors were sleeping. Careless and carefree they slumbered on the benches, heedless of woe, until Grendel's scream tore them from their sleep. Before they could think, he had crashed through their midst, his claws sunk deep in two warriors. Hurriedly he snatched up others, one or two at a time, until he had slaughtered thirty of Hrothgar's doughtiest earls. After the whole company had awakened, he lurched from the hall and took flight, leaving the partially eaten bodies strewn and mangled, among the rushes of the floor.

The deaths were not discovered until dawn. King Hrothgar was appalled. He gathered at once that his strength or that of his earls together could do nothing against the evildoer. The struggle was too uneven. Within a few days Grendel crept back, and again the king awoke to find his fair hall in a shambles, the boards all overturned, and his warriors, torn by the monster's claws, spread about the floor.

Whoever had escaped the ogre's greediness fled for his life across the land of Denmark. In time the great hall was empty. No suppers were held. No scops or gleemen came to Heorot any more. Nor was there any more giving of rings. For twelve long hears Grendel haunted the realm of Hrothgar.

No treaty, no peace, no ransom, no fee—nothing

could allay the wrath of Grendel against the kingdom of Denmark! Night after night the accursed Shadow of Death crept through the woods, prowled about chieftain's dwellings, snatched his prey at random without thought for rank, youth, or years. Stealthily he lay in wait, caught men in his traps, and flung them headlong into an endless darkness.

Men looked for him, straining their eyes fearfully to peer through the rolling fogs of the moors, dreaded the thump of his heavy paw on their shoulders as they hauled in their nets. They scanned the beaches for him at twilight. They saw him behind every bush and stone of the path, or stood stock-still listening for the crunch of his bare pads on the pebbles. So many bloody deaths! So many screeching loved ones! How could a man know where the fiend would turn up next? What does a man know anyway of the fiends that crawl through the black night?

In the dark of evening, Grendel lumbered into the empty hall, hunting for food. One thing alone he could not touch—the throne of Denmark! Only that had God forbidden him to soil.

There was wretchedness in the land, sorrow, wretchedness, and cold fear! Hrothgar and his few trusty earls held meetings and tried to find an answer. They prayed to their idols. They cooked up new magic broths. They called upon their pagan gods to thwart all dragons, all fiends, all evil, all nightmares . . . In their hearts they thought only of hell, not knowing, not having yet heard of the Lord God . . . Cursed is he who slips from the true path and hands his soul back to the hell-fires! Blessed is he who on the day of his death finds peace in the breast of his Maker!

Hrothgar lived on, his days flowing from a cup of sorrow, powerless in the grip of the ogre, beaten and heartsick.

Those were black days shadowed by the awesome blackness of night . . .

*

Meanwhile in the land of the Geats across the sea the bitter news had come. The sorrows of Denmark reached in time the ears of the Geats. King Hygelac heard it and mourned! His earls heard it and shuddered!

Beowulf heard the news.

Of the race of men he was the strongest. Boldest among the bold was this vassal of Hygelac! Greatest in heart among all great hearts was this chief of the Geats, this Beowulf!

"Come! Let us haul down the ship!" cried Beowulf. "Over the path of the sea bird, through the wake of the swan, let us fly to Denmark," he said. "The king of the Danes needs men!"

At first the wise eldermen nearest King Hygelac's throne worried and fretted, for the sea was wide, and Beowulf dear to them all. Finally they yielded, however, and helped him choose fifteen strong warriors. Then they studied their hidden lore and found that their gods were willing. One of their number was called who knew the paths of the sea and who spoke to Beowulf of the tides and the landmarks. He warned him of black rocks and swirling shoals.

Under the sea-girt cliffs the shining ship was readied, laden with coats of mail, swords, and gleaming war harness. Bidding farewell to their king, the sturdy warriors embarked. Last of them all strode their mighty leader, his feet strong and steady on the bobbing craft. Turning their backs on Sweden, the fearless warriors cast off and leaned to the oars.

Like a bird, like a swallow, like a slender gull the glistening ship sped forward. She cut a path through the clear, green sea, her prow wreathed in bubbles and foam. The winds caught her like a bird and blew her swiftly southward. Across unknown waters the light floater lunged and ploughed into the swells. The salt spray blew strong on the warriors' foreheads.

By the first hour of the second day the dark fjords of Denmark rose on the skyline, reaching up toward the clouds from their tide-beaten sands. Sounding cautiously and tacking, the pilot brought the swift craft unharmed to the shore. The sea lanes had been followed aright. The coast had been won.

From his lighthouse on the cliff, the coast guard of Hrothgar saw the Geats disembarking. Spurring his horse, he galloped down the shore and bespoke them.

"Who are you, warriors in war dress who clamber from your seagoing ship? I am an earl of Hrothgar, king of the Danes. Never have shield-bearers so grim of face ever landed before on our shores! Do you at least know the password?"

Then as he spoke, the Danish earl suddenly saw the leader, Beowulf. In fright and amazement he stepped backward. His hand shook on his horse's reins. "Never in my life," stammered the Dane, "have I seen a man like this one! Who in the world is this warrior?" he asked, still staring at Beowulf. "Surely this is a hero, one we must know for his deeds of strength. Please, may I know your kindred and the aim of your trip to this coast."

Beowulf unlocked his word hoard. "We come, indeed, from across the sea. We are folk and vassals of Hygelac, king of the Geats. Perhaps you have heard of my father. His name was Ecgtheow." The Dane gasped. His guess had been right. This was, in truth, a hero and the son of a hero.

"My warriors and I have come to your lands as friends," Beowulf went on. "Have no fear of us! We have heard of some fiend of darkness who is foully mistreating your king. Perhaps we can help him."

"Then hasten back to your ships," bade the coast guard. "Dress yourselves in your coats of mail. Grasp your shields and your axes. Hurry! I will lead you to Heorot Hall. Take no thought for your ship. I shall see that she is well guarded and circled about with hawsers. Her mighty heart shall find rest in our waters."

Setting their boar helmets well over their ears, the fierce warriors from Geatland strode up the sea cliffs after their leader. Shortly the lofty gables and gleaming roof of Heorot Hall came into sight. They stopped and wondered at its cunning workmanship, for truly there was not a building like it in all the world. The coast guard left them. Still gazing up at the high turrets, the warriors drew near the hall over a street of stones. Their swords clanged against mail. On an outer gate to the castle they rested their shields and then climbed the stairs to the door.

They were met by the herald Wulfgar. He curtly craved to know their names, and their will in striding so roughly over the roadway. In one glance he noted their arms and their bearing.

"We are vassals of King Hygelac," answered Beowulf. "We will speak of our errand to your king, that most worthy of men."

Leaving them standing at the door, Wulfgar stepped into the hall and drew near his king. This herald was himself an earl from the highborn kindred of Wendel. He knew how to speak to a king, how to stand behind his chief's shoulder.

"We have here, newly sprung from the sea, a band of Geatish warriors. Their leader is a man named Beowulf. They beg leave to tell you their errand, O King. Do not forbid them entry. They have the mien of earls, and their chieftain is a mighty warrior. Greet them as earls, O Hrothgar!"

King Hrothgar answered his herald at once. "Surely, I know this leader, or knew him when he was a child. He is the son of Ecgtheow. Hrethel the Geat gave that leader his only daughter in wedlock. This is their child Beowulf! Now, indeed, has he come over the sea to me in my sorrow. I heard that this youngster has the strength of thirty men in his handgrip! Call for gifts to be brought at once! Round up our warriors! All you can hail are to come here at once! Go quickly first to the door and make them welcome."

Wulfgar escorted Beowulf and his men into the hall, allowing them to keep on their coats of mail and their helmets, only begging them to leave their swords, axes, and javelins outside the building. With fitting words he led Beowulf to a dais.

In this way Beowulf and King Hrothgar faced each other, each one from his dais on the opposite side of the hall. The younger man spoke first. "Hail to thee, Hrothgar, king of the Danes. You know my kindred, my name, and my rank. In my youth, it is true, I have done some deeds that have been held worthy of my father. We of the Geats have sorrowed to learn how you are beset in Denmark by a bloody fiend named Grendel. My own king and earl has sent us to offer whatever strength we have against fiends. My own kinfolk have watched me, drenched to the skin with foul-smelling blood, struggle to the death with a lemur. I am the one who crushed the wicked Elves. Swimming far under the waves I have oftentimes wrestled with the whales of the deep. In war I overcame the Westerners, who were riding ahead of their own downfall anyway! I crushed those bold warriors out of their lives!

"Today I am ready for Grendel. Grant me this trial, O King! You see that I have come from far over the sea to try it. I would do battle with your Grendel! I would seize your monster barehanded. Without sword or shield I would grapple this fiend as a token of my fealty to King Hygelac. Here in your hall shall sleep whichever one of us our Lord may will. If this beast of yours worsts me, then only send to my uncle and king the gems that are set on my shield. It is the work of Weland the smith; it is thus a priceless heirloom that should be shipped home to my kinfolk."

"This I thought was your errand, dear Beowulf," answered King Hrothgar. "This I thought was the aim of your wandering over the deep. I knew your father back in the days when I was a young man, newly throned. Now I am old and heartsick. My head bows. My eyes weep with shame to have to acknowledge my weakness. My throne, as you see, is almost a barren spot. My lands are becoming a wilderness. What has Grendel wrought in this kingdom! Often at night, swollen with beer, have my warriors sworn to topple this fiend. Then when the bleak, white light of dawn has crept over the misty fields, we have strode through this very hall strewn with their bloodstained bodies!

"Let me speak no more of my woes, great hero. Take

your seat at my board, and let me drink to your health. Eat and be merry, my friend, who have sailed over deep water so boldly to save us all."

Straightforth a bench was drawn out from the wall and a meal set before the warriors from Geatland. Highborn vassals waited on them at the board, poured the sparkling mead into their cups from carved beakers with scrollwork handles. As they ate and drank, Hrothgar's gleemen sang them songs of the bygone works of the Danes.

Then one of Hrothgar's earls, a warrior named Unferth, who sat legs-sprawled at his king's feet, began to bait the guests. He was a spiteful man who could not stand hearing about the wonderful trip over the sea from Sweden. He could not let anyone best him in warwork!

"Say! Are you that Beowulf who swam a race with Breca when both of you, swollen with pride, wanted to fathom the depths of the fjords and risk your lives in deep water? Why, there isn't any man, friend or foe, who wouldn't blame such a shameful feat! Under the wintry waves you swam for a week, sliding the slopes of the sea, learning its hidden kingdoms while the waters boiled and hissed in the storm above you? Breca beat you, though. He was stronger by far than you, Beowulf! So the morning tide swept him to his home shore, where he lived to carve out a realm all by himself. He was a good man, that Breca! He kept his word at least.

"What, you Beowulf," Unferth continued. "I look for a far worse fate for you if you think you dare spend a night in this hall with Grendel!"

"Now listen, friend Unferth," snapped Beowulf. "I have kept still while you, drunk as an earl, have poured forth your flood of words about Breca. Now I'll tell you the truth. So hearken! I happen to have more strength in the sea, more breath for the dive, than any other man.

"If you truly care to hear that tale, I'll be glad to tell you myself how it was. I speak the truth. When Breca and I were boys, in the first hot glow of our manhood, we swore an oath that we would pit our strength against the sea. And so we did. We bore our naked swords in our hands, thinking to use them against whales as we struggled up through the tideraces of the coves. In deep water Breca could neither outswim me nor lose me among the peaks of the swells. Nor did I try to outstrip him. Thus we were together for five days and nights upon the sea until a huge flood swept us asunder. That happened during the height of a storm, through a night so black we couldn't see where we were heading. A wind so fierce, as wild a battle, shrieked down; from the north. It drove tons of gray water into the fjords. The waves were unleashed.

"Then all the daring of the big fishes was awakened. The winds had stirred up their cold blood. Well, against such foes my hand-knotted mail stood me in good stead. My gold-heavy harness buffered my chest, just as in battle. A thousand-hued beast pulled and dragged at my limbs, striving to suck me down to the depths with him. He held me close in a death grip. However, I was happy enough to stab him in the belly with the point of my blade. I gave him the taste of death with this hand of mine that you see.

"Those aren't the only foemen, Unferth, who have threatened me with their snarls. I have known for some years how to wield a weapon. No loathsome fishes, not even all of them together, have yet been able to drag me down against my will.

"Well, dawn broke. The eastern light flooded the sea, and I finally caught glimpses of land. I finally saw bleak crags and the headlands buffeted by the gale. There in shallow beach water rolled my foes of the night, put to sleep as it were, by my sword. True it is, indeed, that they ceased henceforth to prey upon war ships on the shores of my native land.

"Wyrd often saves the earl who is not yet marked for death—when he still helps himself in the fighting. I also had the good luck to kill nine sea prowlers, or nicors. Under heaven I have never heard tell of a mighty battle so hardly waged. Have you, Unferth? . . . Still I kept up my even stroke. The waves bore me ashore amidst the

## THE OGRE

jagged crags of Finland. It was there on a sandy strip that I waded ashore.

"Neither Breca," said Beowulf, "nor any one of you in the flashing of swords has ever done deeds of worth so dearly won. I do not boast before you—even though I know that you, Unferth, have murdered your own brethren. You shall be doomed for it too, to hell, in spite of your cleverness. Let me tell you one more thing. Grendel would never have dared such outrage here in this hall if your might in war were as great as you say it is! Grendel found out long ago that he had nothing to dread here. So has he lusted after this hall, and wanted to suck your blood. He knows he can kill more of the Spear-Danes! He knows he can tumble you all down to death!

"But I, a Geat, have brought a gift for your Grendel. Without his foreknowledge I have here to give him three things: a fighting heart, my dauntless will, and my great strength. After this night whoever may wish to sing in your mead hall may do so. After tomorrow's sun rises in the east upon the sons of men, each one of you may enter this house in freedom. I, Beowulf, swear it."

King Hrothgar heard Beowulf and believed him. He, the aged, baldheaded king of the Danes, felt a hush steal into his heart. So among his heroes there were songs of happiness, and jokes, and toasts drunk to the Geats.

Then through the great hall Queen Wealhtheow walked. She, from whose garments gold dropped, greeted the men in the hall. First she bore a cup of mead to her beloved husband, the king. She begged him to take it from her own hand, and to drink. Hrothgar thanked her and took the goblet. Then the queen passed from earl to earl, young and old alike, bearing to each one a golden gift. She was a queen and the daughter of a queen. Then the highborn lady held out her hand, heavy with rings, to Beowulf. Wise in her words, she thanked him first and then thanked God that her prayers had been answered. She said that she had faith in Beowulf, that she trusted his earlship, and that she was deeply beholden. The freeborn queen held out a cup to the hero.

Beowulf answered the queen, "I wished when I let float my sea-wood on the whale's way, when I set sail with my war-band, to answer with my life the challenge of Grendel. I shall live out my years, as befits an earl, or I shall end up my days right here in your lofty hall."

Queen Wealhtheow was gladdened by his words. Then she took a seat beside the king. After that there were boastings in Heorot! Then did the warriors brag before their stainless queen. Then were they light of heart! Their oaths grew bigger and bigger!

At last King Hrothgar arose. He knew what a fray was shaping up for the small hours of the night. He felt the cold of the evening shrinking his limbs. He felt in his bones that the fiend was even then prowling outside in the misty half-light, searching for men's blood. All the warriors stood as the king bade farewell to Beowulf.

"Never before in my years as a king have I given my realm to another, as I give it now to you, Beowulf, son of Ecgtheow. This night, stand in my stead. Uphold my name with all your might. I give you my hall, this proudest of buildings. Be wakeful, Beowulf, against our foe. He is coming tonight, I feel it . . . if you fulfill this deed, know that no wish of yours during all your lifetime shall go unfulfilled by me."

Then King Hrothgar left the hall with his earls. He wanted to go to bed with his queen.

*

Carls stood ready to take from Beowulf his coat of mail, his helmet, and his heavy sword. Then the Geat lay down on the pile of furs that had been set for him, laid his cheek against the bolster, and waited. His men also lay down to sleep, tired from their long sail and the frightening tales of the day and evening. They could not know whether they would ever see another sunrise, or if they would live through the night to follow the sea tracks home to Sweden. The night was cold and very still. The fire in the central hearth had burned low. Soon all but Beowulf slept . . .

Then through the black moors wreathed in fog, Grendel came creeping, God's ire upon him. Out of the swirling mists he stalked with outstretched claws, hunting toward the dimly lighted hall. To his wonderment the door was barred. Grendel had not foreseen that! With a snarl the fiend stepped backward, stiffening his muscles, and lunged for it. Iron bars sprung loose. Wood splintered. The door burst from its hinges.

Grendel was inside the great hall. All about him the Geatish warriors lay stretched out on their fur beds, sunk in sleep, heedless, unhearing. For a second Grendel stopped to scan them. Darts of red fire shot from his deep-set eyes. Rolling his huge head from side to side, Grendel glared about him. Then he laughed.

From his end of the hall Beowulf watched the ogre, weighed his endowment, and waited to see how Grendel would strike. Quick as a wink the fiend pulled at the warrior nearest him, cracked his bones with one twist, ripped at the body with his talons, split open the jugular and drank the hot blood as it gushed from the torn throat. Then he ravenously broke apart the hands and feet, and swallowed them.

Without warning, Grendel suddenly dropped the mangled body and sprang straight across the hall at Beowulf. The hero had raised himself on his left elbow. Beowulf had just time to stretch forth his right arm as the ogre rushed upon him. He caught Grendel's right hand, and still without rising from his bed, stopped the monster's onrush. For an instant the two stood stock-still. The shepherd of evil then looked down into the ice-cold eyes of the hero. Grendel was chilled. The cold shiver of death ran through his spine as the fingers of Beowulf tightened like steel over his bones.

Wild waves of fear ran over the ogre. His only thought was flight! Without even gathering his strength, he lurched backward, away from the vise, away from the eyes that were working foreign magic on him. As Grendel began to pull, Beowulf sprang to his feet. He did not let go Grendel's hand. On the contrary, he began slowly but surely to push it backward—despite all the strength of Grendel. Of the two Beowulf was the stronger. Grendel felt his hand, his arm, being slowly pushed backward. Great shudders rolled over him. Then Beowulf began to twist the ogre's arm.

With a howl of pain Grendel leaped wildly backward, Beowulf still gripping his hand, into the benches and boards. Back and forth across the hall the two fought, the hunted and the grim hunter. Boards crashed to the floor. The beakers of mead spilled in huge puddles. Against the walls the Geatish warriors huddled in knots or scrambled to safety as the two threw each other against the oak timbers. The outside of Heorot would be burst, as if the roof would cave in at any moment over the din of the struggle. Grendel lurched madly toward the door, hoping to pull Beowulf outside into the black night. Back and forth the two giants wrestled.

Then Grendel began to scream. Mouth open, eyes shooting red fire, he howled in mournful, quivering bursts of pain. Again and again he howled his death shriek until all the ruffians in hell stopped to listen. Beowulf would not let go of the hand. His heart was bent on the ogre's death.

As the twain stood locked together, Beowulf's squire roused himself from his fear and strode forth behind the fiend. Lifting his sharp-biting sword, he tried to rescue his master. Then did the Geatish earls see before them another wonder. Blow after blow of the sword fell upon Grendel's shoulders without even leaving a scratch. Then did the earls know the matchless wisdom of their leader! Beowulf had somehow known to doff his coat of mail and to lay down his weapons. No tool made by man had any strength against Grendel. Daunted and shivering, the squire stole back to his corner. Breathless, blanched with fear, the warriors awaited the outcome.

Beowulf to their amazement had not yet squeezed out the last of his strength. Before their wondering eyes they saw him suddenly wrench the ogre's arm backward and snap the armbone from the shoulder. A gaping wound spurted blood from Grendel's armpit. Beowulf's face, white with anger, flashed back cold fire into the red eyes of the fiend. Eye to eye they glared in unspeakable hatred for one last moment . . . Then the arm gave way utterly. The bones parted, the muscles burst, the flesh tore, and the fiend—at last free from the grip of Beowulf —fled full-tongued into the darkness.

Grendel knew that his days upon earth were numbered.

In the hall Beowulf the Geat stood alone. He had done what he swore to do. He had rid the house of evil. He had saved the kingdom of Denmark. Gladly Beowulf fastened the token of battle, the bloody arm of Grendel, in the rafters of Heorot.

# The High History Of The Sword Gram

## from The Volsunga Saga

### Translated by William Morris

THE *Elder Edda* is the source and fountainhead from which sprang all that we have of the Norse mythology. It was first written down in Iceland (then a Norse colony) in the middle of the 13th Century by a sage or scholar known as Saemund the Wise. But in oral form, as tradition, it is perhaps older by many centuries than this earliest known manuscript.

A second version of most of these stories appears in the *Prose Edda* of Snorri Sturluson, which dates from the same century. Both of the Eddas contain the world-famous story of Siegfried the Dragon-Slayer, but in slightly different forms and with slightly different names. In the *Elder Edda* he is called "Sigurth" while in the *Prose Edda* his name is "Sigurd."

Yet a third writer took this magnificent story and gave

# THE HIGH HISTORY OF THE SWORD GRAM

it another twist. We do not know the name of the unsung genius who composed the *Volsunga Saga*, but he was one of the most brilliant story-tellers since the days of old blind Homer—he who harped of burning Troy.

The *Saga* was also written in Iceland, and it appeared about thirty years after the death of Snorri Sturluson (that is, about 1270 A.D.). The *Volsunga* poet has extracted from the two Eddas the great legend of Sigurd the Volsung and has made that the central theme of his epic; it is not a Bible-like compilation of all Nordic myth (as in Saemund) nor a sophisticated Court-epic which links the primal Norse legendry to the Troy tale and the Old Testament heroes (as in Snorri), but the first and noblest of the great family-sagas of the Northern literatures—a saga which follows the changing fortunes of one particular House down through generations of warfare and wedding, treachery and triumph. In *The Volsunga Saga*, our hero is again named "Sigurd" and here the story takes on grandeur and richness of detail and appears as a great heroic tragedy on the scale of the Greek or Elizabethan dramas.

\*

This story of the Dragon-Slayer—whether he be called Sigurth, or Sigurd, or Siegfried (as in Wagner's *Ring* cycle, based on the same gigantic theme) is certainly one of the most durable and exciting of all the world's stories. The glorious vitality of the tale is such that we see it surging into view out of the dim mists of pre-history. Poet after poet seizes upon it, adding to it something of his own; down through the centuries it passes, ever growing in stature and might; and so tremendous is its appeal and so incredible its longevity that it reappears in half the national literatures of the North. (You will find it related briefly as a lay in the Anglo-Saxon *Beowulf*, and of course it forms the central plot of the German national epic, the *Nibelungenlied;* in the form given it by Richard Wagner—who began writing his cycle of operas in 1850—it achieved at last its final form, no less than a thousand years after it was born.)

Nor has the story yet finished its amazing history: you who have read *The Lord of the Rings* will recognize herein many of the plot-elements and story-devices which Professor Tolkien incorporated into his famous trilogy: the curse on the gold ring, the treasure guarded by a dragon, the invisibility charm on the Helm of Awe (Tolkien has most cleverly combined the ring and the Helm into one, and his characters become invisible when they draw the ring on their finger), the Broken Sword that is made new and whole again, and so on. My recent book, *Tolkien: A Look Behind "The Lord of the Rings"* (Ballantine Books, 1969), discusses in considerable detail the story-elements held in common between the Siegfried legend and the Tolkien trilogy (see pages 157—65 of that book).

It is, for me, a most happy coincidence that the great English novelist, poet and artist, William Morris, created a translation of *The Volsunga Saga*. Those who have followed the Ballantine Adult Fantasy Series thus far will be aware of my thesis that it is to Morris that we must be grateful for the actual invention of the fantasy novel of war, quest or adventure in imaginary worlds of the author's invention. Besides writing his own history-making novels, Morris was one of the most significant forces which brought the ancient Norse saga literature to the attention of the 19th Century, and thus caused an enormous revival of interest in the Northern mythos. It is then most fitting that the work of William Morris the *translator* finds a place in this anthology, as the work of William Morris the *novelist* has also a place in the companion volume to this anthology, which is called *The Young Magicians*.

Morris made his translation with the aid of an Icelandic scholar named Eirikr Magnusson. They had worked together on other translations—*The Saga of Gunnlaug* and the *Grettir's Saga* (1869). But 1870 saw their grestest effort reach print—the first rendering into English of the *Volsunga Saga*. It was the artistic peak of Morris' Icelandic translations, and he was so fascinated with this mighty tale that he returned to it again in later years, to rehandle the materials in the form of an original epic poem, *Sigurd the Volsung*, which Shaw called the greatest epic since Homer.

Here, from Morris' *Volsunga Saga*, I have extracted one strand of the plot, the tale of Sigurd's sword . . .

ꙮ

> (*The tale tells that King Volsung built a noble hall in such a wise that a great oak-tree stood therein, and that the limbs of the tree blossomed fair out over the roof of the hall, while below stood the trunk within the hall; and this tree was called by men the Branstock . . .*)

## Of the Sword That Sigmund, Volsung's Son, Drew from the Branstock

THERE WAS a king called Siggeir, who ruled over Gothland, a mighty king and of many folk; he went to meet Volsung, the king, and prayed him for Signy his daughter to wife; and the king took his talk well, and his sons withal, but she was loth thereto, yet she bade her father rule in this as in all other things that concerned her, sot the king took such rede that he gave her to him, and she was bethrothed to King Siggeir; and for the fulfilling of the feast and the wedding, was King Siggeir to come to the house of King Volsung. The king got ready the feast according to his best might, and when all things were ready, came the king's guest and King Siggeir withal at the day appointed, and many a man of great account had Siggeir with him.

The tale tells that great fires were made endlong the hall and the great tree aforesaid stood midmost thereof; withal folk say that, whenas men sat by the fires in the evening, a certain man came into the hall unknown of aspect to all men; and suchlike array he had, that over him was a spotted cloak, and he was bare-foot, and had linen-breeches knit tight even unto the bone, and he had a sword in his hand as he went up to the Branstock, and a slouched hat upon his head; huge he was, and seeming-ancient, and one-eyed. So he drew his sword and smote it into the tree-trunk so that it sank in up to the hilts; and all held back from greeting the man. Then he took up the word, and said—

"Whoso draweth this sword from this stock, shall have the same as a gift from me, and shall find in good sooth that never bare he better sword in hand than is this."

Therewith out went the old man from the hall, and none knew who he was or whither he went.

Now men stand up, and none would fain be the last to lay hand to the sword, for they deemed that he would have the best of it who might first touch it; so all the noblest went thereto first, and then the others, one after other, but none who came thereto might avail to pull it out, for in nowise would it come away howsoever they tugged at it; but now up comes Sigmund, King Volsung's son, and sets hand to the sword, and pulls it from the stock, even as if it lay loose before him; so good that weapon seemed to all, that none thought he had seen such a sword before, and Siggeir would fain buy it of him at thrice its weight of gold, but Sigmund said—

"Thou mightest have taken the sword no less than I from there whereas it stood, if it had been thy lot to bear it; but now, since it has first of all fallen into my hand, never shalt thou have it, though thou biddest therefor all the gold thou hast."

King Siggeir grew wroth at these words, and deemed Sigmund had answered him scornfully, but whereas he was a wary man and a double-dealing, he made as if he heeded this matter in nowise, yet that same evening he thought how he might reward it, as we was well seen afterwards.

# THE HIGH HISTORY OF THE SWORD GRAM

*(Thus did Gram cause dissention between Volsung and Siggeir of Gothland, who raised war against Volsung and slew him, only to die in his turn under the hand of Sigmund, who became king in his father's place. Years later, Sigmund wins a bride, Hjordis, but his love-rival, Lyngi, raises a host and falls upon the vikings...)*

Now was that battle fierce and fell, and though Sigmund were old, yet most hardily he fought, and was ever the foremost of his men; no shield on byrny might hold against him, and he went ever through the ranks of his foremen on that day, and no man might see how things would fare between them; many an arrow and many a spear was aloft in air that day, and so his spae-wrights wrought for him that he got no wound, and none can tell over the tale of those who fell before him, and both his arms were red with blood, even to the shoulders.

But now whenas the battle had dured a while, there came a man into the fight clad in a blue cloak, and with a slouched hat on his head, one-eyed was he, and bare a bill in his hand; and he came against Sigmund the king, and have up his bill against him, and as Sigmund smote fiercely with the sword it fell upon the bill and burst asunder in the midst: thenceforth the slaughter and dismay turned to his side, for the good-hap of King Sigmund had departed from him, and his men fell fast about him; naught did the king spare himself, but he rather cheered on his men; but even as the saw says, *No might 'gainst many*, so was it now proven; and in this fight fell Sigmund the King, and King Eylimi, his father-in-law, in the fore-front of their battle, and therewith the more part of their folk.

## Of The Shards of the Sword Gram, and How Hjordis Went to King Alf

Now King Lyngi made for the King's abode, and was minded to take the king's daughter there, but failed herein, for there he found neither wife nor wealth: so he fared through all that realm, and gave his men rule thereover, and now deemed that he had slain all the kin of the Volsungs, and that he need dread them no more from henceforth.

Now Hjordis went amidst the slain that night of the battle, and came whereas lay King Sigmund, and asked if he might be healed; but he answered—

"Many a man lives after hope has grown little; but my good-hap has departed from me, nor will I suffer myself to be healed, nor wills Odin that I should ever draw sword again, since this my sword and his is broken; lo now, I have waged war while it was his will."

"Naught ill would I deem matters," said she, "if thou mightest be healed and avenge thy father."

The king said, "That is fated for another man; behold now, thou art great with a man-child; nourish him well and with good heed, and the child shall be the noblest and most famed of all our kin: and keep well withal the shards of the sword: thereof shall a goodly sword be made, and it shall be called Gram, and our son shall bear it, and shall work many a great work therewith, even such as eld shall never minish; for his name shall abide and flourish as long as the world shall endure: and let this be enow for thee. But now I grow weary with my wounds, and I will go see our kin that have gone before me."

So Hjordis sat over him till he died at the day-dawning; and then she looked, and behold, there came many ships sailing to the land: then she spake to the handmaid—

"Let us now change raiment, and be thou called by my name, and say that thou art the king's daughter."

And thus they did; but now the vikings behold the great slaughter of men there, and see where two women fare away thence into the wood; and they deem that some great tidings must have befallen, and they leaped ashore from out their ships. Now the captain of these folks was Alf, son of Hjalprek, king of Denmark, who was sailing with his power along the land. So they came into the field among the slain, and saw how many men lay dead there; then the king bade go seek for the women and bring them thither, and they did so. He asked them what women they were; and, little as the thing seems like to be, the bondmaid answered for the twain, telling of the fall of King Sigmund and King Eylimi, and many another great man, and who they were withal who had wrought the deed. Then the king asks if they wotted where the wealth of the king was bestowed; and then says the bondmaid—

"It may well be deemed that we know full surely thereof."

And therewith she guides them to the place where the treasure lay: and there they found exceeding great wealth; so that men deem they have never seen so many things of price heaped up together in one place. All this they bore to the ships of King Alf, and Hjordis and the bondmaid went with them. Therewith these sail away to their own realm, and talk how that surely on that field had fallen the most renowned of kings.

So the king sits by the tiller, but the women abide in the forecastle; but talk he had with the women and held their counsels of much account.

In such wise the king came home to his realm with great wealth, and he himself was a man exceeding goodly to look on. But when he had been but a little while at home, the queen, his mother, asked him why the fairest of the two women had the fewer rings and the less worthy attire.

"I deem," she said, "that she whom we have held of least account is the noblest of the twain."

He answered: "I too have misdoubted me, that she is little like a bondwoman, and when we first met, in seemly wise she greeted noble men. Lo now, we will make a trial of the thing."

So on a time as men sat at the drink, the king sat down to talk with the women, and said—

"In what wise do ye note the wearing of the hours, whenas night grows old, if ye may not see the lights of heaven?"

Then says the bondwoman, "This sign have I, that whenas in my youth I was wont to drink much in the dawn, so now when I no longer use that manner, I am yet wont to wake up at the very same tide, and by that token do I know thereof."

Then the king laughed and said, "Ill manners for king's daughter!" And therewith he turned to Hjordis, and asked her even the same question; but she answered—

"My father erst gave me a little gold ring of such nature, that it groweth cold on my finger in the day-dawning; and that is the sign that I have to know thereof."

The king as answered: "Enow of gold there, where a very bondmaid bore it! but come now, thou has been long enow hid from me; yet if thou hadst told me all from the beginning, I would have done to thee as though we had both been one king's children: but better than thy deeds will I deal with thee, for thou shalt be my wife, and due jointure will I pay thee whenas thou hast borne me a child."

She spake therewith and told out the whole truth, about herself: so there was she held in great honour, and deemed the worthiest of women.

## Of the Birth and Waxing of Sigurd Fafnir's-Bane

The tale tells that Hjordis brought forth a man-child, who was straightly borne before King Hjalprek, and then was the king glad thereof, when he saw the keen eyes in the head of him, and he said that few men would be equal to him or like unto him in any wise. So he was sprinkled with water, and had to name Sigurd, of whom all men speak with one speech and say that none was ever his like for growth and goodliness. He was brought up in the house of King Hjalprek in great love and honour; and so it is, that whenso all the noblest men and greatest kings are named in the olden tales, Sigurd is ever put before them all, for might and prowess, for high mind and stout heart, wherewith he was far more abundantly gifted than any man of the northern parts of the wide world.

So Sigurd waxed in King Hjalprek's house, and there was no child but loved him; through him was Hjordis bethrothed to King Alf, and jointure meted to her.

Now Sigurd's foster-father was hight Regin, the son of Hreidmar; he taught him all manner of arts, the chess play, and the lore of runes, and the talking of many tongues, even as the wont was with kings' sons in those days. But on a day when they were together, Regin asked Sigurd, if he knew how much wealth his father had owned, and who had the ward thereof; Sigurd answered, and said that the kings kept the ward thereof.

Said Regin, "Dost thou trust them all utterly?"

Sigurd said, "It is seemly that they keep it till I may do somewhat therewith, for better they wot how to guard it than I do."

Another time came Regin to talk to Sigurd, and said—

"A marvellous thing truly that thou must needs be a horseboy to the kings, and go about like a running knave."

"Nay," said Sigurd, "it is not so, for in all things I have my will, and whatso thing I desire is granted me with good will."

"Well then," said Regin, "ask for a horse of them."

"Yea," quoth Sigurd, "and that shall I have, whenso I have need thereof."

Thereafter Sigurd went to the king, and the king said—
"What wilt thou have of us?"

Then said Sigurd, "I would even a horse of thee for my disport."

Then said the king, "Choose for thyself a horse, and whatso thing else thou desirest among my matters."

So the next day went Sigurd to the wood, and met on the way an old man, long-bearded, that he knew not, who asked him whither away.

Sigurd said, "I am minded to choose me a horse; come thou, and counsel me thereon."

"Well then," said he, "go we and drive them to the river which is called Busil-tarn."

They did so, and drave the horses down into the deeps of the river, and all swam back to land but one horse; and that horse Sigurd chose for himself; grey he was of hue, and young of years, great of growth, and fair to look on, nor had any man yet crossed his back.

Then spake the grey-beard, "From Sleipnir's kin in this horse come, and he must be nourished heedfully, for it will be the best of all horses"; and therewithal he vanished away.

So Sigurd called the horse Grani, the best of all the horses of the world; nor was the man he met other than Odin himself.

Now yet again spake Regin to Sigurd, and said—

"Not enough is thy wealth, and I grieve right sore that thou must needs run here and there like a churl's son; but I can tell thee where there is much wealth for the winning, and great name and honour to be won in the getting of it."

Sigurd asked where that might be, and who had watch and ward over it.

Regin answered, "Fafnir is his name, and but a little way hence he lies, on the waste of Gnita-heath; and when thou comest here thou mayst well say that thou hast never seen more gold heaped together in one place, and that none might desire more treasure, though he were the most ancient and famed of all kings."

"Young am I," said Sigurd, "yet still know I the fashion of this worm, and how that none durst go against him, so huge and evil is he."

Regin said, "Nay, it is not so, the fashion and the growth of him is even as if other lingworms, and an over great tale men make of it; and even so would thy forefathers have deemed; but thou, though thou be of the kin of the Volsungs, shalt scarce have the heart and mind of those, who are told of as the first in all deeds of fame."

Sigurd said, "Yea, belike I have little of their hardihood and prowess, but thou has naught to do, to lay a coward's name upon me, when I am scarce out of my childish years. Why dost thou egg me on hereto so busily?"

Regin said, "Therein lies a tale whih which I must needs tell thee."

"Let me hear the same," said Sigurd.

*Regin's Tale of his Brothers,*
*and of the Gold called*
*Andvari's Hoard*

"Thus the tale begins," said Regin. "Hreidmar was my father's name, a mighty man and a wealthy: and his first son was named Fafnir, his second Ottar, and I was the third, and the least of them both for prowess and good conditions, but I was cunning to work in iron, and silver, and gold, whereof I could make matters that availed somewhat. Other skill my brother Ottar followed, and had another nature withal, for he was a great fisher, and above other men herein; in that he had the likeness of an otter by day, and dwelt ever in the river, and bare fish to bank in his mouth, and his prey would he ever bring to our father, and that availed him much: for the most part he kept him in his otter-gear, and then he would come home, and eat alone, and slumbering, for on the dry land he might see naught. But Fafnir was by far the greatest and grimmest, and would have all things about called his.

"Now," says Regin, "there was a dwarf called Andvari, who ever abode in that force, which was called Andvari's force, in the likeness of a pike, and got meat for himself, for many fish there were in the force; now Ottar, my brother, was ever wont to enter into the force, and bring fish aland, and lay them one by one on the bank. And so it befell that Odin, Loki, and Hoenir, as they went their ways, came to Andvari's force, and Ottar had taken a salmon, and ate it slumbering upon the river bank; then Loki took a stone and cast it at Ottar, so that he got his death thereby; the gods were well content with their prey, and fell to flaying off the otter's skin; and in the evening they came to Hreidmar's house, and showed him what they had taken: thereon he laid hands on them, and doomed them to such ransom, as that they should fill the otter skin with gold, and cover it over without with red gold; so they sent Loki to gather gold together for them; he came to Ran, and got her net, and went therewith to Andvari's force, and cast the net before the pike, and the pike ran into the net and was taken. Then said Loki—

> What fish of all fishes,
> Swims strong in the flood,
> But hath learnt little wit to beware?
> Thine head must thou buy,
> From abiding in hell,
> And find me the wan waters flame.

"He answered—

> Andvari folk call me,
>   Call Odin my father,
> Over many a force have I fared;
>   For a Norn of ill-luck,
>   This life on me lay
> Through wet ways ever to wade.

"So Loki beheld the gold of Andvari, and when he had given up the gold, he had but one ring left, and that also Loki took from him; then the dwarf went into a hollow of the rocks, and cried out, that the gold-ring, yes, and all the gold withal, should be the bane of every man who should own it thereafter.

"Now the gods rode with the treasure to Hreidmar, and fulfilled the otter-skin, and set it on its feet, and they must cover it over utterly with gold: but when this was done then Hreidmar came forth, and beheld yet one of the muzzle hairs, and bade them cover that withal; then Odin drew the ring, Andvari's loom, from his hand, and covered up the hair therewith; then sang Loki—

> Gold enow, gold enow,
>   A great weregild, thou hast,
> That my head in good hap I may hold;
>   But thou and thy son
>   Are naught fated to thrive,
> The bane shall it be of you both.

"Thereafter," says Regin, "Fafnir slew his father and murdered him, nor got I aught of the treasure, and so evil he grew, that he fell to lying abroad, and begrudged any share in the wealth to any man, and so became the worst of all worms, and even now lies brooding upon that treasure: but for me, I went to the king and became his master-smith; and thus is the tale told of how I lost the heritage of my father, and the weregild for my brother."

So spake Regin; but since that time gold is called Ottargild, and for no other cause than this.

But Sigurd answered, "Much hast thou lost, and exceeding evil have thy kinsmen been! but now, make a sword by thy craft, such a sword as that none can be made like unto it; so that I may do great deeds therewith, if my heart avail thereto, and thou wouldst have me slay this mighty dragon."

Regin says, "Trust me well herein; and with that same sword shalt thou slay Fafnir."

*Of the Welding Together of
the Shards of the Sword Gram*

So Regin makes a sword, and gives it into Sigurd's hands. He took the sword, and said—

"Behold thy smithying, Regin!" and therewith smote it into the anvil, and the sword brake; so he cast down the brand, and bade him forge a better.

Then Regin forged another sword, and brought it to Sigurd, who looked thereon.

Then said Regin, "Belike thou art well content therewith, hard master though thou be in smithying."

So Sigurd proved the sword, and brake it even as the first; then he said to Regin—

"Ah, art thou, mayhappen, a traitor and a liar like to those former kin of thine?"

Therewith he went to his mother, and she welcomed him in seemly wise, and they talked and drank together.

Then spake Sigurd, "Have I heard aright, that King Sigmund gave thee the good sword Gram in two pieces?"

"True enough," she said.

So Sigurd said, "Deliver them into my hands, for I would have them."

She said he looked like to win great fame, and gave him the sword. Therewith went Sigurd to Regin, and bade him make a good sword thereof as he best might; Regin grew wroth thereat, but went into the smithy with the pieces of the sword, thinking well meanwhile that Sigurd pushed his head far enow into the matter of smithying. So he made a sword, and as he bore it forth from the forge, it seemed to the smiths as though fire burned along the edges thereof. Now he bade Sigurd take the sword, and said he knew not how to make a sword if this one failed. Then Sigurd smote it into the anvil, and cleft it down to the stock thereof, and neither burst the sword nor brake it. Then he praised the sword much, and thereafter went up to the river with a lock of wool, and threw it up against the stream, and it fell asunder when it met the sword. Then was Sigurd glad, and went home.

But Regin said, "Now whereas I have made the sword for thee, belike thou wilt hold to thy troth given, and wilt go meet Fafnir?"

"Surely will I hold thereto," said Sigurd, "yet first must I avenge my father."

Now Sigurd the older he grew, the more he grew in the love of all men, so that every child loved him well.

## The Prophecy of Grifir

There was a man hight Grifir, who was Sigurd's mother's brother, and a little after the forging of the sword Gram Sigurd went to Grifir, because he was a man who knew things to come, and what was fated to men: of him Sigurd asked diligently how his life should go; but Grifir was long or he spake, yet at the last, by reason of Sigurd's exceeding great prayers, he told him all his life and the fate thereof, even as afterwards came to pass. So when Grifir had told him all even as he would, he went back home; and a little after he and Regin met.

Then said Regin, "Go thou and slay Fafnir, even as thou hast given thy word."

Sigurd said, "That work shall be wrought."

> *(But ere the undertaking of the adventure against the mighty lingworm, Fafnir, Sigurd went up against them had slain his father in war, and slew them all. King Lyngi he slew, and his brother, and all the sons of Hunding: then was he ready to try the steel of Gram the Mighty against the scales of Fafnir . . .*

## Of the Slaying of the Worm Fafnir

Now Sigurd Regin ride up the heath along that same way wherein Fafnir was wont to creep when he fared to the water; and folk say that thirty fathoms was the height of that cliff along which he lay when he drank of the water below. Then Sigurd spake—

"How sayedst thou, Regin, that this drake was no greater than other lingworms; methinks the track of him is marvellous great?"

Then said Regin, "Make thee a hole, and sit down therein, and whenas the worm comes to the water, smite him into the heart, and so do him to death, and win for thee great fame thereby."

But Sigurd said, "What will betide me if I be before the blood of the worm?"

Says Regin, "Of what avail to counsel thee if thou art still afeard of everything? Little art thou like thy kin in stoutness of heart."

Then Sigurd rides right over the heath; but Regin gets him gone, sore afeard.

But Sigurd fell to digging him a pit, and whiles he was at that work, there came to him an old man with a long beard, and asked what he wrought there, and he told him.

Then answered the old man and said, "Thou doest after sorry counsel: rather dig thee many pits, and let the blood run therein; but sit thee down in one thereof, and so thrust the worm's heart through."

And therewithal he vanished away; but Sigurd made the pits even as it was shown to him.

Now crept the worm down to his place of watering, and the earth shook all about him, and he snorted forth venom on all the way before him as he went; but Sigurd neither trembled nor was adrad at the roaring of him. So whenas the worm crept over the pits, Sigurd thrust his sword under his left shoulder, so that it sank in up to the hilts; then up leapt Sigurd from the pit and drew the sword back again unto him, and therewith with his arm all bloody, up to the very shoulder.

Now when that mighty worm was ware that he had his death-wound, then he lashed out head and tail, so that all things soever that were before him were broken to pieces.

So whenas Fafnir had his death-wound, he asked, "Who art thou? and who is thy father? and what thy kin, that thou wert so hardy as to bear weapons against me?"

Sigurd answered, "Unknown to men is my kin. I am called a noble beast: neither father have I nor mother, and all alone have I fared hither."

Said Fafnir, "Whereas thou hast neither father nor mother, of what wonder wert thou born then? But now, though thou tellest me not thy name on this my death-day, yet thou knowest verily that thou liest unto me."

He answered, "Sigurd am I called, and my father was Sigmund."

Says Fafnir, "Who egged thee on to this deed, and why wouldst thou be driven to it? Hadst thou never heard how that all folks were adrad of me, and of the awe of my countenance. But an eager father thou hadst, O bright-eyed swain!"

Sigurd answered, "A hardy heart urged me on hereto; and a strong hand and this sharp sword, which well thou knowest now, stood me in stead in the doing of the deed; *Seldom hath hardy eld a faint-heart youth.*"

Fafnir said, "Well, I wot that hadst thou waxed amid thy kin, thou mightest have good skill to slay folk in thine anger; but more of a marvel is it, that thou, a bondsman taken in war, shouldst have the heart to set on me, *for few among bondsmen have heart for the fight.*"

Said Sigurd, "Wilt thou then cast it in my teeth that I am far away from my kin? Albeit I was a bondsman, yet was I never shackled. God wot thou hast found me free enow."

Fafnir answered, "In angry wise dost thou take my speech; but harken, for that same gold which I have owned shall be thy bane too."

Quoth Sigurd, "Fain would we keep all our wealth till that day of days; yet shall each man die once for all."

Said Fafnir, "Few things wilt thou do after my counsel; but take heed that thou shalt be drowned if thou farest unwarily over the sea, so bide thou rather on the dry land, for the coming of the calm tide."

Then said Sigurd, "Speak, Fafnir, and say, if thou art so exceeding wise, who are the Norns who rule the lot of all mother's sons."

Fafnir answers, "Many there be and wide apart; for some are of the kin of the Aesir, and some are of Elfin kin, and some there are who are daughters of Dvalin."

Said Sigurd, "How namest thou the holm whereon Surt and the Aesir mix and mingle the water of the sword?"

"Unshapen is that holm hight," said Fafnir.

And yet again he said, "Regin, my brother, has brought about my end, and it gladdens my heart that thine too he bringest about; for thus will things be according to his will."

And once again he spake, "A countenance of terror I bore up before all folk, after that I brooded over the heritage of my brother, and on every side didst I spout

out poison, so that none durst come anigh me, and of no weapon was I adrad, nor ever had I so many men before me, as I deemed myself not stronger than all; for all men were sore afeard of me."

Sigurd answered and said, "Few may have victory by means of that same countenance of terror, for whoso comes amongst many shall one day find that no one man is by so far the mightiest of all."

Then says Fafnir, "Such counsel I give thee, that thou take thy horse and ride away at thy speediest, for ofttimes it falls out so, that he who gets a death-wound avenges himself none the less."

Sigurd answered, "Such as thy redes are I will nowise do after them; nay, I will ride now to thy lair and take to me that great treasure of thy kin."

"Ride there then," said Fafnir, "and thou shalt find gold enow to suffice thee for all thy life-days; yet shall that gold be thy bane, and the bane of every one soever who owns it."

Then stood up Sigurd, and said, "Home would I ride and lose all that wealth, if I deemed that by the losing thereof I should never die; but every brave and true man will fain have his hand on wealth till that last day; but thou, O Fafnir, wallow in the death-pain till Death and Hell have thee."

And therewithal Fafnir died.

## Of the Slaying of Regin, Son of Hreidmar

Thereafter came Regin to Sigurd, and said, "Hail, lord and master, a noble victory hast thou won in the slaying of Fafnir, whereas none durst heretofore abide in the path of him; and now shall this deed of fame be of renown while the world stands fast."

Then stood Regin staring on the earth a long while, and presently thereafter spake from heavy mood: "Mine own brother has thou slain, and scarce may I be called sackless of the deed."

Then Sigurd took his sword Gram and dried it upon the earth, and spake to Regin—

"Afar thou faredst when I wrought this deed and tried this sharp sword with the hand and the might of me; with all the might and main of a dragon must I strive, while thou wert laid alow in the heather-bush, wotting not it if it were earth or heaven."

Said Regin, "Long might this worm have lain in his lair, if the sharp sword I forged with my hand had not been good at need to thee; had that not been, neither thou nor any man would have prevailed against him as at this time."

Sigurd answers, "Whenas men meet foes in fight, better is stout heart than sharp sword."

Then said Regin, exceeding heavily, "Thou hast slain my brother, and scarce may I be called sackless of the deed."

Therewith Sigurd cut out the heart of the worm with the sword called Ridil; but Regin drank of Fafnir's blood, and spake—

"Grant me a boon, and do a thing like for thee to do. Bear the heart to the fire, and roast it, and give me thereof to eat."

Then Sigurd went his ways and roasted it upon a rod; and when the blood bubbled out he laid his finger thereon to essay it, if it were fully done; and then he set his finger in his mouth, and lo, when the heart-blood of the worm touched his tongue, straightway he knew the voice of all fowls, and heard withal how the wood-peckers chattered in the brake beside him—

"There sittest thou, Sigurd, roasting Fafnir's heart for another, that thou shouldst eat thine ownself, and then thou shouldest become the wisest of all men."

And another spake: "There lies Regin, minded to beguile the man who trusts in him."

But yet again said the third, "Let him smite the head from off him then, and be only lord of all that gold."

And once more the fourth spake and said, "Ah, the wiser were he if he followed after that good counsel, and rode thereafter to Fafnir's lair, and took to him that mighty treasure that lieth there, and then rode over Hindfell, whereas sleeps Brynhild; for there would he get great wisdom. Ah, wise he were, if he did after your redes, and bethought him of his own weal; *for where wolf's ears are, wolf's teeth are near.*"

Then cried the fifth: "Yea, yea, not so wise is he as I deem him, if he spareth him whose brother he hath slain already."

At last spake the sixth: "Handy and good rede to slay him, and be lord of the treasure!"

Then said Sigurd, "The time is unborn wherein Regin shall be my bane; nay, rather one road shall both these brothers fare."

And therewith he drew his sword Gram and struck off Regin's head.

Then heard Sigurd the wood-peckers a-singing, even as the song says.

For the first sang:

Bind thou, Sigurd,
The bright red rings!
Not meet it is
Many things to fear.
A fair may know I,
Fair of all the fairest
Girt about with gold,
Good for thy getting.

And the second:

Green go the ways
Toward the hall of Giuki
That the fates show forth
To those who fare thither;

> There the rich king
> Reareth a daughter;
> Thou shalt deal, Sigurd,
> With gold for thy sweetling.

And the third:

> A high hall is there
> Reared upon Hindfell,
> Without all around it
> Sweeps the red flame aloft
> Wise men wrought
> That wonder of halls
> With the unhidden gleam
> Of the glory of gold.

Then the fourth sang:

> Soft on the fell
> A shield-may sleepeth
> The lime-tree's red plague
> Playing about her:
> The sleep-thorn set Odin
> Into that maiden
> For her choosing in war
> The one he willed not.
>
> Go, son, behold
> That may under helm
> Whom from battle
> Vinskornir bore,
> From her may not turn
> The torment of sleep.
> Dear offspring of kings
> In the dread Norns' despite.

Then Sigurd ate some deal of Fafnir's heart, and the remnant he kept. Then he leapt on his horse and rode along the trail of the worm Fafnir, and so right unto his abiding-place; and he found it open, and beheld all the doors and the gear of them that they were wrought of iron: yea, and all the beams of the house; and it was dug down deep into the earth: there found Sigurd gold exceeding plenteous, and the sword Rotti; and thence he took the Helm of Awe, and the Gold Byrny, and many things fair and good. So much gold he found there, that he thought verily that scarce might two horses, or three belike, bear it thence. So he took all the gold and laid it in two great chests, and set them on the horse Grani, and took the reins of him, but nowise will he stir, neither will he abide smiting. Then Sigurd knows the mind of the horse, and leaps on the back of him, and smites and spurs into him, and off the horse goes even as if it were unladen.

# Manawyddan Son of the Boundless

## Kenneth Morris

THE SMALL, MOUNTAINOUS and coal-rich country of Wales has never played a major role in world history, although it gave England her dynasty of Tudor monarchs, and gave the world the brilliant lyric genius of Dylan Thomas. These to one side, the Welsh have vastly enriched the world's treasury of mythology with a slender collection of eleven prose narratives we call *The Mabinogion*.

These tales are found in two major versions, first in an ancient codex called *The White Book of Rhydderch* (written between 1300 and 1325 A.D.), and, most importantly, in a great volume called *Llyfr Coch Hergest—The Red Book of Hergest*, which is probably the origin of Professor Tolkien's "Red Book of Westmarch," his pretended source-text for *The Lord of the Rings*.

The eleven mythic tales extracted from these two codices have been given the name of *Mabinogion*. This word has long been considered the plural of the Welsh *mabinogi*, which derives from *mabinog*, which is what apprentice bards were called; but more recently, the scholarly experts on the Cymraeg language (which is what those who speak Welsh call it) say the term is derived from a scribal error and is actually meaningless; it is, however, a convenient title for these inter-related tales

# MANAWYDDAN SON OF THE BOUNDLESS

which date from the second half of the 11th Century to the close of the 13th.

Since the *Mabinogion* was first translated into English about a century ago, it has proved a splendid source for story-tellers in general and fantasy writers in particular, such as the American novelist, Evangeline Walton, whose gorgeous fantasy novel *The Virgin and the Swine* (1936) is drawn from *Mabinogion* sources, or that volume of dark splendor, *Porius: A Romance of the Dark Ages* (1952), by the brilliant Welsh novelist John Cowper Powys. Most recently, the foremost of the "post-Tolkienian" writers, Lloyd Alexander, has utilized the world of Welsh mythology as the scene of his Prydain Series, a group of five novels which opened with *The Book of Three* (1964) and ended with *The High King* (1968).

I chose part of the epic story of Manawyddan, one of the great Welsh heroes, for my selection for this anthology from *The Mabinogion*. Manawyddan was born a mortal man and reigned as one of the kings, but the Gods purified him through many harsh trials and raised him up to a place amongst them atop Mount Snowdon, the Welsh Olympus, in the end. Out of the many different versions, translations and retellings of the Manawyddan saga, I chose this version by Kenneth Morris from *The Book of the Three Dragons;* the Morris version is fuller and more explicit than some I might have selected, for he used other early Welsh mythological sources, not *The Mabinogion* alone, in recreating the mighty tale of the Son of the Boundless . . .

A⊤ one time there was no Crowned King in London; and for lack of one, often there would be confusion and the failure of crops. So Six Chieftains of the Cymry consulted among themselves who should get the crown. Taliesin the Chief of Bards was at the head of them: his forehead shone like the Morning Star.

"If you will take advice of mine," said he, "the one to wear the crown will be the Blessed Bran."

"The best advice in the world," they agreed, "if there be any getting him." He had been crowned King of London none knew how many ages before; and there would be no finding him but in the Islands of the Blessed in the West of the World; and the journey thither they were for making.

"It would be beneath his dignity to have less than seven men come to him on an embassy," said Heilyn ab Gwyn Hen. (He was the most impatient of all warriors and horsemen.)

"That is true," said Taliesin Benbardd. "We shall meet the seventh in Mon as we go forward; he will be a son of the Boundless as Bran Fendigaid is; he will be at the head of us."

In Mon they met Manawyddan; and all could see that he was to be their leader. Now here is who this Manawyddan son of the Boundless was:

It happened of old that the Gods of the Island of the Mighty desired to raise auxiliar godhood from the ranks of the Cymry, the men of that island. So Hu the Mighty called them into council; and in the council they decided that Pwyll, Prince of Dyfed in Wales, should be the man they would make a god of, if he were capable of it. So first they sent him to reign in Annwn the Great Deep, and a year and a day he was king there, and undergoing the trials incident to the place, and nowise failing in them. They sent one of their own divine kindred, Rhianon Ren the daughter of Hefeydd, into Wales to become his wife; that she might help him towards godhood as only a goddess could.

But it was when his son Pryderi was born that they put the heaviest trial on him; and in that he failed. So they did what they had to do by him: took the memory from his mind, and himself from his kin and his kingdom; and cast him loose on Wales and the world. Whatever misfortune they could devise, they brought him deep into the midst of it, and poured it out over the head of him, and set it howling and fanged at his heels;

and all for no reason but that bound they were to make a god of him, and to have him fighting in their ranks with them against Hell and Chaos along the borders of space.

He knew nothing, at that time, of his having been Pwyll Pen Annwn, Lord of Dyfed and the Great Deep; style or title he had none; the best name there was for him was Dienw'r Anffodion, the Nameless One with the Misfortunes; and to get a better he would have to come into Pair Dadeni, the Caldron of Ceridwen, the Mother of the World; but he knew nothing of that. In it the dead come by new life and the nameless by a name; and the Gods were guiding him towards it always, by the shortest path there was. For Hu Gadarn sent Gwydion ab, Don the God of Wisdom and Laughter, to guide him; and by reason of that, towards Pair Dadeni his face was set. Gwydion ab Don was beside him on all his wanderings: through Eruope and through Africa and the Islands of Corsica, and through Sach and Salach, and Lotor and Ffotor, and India the Greater and India the Less, and Powys and Meirion and Arfon.

And there, one day, he was traversing the mountains towards Mon and Ireland; and it seemed to him he had never been anything but fortunate, compared to what he was then.

It was long since he had passed any habitation, or looked on the faces of men. The fields bore no mushrooms for him, nor the thorns blackberries, although it was the beginning of Autumn; and if there were eels or trout in the streams, he could get no news of them. Three days before he had shot an old lean rabbit; and had seen neither bird nor beast to shoot at since. Nothing was left of it but the right hind leg; and the best that could be said for that was that it was dry and tough and withered. He was shoeless and in rags; and lame with a wounded foot a sharp rock had torn the day before and that now was festering.

He had risen from the heather at dawn after a night of rain and fever; and thought that death could not be far from him. Now and again hunger tormented him;

but he took no thought for the rabbit leg in his wallet. Through the morning he limped on, and the rain drove down on him; and the thoughts in his mind were either numb and silent or else fantastic and beyond control; and the one thing he hoped for in his heart was death.

And then suddenly he became aware of that which had already driven the clouds from the sky, and the rain from mid air, and now the grief and confusion from his mind. It was harping and song that filled the mountain world with wonder, and made the morning wholly beautiful, with sunlit raindrops sparkling everywhere on the fern. The rabbits came hurrying from their burrows to listen, and paid no heed to him as he passed. An old gray wolf, sauntering down the hillside, turned, and stood still with trembling ears. Three eagles came down out of the sky, and lighted on boulders, intent. Wild goats on the crags above stood motionless. Nothing living moved but himself; and, he, as best he could, hurried forward to come to the heart of the enchantment.

A hundred paces brought him to it. A youth sat on a rock, his harp at his breast, floating out the music on the sunlight. A motion of his eyes bade Dienw be seated; and so he kept him until the song was sung. It was healing and happiness to listen to it. The singer was hardly more than a boy; yet had the blue robe of an Institutional Bard of that island on him.

He ended the song and set down the harp, and picked up his wand of alderwood studded with gold. "The greeting of the god and the man to you, pleasantly and kindly!" said he. It was the best greeting Dienw had had, so far as he knew, during the whole of his life.

"And better be it with you than it is with me—better and more copious!" he answered. "It would be a delight to me to remember, in after times, the name of the one who could so ingratiate these mountains with his harping and his vocal song."

"As to the name, it will be Goreu fab Ser," said the Bard; and clear it was he would be of starry lineage, and few his betsters throughout the worlds. "It was foretold to me that I should meet here the man I desired to meet; and I made the music to attract him to me."

"It would be pleasant to know who that one might be," said Dienw.

"It is a Prince of the Cymry, a Son of the Boundless, to go with Taliesin Benbardd into the Western World. Is it you who are the man?"

"Dear, help me better!" said Dienw. "Is it the look of a Prince of the Cymry or a Son of the Boundless is with me?"

"Whether it is or not," said Goreu, "the fate is on any man who heard the music, that he shall accompany me today until I find that man; if it is all Arfon and Mon itself I must travel."

"I will do that gladly," said Dienw.

"That is well," said Goreu fab Ser. "We will go forward."

They journeyed on; and what with Goreu's songs and his stories, and his laughter and diverting conversation, Dienw had no memory of his sorrows and pain; and was happy for the first time in his life, so far as he knew. At noon Goreu stopped, and said:

"The hunger of the world has overtaken me. Is there food with you in the wallet?"

Dienw remembered the rabbit's leg, and was overcome with shame. "Such food as it is," said he. He opened the wallet and brought out what it contained.

"Dear, a miserable provision is this, for such a one as I am," said Goreu. "In your deed, is there nothing better with you than this poor and dilapidated meat?"

"There is not," said Dienw, sighing.

"Detestable to me, truly, is loathsome hunger; abominable an insufficiency of food upon a journey. Mournful, I declare to you is such a fate as this, to one of my lineage and nurture!"

"Well, well," said Dienw'r Anffodion, with the bitter hunger awaking in him again; "common with me is knowledge of famine. Take you the whole of the food, if you will."

"Yes," said Goreu, "that will be better." With that he

ate the meat and gnawed the bone and flung it from him. "Now that I have partaken of food," said he, "I am refreshed, and grief and fatigue have forsaken me; and I am filled with a desire for music. Play you the harp for my diversion!"

Dienw took it, and played *The Little Mountain Bird* on it, singing the song as best he could. When he came to, "God fired with song his wild prophetic tongue," Goreu fab Ser, groaning piteously, snatched the harp from him.

"Music I desired, and not this soul-piercing cacophony!" he cried. "A poor return is this for my kindness! Listen you now, and be silent."

Then he struck chords from the harp and began singing; and hurried forward as he played and sang; and the harping was a ruthless torment, and the song, hideous screeching: the birds in the air hearing it fell dead, and the rabbits perished in their burrows; the wolves fled howling, and the winds' of heaven moaned and mourned. And as for Dienw, his pains and sorrows came back to him a thousandfold, and there was nothing for him to do but mourn and follow: over the mountains and the wild places, by sharp crag and raging torrent: his legs jerked miserably into speed by the harping; his mind and body in anguish.

"Come!" cried Goreu fab Ser augustly; "I am refreshed with good and glorious music; I loathe this dawdling unenterprise; it is a poor return for my kindness to you, that you should delay me thus on the road!" Thus he dragged him on and never spared him; but to gorse-grown level and jagged steep; trailing the way with crimson from Dienw's wounds, but going weightless and dauntless himself: until they came to the shore of the Menai and the house of the ferryman.

"Soul," said Goreu fab Ser; "is there food in the house with you, to appease the enormous hunger of the world that afflicts me?"

"Such as it is," said the ferryman; "and little enough of it." He brought out half an oatcake and a thumb's weight of cheese; and it was Goreu who took them from him.

"Better for one to be filled than for two to go hungry," said he to Dienw. "Is it grudge me the provisions you do?"

"No I," said Dienw. "Hunger and famine I am familiar with."

"It will be the better for you," said Goreu; and compassion in his voice instead of mockery and merriment; if anyone had been listening for it.

The ferryman launched his coracle, and the three of them went into it and began the crossing. And now a mood of restlessness came on Goreu, and he became wilder and merrier than ever he had been; yet losing nothing of his augustness of mien and tone. Night was drifting westward at that time, and the deep gray of the twilight over the waters of Menai.

"Dear, help thee better!" he cried, leaping to his feet, "behold yonder!" What was there to be beheld, none was to know: for no man may leap to his feet in a coracle without overturning it. The three of them were in the water; the ferryman swimming back towards Arfon, and pushing his boat before him as he swam.

"Peace now to drown and forget," thought Dienw with the Misfortunes. But there was no peace for him. "On me is the sorrow of all my race!" cried Goreu son of the Stars. "Never have I feared anything so much as death by loathsome drowning—a watery and evil death, and to end my life beneath Menai waves. Were there one here better than a poltroon and a braggart, he would quit his extreme selfishness and save me from the fury of the deep sea!"

"I am here," gasped Dienw; "it is not fated that you should drown." He gathered what strength he had, and made the best use of it, and held Goreu up in the water, and began swimming with him towards Mon. Whilst he swam, Goreu struggled and encumbered his limbs, and made no end of his august lamentations and reproofs. "If I save him, it is as much as I shall do," thought Dienw. "As for me, there will be peace when the waves have closed over me." Night fell, and the stars shone fitfully through gaps in the clouds. "I will save him," thought Dienw; "in my deed to Heaven I will." Then he thought, "It is a hundred miles between me and Mon"; and with that a wave lifted the two of them, and cast them up upon the beach. Mind and thought were gone from him, as if death had taken him.

Goreu son of the Stars arose, and lifted him beyond reach of the tide, and laid him down in a hollow between the sand-hills; and then the likeness of human flesh and bone departed from Goreu, and he took fire-form and god-form, and rose up flaming into mountain stature till the peak of the Wyddfa was less lofty than he; and turned his face southward and east toward that holy mountaintop; and he said:

"Lord Mighty One, he is ready; the breath is gone from him; the Nameless One with the Misfortunes is ready; Pwyll Pen Annwn is ready at last."

Out of the peak of the Wyddfa rose Hu Gadarn, who was appointed in those days to be Emperor of the Gods and the Cymry of Ynys Wen. He too flamed skyward, his crest burning among the stars of Capricorn, his eyes shining with wisdom and beneficence, his White Shield better than seven moons in the heavens.

"I commend you, Lord Gwydion ab Don," said he. "Let him be brought now into the Caldron of Ceridwen my daughter; let his body be laid in Pair Dadeni, that new life and name may be his."

From the midst of Mon, light streamed up into the sky; flame-flakes of rainbow hues; and thence came nine dragons through the air, and lighted down among the sand dunes, and became the Nine Faery Princes that watch the fires under Ceridwen's Caldron. They picked up the body of the Nameless One, and bore it to the Caldron.

In the morning when Dienw awoke, not an ache nor wound was in his body, nor any sorrow in his mind. One stood over him of immortal beauty, whose forehead shone like the Morning Star; five others came up the beach toward them.

"The greeting of heaven and man to you, Manawyddan son of the Boundless!" said Taliesin the Chief of Bards.

"And better be it with you than with me, Lord Taliesin!" said he, arising from the sand. "And better be it with the other five Chief Chieftains that are approaching us. It is I who will go with you into the Western World."

"Yes, it is you," said Taliesin Benbardd. "Behold here, the seventh who will be at the head of us!" said he, "son of the Boundless, as befits the Blessed One's dignity!"

He went with them towards the Malltraeth; remembering how he had come by the name Taliesin had called him by, in the Caldron of Ceridwen in the night. "Goreu fab Ser," said he; "the Beset One, the son of the Stars; and Gwydion ab Don he was, whatever. And I that was Pwyll Pen Annwn, am Manawyddan son of the Boundless."

# Puck's Song

## from Puck of Pook's Hill

## Rudyard Kipling

I suppose Rudyard Kipling must be one of the world's favorite story-tellers: his *Jungle Book* is among the most beloved of books, to say nothing of *The Just So Stories* or my own favorite, *Kim*. While many of his tales and novels seem to have found a permanent place in the world's affections, the poetry which originally won him his fame seems to have lost much of its popularity. This may be more the fault of the reader than the poet; the casual reader, when he thinks of Kipling's verse, may remember only the humorous dialect poems of early collections like *Departmental Ditties* or *Barrack-Room Ballads*.

This is perhaps unfortunate, for the bulk of Kipling's verse is perfectly straight-forward English poetry, written with passion, poignancy and power by a brilliant writer with a remarkable command of the language, such as the pure and simple and moving lyric I include here, which is filled with an honest love for the English earth and its rich history.

Unknown to many readers, Kipling wrote two volumes of remarkable fairy lore: *Puck of Pook's Hill* (1906) and a sequel, *Rewards and Fairies* (1910). The central figure of these two collections of tales is Puck himself—transfigured in Kipling's imagination from the cute, mischievous, tiny sprite of Shakespeare's *A Midsummer Night's*

*Dream* to a strong nature-elemental of the English earth, "the oldest Old Thing in England" and the last of the People of the Hills, as Kipling calls him.

In so doing, Kipling is not distorting a Shakespearean creation, but restoring it to something like its original form. For Puck, or Robin Goodfellow, was an ancient figure in traditional British folklore long centuries before Shakespeare ever wrote of him.

The poem I have selected to include in this collection is drawn from *Puck of Pook's Hill*, where it appears in conjunction with the first of the Puck tales, "Weland's Sword." I chose this poem, not only because of its simple and honest beauty, but because it commemorates the ancientry and holiness of the British earth—an emotion which permeates the work of Professor Tolkien—a sentiment with which, I am sure, he heartily agrees.

And the last verse is one of the loveliest things I know. It still has power to send chills up my spine . . .

◈

See you the dimpled track that runs,
    All hollow through the wheat?
O that was where they hauled the guns
    That smote King Philip's fleet.

See you our little mill that clacks,
    So busy by the brook?
She has ground her corn and paid her tax
    Ever since Domesday Book.

See you our stilly woods of oak,
    And the dread ditch beside?
O that was where the Saxons broke,
    On the day that Harold died.

See you the windy levels spread
    About the gates of Rye?
O that was where the Northmen fled,
    When Alfred's ships came by.

See you our pastures wide and lone,
  Where the red oxen browse?
O there was a City thronged and known,
  Ere London boasted a house.

And see you, after rain, the trace
  Of mound and ditch and wall?
O that was a Legion's camping-place,
  When Caesar sailed from Gaul.

And see you marks that show and fade,
  Like shadows on the Downs?
O they are the lines the Flint Men made,
  To guard their wondrous towns.

Trackway and Camp and City lost,
  Salt Marsh where now is corn;
Old Wars, old Peace, old Arts that cease,
  And so was England born!

*She is not any common Earth,*
  *Water or wood or air,*
*But Merlin's Isle of Gramarye,*
  *Where you and I will fare.*

# Barrow-Wight

## from The Grettir Saga

### S. Baring-Gould

THE NORSE SAGAS form one of the richest traditional literatures of the Dark Ages. They are ringing and heroic adventure-tales of stalwart warriors laid against the stark backdrop of ancient Scandinavia. The grim and wintry North permeates them with a shadowy sense of foreboding and many of their epic heroes are towering tragic figures, inexorably doomed through some twist or flaw in their character. In this, they are not unlike the greatest of the Greek tragedies, with which they are often compared. While many of the sagas abound in supernatural incident, many others are set in realistic backgrounds and are told with a mature restraint of style and a degree of psychological realism most astonishing for such an ancient literature. Indeed, some of the sagas—the *Laxdale*, for instance—have been called "the first modern novels."

It was largely due to the pioneering translations of William Morris in the late 19th Century that the sagas were rediscovered and became part of popular literature. They have exerted a broad and deep influence on many fantasy writers (including Morris himself). You will find traces of the saga influence in Fletcher Pratt's *The Well of the Unicorn* and Poul Anderson's *The Broken Sword* and *Three Hearts and Three Lions,* and in both Tolkien and Eddison, who were entranced by "the Northern

Thing," as was C. S. Lewis as a boy, although the influence left little discernible mark on his mature writings. As for Eddison, it is neither unmeaningful nor accidental that the first chapter of his greatest romance, *The Worm Ouroboros,* quotes a passage from the mightiest of all the sagas, *Burnt Njal.*

When I first began thinking about this anthology, I knew I must have a good sample from one or another of the sagas. So I wrote to Poul Anderson, who, besides being the only Dane I know, is a great enthusiast of saga literature and has written a gigantic historical novel about the Viking Age, a novel that has not as yet found a publisher. I asked Poul to suggest scenes of fantasy from the sagas, and he called my attention to the *Grettir Saga,* for which I am very grateful.

I compared several different translations of the *Grettir* before settling on this version, by S. Baring-Gould. Baring-Gould so deeply loved the marvelous adventures of Grettir that he spent thirty years in preparation for his prose version. He tells us that he learned both Icelandic and Danish in order to study the saga in its original language, and his version remains—to my taste—the fullest and most satisfying rendition of the ancient tale. Baring-Gould uses an expansive English prose, and he is not without his eccentricities (he incorporates his footnotes into the text, for example, and interrupts his tale from time to time to inject a note of personal experience, for he explored on foot the lands that Grettir knew centuries before), but his own enduring love and enthusiasm for his tale shines through and adds luster to his retelling.

The *Grettir* dates from the closing years of the 13th Century, when a taste for the fantastic and the romantic was rife. It is a magnificent yarn, filled with gruesome and gory battles against trolls and giants, ghosts and ogres. The *Grettir,* as we now have it, seems to have been based on a much earlier original, and scholars have traced it to a version attributed to Sturla Thórdarson, written sometime before 1284 A.D. With the *Njal* and the *Volsunga,* it is one of the most popular and beloved of all the sagas.

I have selected the episode in which Grettir the Strong gets his magic sword from the tomb of a long-dead king. I could equally well have chosen an episode a little further along, in which he battles an ogre named Glam in a horrendous hand-to-hand battle; this scene, however, is very similar to Beowulf's battle with the monster Grendel, elsewhere included in *Dragons, Elves and Heroes*, so I will let my first choice stand.

※ ※ ※

Some little while before the slaying of the Red Rovers, a strange event had taken place.

Grettir had made the acquaintance of a man called Audun, who lived at a little farm at some distance from the house of Thorfin, and he walked over there occasionally to sit and talk with his friend. As he returned late at night he noticed that a strange light used to dance at the end of a cliff that overhung the sea, at the end of a headland; a lonely desolate headland it was, without house or stall near it. Grettir had never been there, and as it was so bare, he knew that no one lived on that headland, so he could not account for the light. One day he said to Audun that he had seen this strange light, which was not steady but flickered; and he asked him what it meant.

Audun at once became very grave, and after a moment's hesitation said, "You are right. No one lives on that ness, but there is a great mound there, under which is buried Karr the Old, the forefather of your host Thorfin; and it is said that much treasure was buried with him. That is why the ghostly light burns above the mound; for—you must know that flames dance over hidden treasure."

"If treasure be hidden there, I will dig it up," said Grettir.

"Attempt nothing of the kind," said Audun, "or Thorfin will be angry. Besides, Karr the Old is a dangerous fellow to have to deal with. He walks at night, and haunts all that headland and has scared away the dwellers in the nearest farms. No one dare live there because of him. That is why the Ness is all desolate without houses."

"I will stay the night here," said Grettir, "and to-morrow we will go together to the Ness, and take spade and pick and a rope, and I will see what can be found."

Audun did not relish the proposal, but he did not like to seem behindhand with Grettir, and he reluctantly agreed to go with him.

So next day the two went out on the Ness together. They passed two ruined farmhouses, the buildings rotting, the roofs fallen in. Those who had lived in them had been driven away by the dweller in the old burial mound, or barrow. The Norse name for these sepulchral mounds is *Haug*, pronounced almost like How; and where in England we have places with the names ending in *hoe*, there undoubtedly in former times were such mounds. Thus, in Essex are Langenhoe and Fingringhoe, that is to say the Long Barrow and Fingar's How. Also, the Hoe, the great walk at Plymouth above the sea, derives its name from some old burial mound now long ago destroyed.

The Ness was a finger of land running out into the sea, and on it grew no trees, only a little coarse grass; at the end rose a great circular bell-shaped mound, with a ring of stones set round it, to mark its circumference. Grettir began to dig at the summit, and he worked hard. The day was short, and the sun was touching the sea as his pickaxe went through an oak plank, into a hollow space beneath, and he knew at once that he had struck into the chamber of the dead. He worked with redoubled energy, and tore away the planks, leaving a black hole beneath of unknown depth, but which to his thinking could not be more than seven feet beneath him. Then he called to Audun for the rope. The end he fastened round his waist, and bade his friend secure the other end to a pole thrown across the pit mouth. When this was done, Audun cautiously let Grettir down into the chamber of the dead.

Now, you must know that in heathen times what was often done with old warriors was to draw up a boat on the shore, and to seat the dead man in the cabin, with his horse slain beside him, sometimes some of his slaves or thralls were also killed and put in with him, and his choicest treasures were heaped about him. This men did because they thought that the dead man would want his weapons, his raiment, his ornaments, his horse and his servants in the spirit world. Of late years such a mound has been opened in Norway, and a great ship found in it, well preserved, with the old dead chief's bones in it. When a ship was not buried, then a chamber of strong planks was built, and he was put in that, and the earth heaped over him. Into such a chamber had Grettir now dug.

He soon reached the bottom, and was in darkness, only a little light came in from above, through the hole he had broken in the roof of the cabin or chamber. His feet were among bones, and these he was quite sure were horse bones. Then he groped about.

As his eyes became more accustomed to the darkness, he discerned a figure seated in a throne. It was the long-dead Karr the Old. He was in full harness, with a helmet on his head with bull's horns sticking out, one on each side; his hands were on his knees, and his feet on a great chest. Round his neck was a gold torque or necklet, made of bars of twisted gold, hooked together behind the head. Grettir in the dark could only just make out the glimmer of the gold, but it seemed to him that a phosphorescent light played about the face of the dead chief.

So little light was left, that Grettir hasted to collect what he could. There stood a brazen vessel near the chair, in which were various articles, probably of worth, but it was too dark for Grettir to see what they were. He brought the vessel to the rope and fastened the end of the cord to its handle. Then he went back to the old dead man and drew away a short sword that lay on his lap, and this he placed in the brass vessel. Next he began to unhook the gold torque from his neck, and as he did this the phosphorescent flame glared strangely about the dead man's face.

Then, all at once, as both his hands were engaged undoing the hook behind Karr's neck, he was clipped. The dead man's arms had clutched him, and with a roar like a bull Karr the Old stood up, holding him fast, and now all the light that had played over his features gathered into and glared out of his eyes.

When Audun heard the roar, he was so frightened that he ran from the barrow, and did not stay his feet till he reached home, feeling convinced that the ghost or whatever it was that lived in the tomb had torn Grettir to pieces.

Then began in the chamber of the dead a fearful wrestle. Grettir was at times nigh on smothered by the gray beard of the dead chief, that had been growing, growing, in the vault, ever since he had been buried.

How long that terrible struggle continued no one can tell. Grettir had to use his utmost force to stand against Karr the Old. The two wrestled up and down in the chamber, kicking the horse bones about from side to side, stumbling over the coffer, and the brass vessel, and the horse's skull, striking against the sides, and when they did this then masses of earth and portions of broken plank fell in from above.

At last Karr's feet gave way under him and he fell, and Grettir fell over him. Then instantly he laid hold of his sword, and smote off Old Karr's head and laid it beside his thigh.

This, according to Norse belief, was the only way in which to prevent a dead man from walking, who had haunted the neighbourhood of his tomb, and in the Icelandic sagas we hear of other cases where the same proceeding was gone through. The Norsemen held to something more dreadful than ghosts walking; they thought that some evil spirit entered into the bodies of the dead, that when this happened the dead no longer decayed, but walked, and ate, and drank, and fought, very much like living ruffians, but with redoubled strength. Then, when this happened, nothing was of any avail save the digging up of the dead man, cutting off his head and laying it at his thigh.

When Grettir had done this, he despoiled Karr the Old of his helm, his breast-plate, his torque, and he took the box on which the feet had rested. He fastened all together to the rope, and called to Audun to haul up. He received no answer, so he swarmed up himself, and finding that his friend had run away he pulled up what he had tied together, and carried the whole lot in his arms to the house of Thorfin. Thorfin and his party were at supper; and when Grettir came in, the bonder looked up, and asked why he did not keep regular hours, and be at the table when the meal began. Grettir made no other answer than to throw all he carried down on the supper-table before the master. Thorfin raised his eyebrows when he saw so much treasure.

"Where did you get all this?" he asked.

Then Grettir answered in one of his enigmatical songs:

> Thou who dost the wave-shine shorten,
>   My attempt has been to find
> In the barrow what was hidden,
>   Deep in darkness black and blind.
> Nothing of the dragon's treasure
>   With the dead is left behind.

By the wave-shine shortener he meant Thorfin; the dragon's treasure meant gold, because dragons were thought to line their lairs with that metal.

Thorfin saw that Grettir's eye looked longingly at the short sword that had lain on the knees of Karr. He said: "It was a heathen custom in old times to bury very much that was precious along with the dead. I do not blame you for what you have done; but this I will say, that there is no one else about this place who would have ventured to attempt what you have done. As for that sword on which you cast your eyes so longingly, it has ever been in our family, and I cannot part with it till you have shown that you are worthy to wear it."

Then that sword was hung up over Thorfin's bed. You have heard how Grettir did show that he was worthy to wear it, and also how Thorfin gave it him.

Now, this tale about the sword will very well illustrate what was said at the beginning, that the history of Grettir contains, in the main, truth; but that this substance of truth has been embroidered over by fancy. What is true is, that during the winter in which he was with Thorfin he did dig into the mound in which Karr was buried, and did take thence his treasures and his sword. But all the story of his fight with the dead man was added. The same story occurs in a good many other sagas, as in that of Hromund Greip's son, who also got a sword by digging into a barrow for it. When the history of Grettir was told, and this adventure of his was related, those who told the story imported into it the legend of the fight of Hromund in the grave with the dead man, so as to make the history of Grettir more amusing. As you will see by the tale, no one else was present when it happened, for Audun had run away, and it was not like Grettir to boast of what he had done. This was an embellishment added by the story-teller, and from the story-teller the incident passed into the volume of the story-writer.

Grettir had now two good swords; one long, which he called Jokull's Gift, that he had received from his mother, and this short one that he wore at his girdle, which he had taken out of the grave of Karr the Old, and which he had won fairly by his bravery in the defence of the house and family of Thorfin.

# Fingal At The Siege Of Carric-thura

## from The Poems of Ossian

## James Macpherson

JAMES MACPHERSON was one of those colorful and extraordinary characters who come along every once in a while to keep things from getting too dull. He was a bit of an eccentric, like William Beckford, the author of *Vathek,* and a bit of a charlatan, like Aleister Crowley, the notorious English black magician.

He was a Scotsman, born at Ruthven, Inverness, forty years before the Declaration of Independence was signed and the American Revolution was launched. He did a little of everything in his time: for a time he was in Pensacola, Florida, as secretary to General Johnstone; for a while he played at being a statesman in the halls of Parliament; for a while he held down "the most astonishing job in London," as London agent for the Nabob of Arcot. And for a while he turned the literary world upside down by making the most momentous and history-making literary discovery in centuries.

He claimed he had discovered the lost literature of the primitive Gaels of Scotland—a titanic cycle of magnificent heroic poems lost for one thousand and five hundred years—the long-forgotten works of a Gaelic Homer of the 3rd Century, called Ossian. And to prove it he published *Fingal* and *Temora* and *Cath-Loda* and the *War of Inis-Thona* and eighteen other epics of astounding dramatic power and poetic beauty.

He set the literary world on its ear. Poets of the day praised the discovery of an authentic native genius. Word spread like wildfire across the continent. The epics were widely translated. Goethe enthused over them; so did Herder; the Emperor Napoleon read Ossian in the Italian translation and called it one of his favorite books; whole schools of poets were inspired by Ossian; the epics did as much as any other literary work to initiate the rise of the Romantic movement in European literature.

But Macpherson was in trouble from the first. Canny old Samuel Johnson, a tough man to hoodwink, was not fooled. He simply sat back and blandly asked to see the original Gaelic manuscripts before giving an opinion on the authenticity of the epics. Macpherson fumbled and flustered, hemmed and hawed: it was too inconvenient; he was too busy; he could not afford to publish the texts, and so on. Eventually the whole thing fell through and Macpherson was revealed as a fraud—albeit a fraud of genius.

It is now the consensus of scholars that, while Macpherson may have woven some genuine scraps of old Gaelic verse into the epics, they are very largely the work of his own hand. This should not be of any particular importance—phoney or no, the epics are extraordinary works of literary power. One is tempted to call them works of genius; they are quite Homeric in their internal unity, purity of phrasing, clear, ringing music of language and dramatic coloring. Unfortunately, they are almost forgotten today: the most recent edition I could find for this selection was printed in Leipzig in 1847.

I have somewhat shortened the text and slightly modernized the punctuation for the purpose of clarity and to make it easier for the modern reader to appreciate.

## FINGAL AT THE SIEGE OF CARRIC-THURA

The following is selected from one of the shorter of the Ossianic epics, the poem *Carric-thura*.

The mighty hero, Fingal, returning home from a war expedition, turns aside to visit his friend Cathulla, King of Inistore, before continuing on to his own realm of Morven.

As he nears Carric-thura, the citadel of Cathulla, he discovers that it is under siege by the host of Frothal, King of Sora, who bears an ancient grudge against Cathulla. A signal-fire has been lit upon the heights of the citadel. Fingal sees the warning lights and lands on the coast with all his warriors.

They encamp for the night. Fingal, distressed over the safety of his friend, cannot sleep. He puts on his armor, takes up his spear and climbs the hills to look upon the beleaguered citadel. But the crest of the hills is a place sacred to the god Loda: a ring of standing stones marks the holy ground, and in the center lies the potent Stone of Power. As Fingal enters the ring, the ghostly apparition of Loda arises to challenge him. Loda is the father of Frothal, and he warns Fingal to retire lest he rouse the wrath of the gods . . .

&ast;&ast;&ast;

Morning rose in the east. The blue waters rolled in light. Fingal bade his sails to rise; the winds came rustling from their hills. Inistore rose to sight, and Carric-thura's mossy towers. But the sign of distress was on their top; the warning came edged with smoke.

The king of Morven smote his breast. He assumed at once his spear. His darkened brow bends forward to the coast. He looks back to the lagging winds. His hair is disordered on his back. The silence of the king is terrible.

Night came down on the sea; Rotha's bay received the ship. A rock bends along the coast with all its echoing woods. On the top is the Circle of Loda, the mossy stone of power. A narrow plain spreads beneath, covered with grass and aged trees, which the midnight winds in their wrath had torn from the shaggy rock.

The blue course of a stream is there. The lonely blast of ocean pursues the thistle's beard. The flame of three oaks arose; the feast is spread around; but the soul of the king is sad, for Carric-thura's chief distressed.

\*

The wan cold moon rose in the east. Sleep descended on the youths. Their blue helmets glitter to the beam. The fading fire decays. But sleep did not rest on the king: he rose in the midst of his arms and slowly ascended the hill, to behold the flame of Sarno's tower.

The flame was dim and distant, and the moon hid her red face in the east. A blast came from the mountain, and on its wings the spirit of Loda rode.

Loda came to his place in his terrors and shook his dusky spear. His eyes appear like flames in his dark face; his voice is like distant thunder.

Fingal advanced his spear in night and raised his voice on high:

"Son of Night, retire: call thy winds, and fly! Why dost thou come to my presence with thy shadowy arms? Do I fear thy gloomy form, spirit of dismal Loda? Weak is thy cloudy shield! Feeble is that meteor, thy fiery sword! Fly from my presence, Son of Night: call thy winds and fly!"

\*

"Does thou force me from my place?" replied the hollow voice. "The people bend before me. I turn the battle in the field of the brave. I look upon the nations, and they vanish. My nostrils pour the blast of death. I come abroad on the winds: the tempests are before my face.

But my dwelling is calm, above the clouds, and the fields of my rest are pleasant."

"Dwell in thy pleasant fields," said the king. "Let Comhal's son be forgot. Do my steps ascend from my hills into thy peaceful plains? Do I meet thee with a spear on thy cloud, spirit of dismal Loda? Why, then, dost thou frown on me? Why shake thine airy spear? Thou frownest in vain: I never fled from the mighty in war. And shall the Sons of the Wind frighten the king of Morven? No—he knows the weakness of their arms!"

\*

"Fly to thy land," replied the form. "Receive thy wind, and fly! The blasts are in the hollow of my hand; the course of the storm is mine. The king of Sora is my son; he bends at the stone of my power. His battle is around Carric-thura and he will prevail. Fly to thy land, Son of Comhal, or feel my flaming wrath!"

He lifted high his shadowy spear. He bent forward his dreadful height. Fingal, advancing, drew his sword, the blade of dark-brown Luno. The gleaming path of the steel winds through the gloomy ghost. The form fell shapeless into air, like a column of smoke which the staff of the boy disturbs as it riseth from the half-extinguished furnace.

The Spirit of Loda shrieked as, rolled into himself, he rose on the wind. Inistore shook at the sound. The waves heard it upon the deep; they stopped in their course with fear.

\*

The friends of Fingal started at once, and took up their heavy spears. They missed the king. They rose in rage and all their arms resound.

The moon came forth in the east. Fingal returned in the gleam of his armor. The joy of his youth was great, and their souls settled as a sea after a storm. Ullin raised the song of gladness. The hills of Inistore rejoiced.

The flame of the oak arose, and the tales of heroes are told.

\*

But Frothal, Sora's wrathful king, sits in a sadness beneath a tree. The host spreads around Carric-thura. He looks towards the walls with rage. He longs for the blood of Cathulla, who once overcame him in war; wrath darkened in his soul against the noble Cathulla.

Morning rose on Inistore. Frothal struck his dark-brown shield. His chiefs started at the sound. They stood, but their eyes were turned to the sea.

They saw Fingal coming in his strength, and first the noble Thubar spoke.

"Who come like the stag of the wilderness, with all his herd behind him? Frothal, it is a foe! I see his forward spear. Perhaps it is the king of Morven, Fingal, the first of men. His deeds are well known in Lochlin; the blood of his foes is in Starno's halls. Shall I ask the peace of kings? His sword is like the bolt of heaven!"

"Son of a feeble hand," said Frothal, "shall my days begin in a cloud? Shall I yield before I have conquered, chief of streamy Tora? The people would say in Sora, Frothal flew forth like a meteor, but a darkness has met him and his fame is no more. No, Thubar, I will never yield. My fame shall surround me like light."

\*

He went forth with the stream of his people, but they met a rock: Fingal stood unmoved. Broken they rolled back from his side. Nor did they safely fly: the spear of the king pursued their steps.

The field is covered with heroes. A rising hill preserved the foe.

Frothal saw their flight. The rage of his bosom rose. He bent his eyes to the ground and called the noble Thubar.

"Thubar! my people are fled. My fame has ceased to

## FINGAL AT THE SIEGE OF CARRIC-THURA

rise. I will fight the king; I feel my burning soul! Send a bard to demand the combat. Speak not against Frothal's words!"

*

Fingal heard the words of the bard. He came in the strength of his steel. They mixed their deathful spears. They raised the gleam of their arms.

But the sword of Fingal descended and cut Frothal's shield in twain. His side is exposed: half bent, he foresees his death.

The white-bosomed daughter of Heran, Utha, with soft-rolling eyes, was near! She had followed her hero in the armour of a man. Her loose hair flew on the wind. Darkness gathered on Utha's soul. The tear rolled down her cheek. She rushed to cover the chief with her shield, but a fallen oak met her steps.

She fell on her arm in the snow; her shield, her helmet, flew wide. Her white bosom heaved to the sight. Her dark-brown hair is spread on the earth.

Fingal pitied the white-armed maid. He stayed the uplifted sword. He spoke:

"King of streamy Sora! fear not the sword of Fingal. It was never stained with the blood of the vanquished; it never pierced the breast of a fallen foe. Let thy people rejoice by their native streams; let the maiden of thy love be glad. Why shouldst thou fall in thy youth, king of streamy Sora?"

*

Frothal heard the words of Fingal and saw the rising maid. They stood in silence in their beauty, like two young trees of the plain when the shower of spring is on their leaves and the loud winds are laid.

"Terrible art thou, O king of Morven, in battles of the spear," said Frothal. "But in peace thou art like the sun when he looks through a shower and the flowers lift their fair heads before him."

Fingal said: "Come thou, O Frothal! to the feast of Inistore; let the maid of thy love be there; let our faces brighten with joy!"

\*

Fingal took his spear, moving in the steps of his might. The gates of Carric-thura are opened wide. The feast of shells is spread; the soft sound of music arose and gladness brightened the hall.

The voice of Ullin was heard and the harp of Selma was strung. And Utha rejoiced, but demanded a song of grief for the fallen.

Ullin saw the virgin's tear. He took the softly-trembling harp. His song was lovely, but sad, and silence was in Carric-thura.

\*

Three days feasted the kings: on the fourth their white sails arose. The winds of the north drove Fingal to Morven's woody land.

But the Spirit of Loda sat in his cloud behind the ships of Frothal. He hung forward with all his blasts, and spread the white-bosomed sails.

The wounds of his form were not forgot.

But he feared the hand of Fingal the king.

# The Sword Of Avalon
## from Le Morte d'Arthur

### Sir Thomas Malory

IT's AN odd fact, but quite a number of the world's most wonderful books were written in jail. Perhaps the enforcement of leisure and the utter lack of anything else to do works a certain stimulus on the creative mind. I don't know. But if it hadn't been for that year he spent in the Genoa prison, Marco Polo might never have written his mighty *Book*. And Cervantes tells us that it was during those years he lay in the prison of the Dey of Algiers that he conceived of the character of the Ingenious Gentleman of La Mancha, and began to write the First Part of *Don Quixote*.

Much the same sort of thing happened to an otherwise obscure Lancastrian knight who flourished (if that's the right word) during the War of the Roses. His name was Sir Thomas Malorie or Malory, and we know little about his life, except that he was among those Lancastrian supporters who were denied a pardon when King Edward IV issued his general amnesty in 1468. Malory languished in prison in ill-health for some considerable length of time. To while away the weary hours, he worked on a mammoth book about the fabulous age of King Arthur. The Arthurian Cycle had already become, by Malory's day, the central subject of English literature —the "Matter of Britain." Malory drew from a number of earlier sources, reconciling various differing accounts of the Arthurian Age, and produced a masterpiece of English prose.

He called his book *Le Morte d'Arthur*, the Death of Arthur, and from the very beginning of its history it was destined to be a very important and central classic of English literature. For one thing, the book is a composite, a synthesis, a final reworking of the many different versions of the Tale of Arthur that had been done before. Wace and Layamon and Chrétien and Geoffrey of Monmouth and Robert de Borron and all sorts of other romancers had written of Arthur, but Malory drew everything into focus and produced *the* final, definitive version of the Matter of Britain (just as Firdausi, elsewhere in this anthology, was the master poet who drew into its final form the great Persian *Shah Namah*). No writer after Malory has ever been able to supersede him as the author of the definitive *Morte d'Arthur*.

The book has a most illustrious history. It was completed in the ninth year of the reign of Edward IV, that is, between March 4, 1469, and March 4, 1470. It was the last great English book written before the introduction of printing, and it was printed by the first great English printer, William Caxton, who also edited it, dividing Malory's manuscript into separate books and chapters. Caxton finished his edition in July, 1485: Malory by then had died, and Caxton seems to have simply chucked out the manuscript, which is a great pity, and which also makes this the first classic in English literature our knowledge of which depends *completely* on a printed text.

Malory's masterpiece has been closely studied by many generations of scholars and by now we have a pretty good idea of just what books he used in prison. Some of *Le Morte d'Arthur* seems to have been completely invented by Malory (for instance, no original has ever been found for Book vii, and it is believed he also made up Chapter 20 of Book xviii, which describes how the body of the Lily Maid of Astolat floated down river on a barge to the court of King Arthur), but most of the rest of the book has been traced, almost chapter by chapter, to the *Merlin* of Robert de Borron and the writers who took over after him. Malory also used an English metrical romance called *La Morte Arthur* (the "Thornton manuscript"), several French romances about Tristan and Launcelot, and the great English prose romance, the *Morte Arthur* of Harley MS. 2252. And, by the way, Malory did not always "improve" on his sources, and often worked from the worst possible texts. Of course, the poor old knight was stuck in jail at the time and had to work with what was at hand: he could hardly order a complete set of the Arthuriana from his local bookseller. If he had, doubtless his version would have been much better than it is, for as it stands his handling of his sources is often done with such skill and finesse as to approach original authentic genius.

And Malory's prose is incredibly beautiful: pure, limpid, crystalline. I think this was the original influence that molded the lucent prose of William Morris: at least I seem to see in the shadowy twilights, the dim forests, the dewy meadows, the crumbling old abbeys and the haunted palaces of Malory more than a trace of the mysterious dim world of Morris' great fantasy novels—"the water-color world of William Morris," as C. S. Lewis put it.

I have chosen my selection from the second book of *Le Morte d'Arthur*, because this portion, which relates the tale of Balin and Balan and of Sir Lanceor, is a typical passage. It is filled with magical swords, mysterious dwarves, strange witch ladies and romantic battles. The dim shadowy air of mystery and enchantment through which these stately figures move is the essence of the magic of Malory. The spelling and grammar have been slightly—but only slightly—modernized, and the punctuation has been somewhat simplified. I have also rendered some of the names into versions that will be more familiar to my readers: Malory may say "Aveilion," but we call the Enchanted Isle "Avalon," hence I see no reason not to alter the spelling for greater ease in reading.

But I have not changed much. It is a tribute to, and a measure of, the genius of Sir Thomas Malory that his book—now almost exactly five hundred years old—is still every bit as charming and mysterious and completely readable as it was when he wrote it . . .

I

*Of a damosel which came girt with a sword for to find a man of such virtue to draw it out of the scabbard*

AFTER THE death of Uther Pendragon reigned Arthur his son, the which had great war in his days for to get all England into his hand. For there were many kings within the realm of England, and in Wales, Scotland, and Cornwall. So it befell on a time when King Arthur was at London, there came a knight and told the king tidings how that the King Rience of North Wales had reared a great number of people, and were entered into the land, and burnt and slew the king's true liege people. If this be true, said Arthur, it were great shame unto mine estate but that he were mightily withstood. It is truth, said the knight, for I saw the host myself. Well, said the king, let make a cry, that all the lords, knights, and gentlemen of arms, should draw unto a castle, called Camelot in those days, and there the king would let make a council-general and a great jousting.

So when the king was come thither with all his baronage, and lodged as they seemed best, there was come a damosel the which was sent on message from the great lady Lile of Avalon. And when she came before King Arthur, she told from whom she came, and how she was sent on message unto him for these causes. Then she let fall her richly-furred mantle, and they saw that she was girt with a noble sword whereof the king had marvel, and said, Damosel, for what cause are ye girt with that sword? it beseemeth you not.

## THE SWORD OF AVALON

Now shall I tell you, said the damosel: this sword that I am girt withal doth me great sorrow and cumbrance, for I may not be delivered of this sword but by a knight, and he must be a passing good man of his hands and of his deeds, and without villainy or treachery, and without evil. And if I may find such a knight that hath all these virtues, he may draw this sword out of the sheath, for I have been at the lands of King Rience, where are said to dwell passing good knights and brave, but he and all his knights have assayed the deed and none could do it.

This is a great marvel, said Arthur, if this be sooth; I will myself assay to draw out the sword, not presuming upon myself that I am the best knight, but that I will begin to draw at your sword in giving example to all the barons that they shall assay every one after other when I have assayed it.

Then Arthur took the sword by the sheath and by the girdle and pulled at it eagerly, and with all the strength of his good right arm, but the sword would not out of the scabbard thereof.

Sir, said the damosel from Avalon, you need not to pull half so hard, for he that shall achieve the deed shall do it with little might. Ye say well, said Arthur; now assay ye all my barons, but beware ye be not defiled with shame, treachery, nor guile. Then it will not avail, said the damosel, for he must be a clean knight with outen villainy, and of a gentle strain of father-side and of mother-side.

Most of all the barons of the Round Table that were there at Camelot Castle that day assayed the deed, but there were none that might do it. Wherefore the damosel made great sorrow out of measure, and said, Alas! I weened that in this court had been the best knights of all the world, without treachery or treason.

By my faith, said Arthur, here are good knights, as I deem, as any be in the world, but their grace is not to help you, wherefore I am displeased.

## II

*How Balin, arrayed like a poor knight, pulled out the sword, which afterwards was the cause of his death*

Then fell it so that time there was a poor knight with King Arthur, that had been prisoner with him half a year and more for slaying of a knight, the which was cousin to King Arthur. The name of this knight was called Balin, and by good means of the barons he was delivered out of prison, for he was a good man named of his body, and he was born in Northumberland. And so he went privily into the court, and saw this adventure, whereof it raised his heart, and he would assay it as other knights did, but for he was poor and poorly arrayed he put him not far in press. But in his heart he was fully assured to do as well, if his grace happed him, as any knight that there was.

And as the damosel took her leave of Arthur and of all the barons, so departing, this knight Balin called unto her, and said, Damosel, I pray you of your courtesy, suffer me as well to assay the deed as these lords, though that I be so poorly clothed, for in my heart meseemeth I am fully assured as some of these others, and meseemeth in my heart to do right well.

The damosel beheld the poor knight, and saw he was a likely man, but for his poor arrayment she thought he would be of no worship without villainy or treachery. And then she said unto the knight, Sir, it needeth not to put me to more pain or labour, for it seemeth not you to speed there as others have failed.

Ah! fair damosel, said Balin, worthiness and good tatches and good deeds are not only in arrayment, but manhood and worship in his within man's person, and many a worshipful knight is not known unto all people, and therefore worship and hardiness is not in arrayment.

By God, said the damosel, ye say sooth: therefore ye shall assay to do what ye may.

## THE SWORD OF AVALON

Then Balin took the sword by the girdle and sheath, and drew it out easily; and when he looked on the sword it pleased him much. Then had the king and all the barons great marvel that Balin had done that adventure, and many knights had great despite of Balin. Certes, said the damosel, this is a passing good knight, and the best that ever I found, and most of worship withouten treason, treachery, or villainy, and many marvels shall he do. Now, gentle and courteous knight, give me the sword again.

Nay, said Balin, for this sword will I keep, but it be taken from me with force. Well, said the damosel, ye are not wise to keep the sword from me, for ye shall slay with the sword the best friend that ye have, and the man that most ye love in the world, and the sword from Avalon shall be your destruction.

I shall take the adventure that God will ordain to me, said Balin, but the sword ye shall not have at this time, by the faith of my body. Ye shall repent it within short time, said the damosel, for I would have the sword more for your avail than for mine, for I am passing heavy for your sake; for ye will not believe that the sword shall be your destruction, and that is great pity. With that the damosel departed, making great sorrow.

After this, Balin sent for his horse and armour, and so would depart from the court, and took his leave of King Arthur. Nay, said the king, I suppose ye will not depart so lightly from this fellowship, I suppose ye are displeased that I have shewed you unkindness; blame me the less, for I was misinformed against you, but I weened ye had not been such a knight as ye are, of worship and prowess, and if ye will abide in this court among my fellowship, I shall so advance you as ye shall be pleased.

God thank your highness, said Balin, your bounty may no man praise half to the value; but at this time I must needs depart, beseeching you alway of your good grace. Truly, said the king, I am right wroth for your departing; I pray you, fair knight, that ye tarry not long, and ye shall be right welcome to me, and to my barons, and

I shall amend all amiss that I have done against you. God thank our great lordship, said Balin, and therewith made him ready to depart.

Then the most part of the knights of the Round Table said that Balin did not this adventure all only by might, but by witchcraft and sorcery.

## III

*How the Lady of the Lake demanded the knight's head that had won the sword, or the maiden's head*

The meanwhile, that this knight was making him ready to depart, there came into the court a lady that hight the Lady of the Lake. And she came on horseback, richly beseen, and saluted King Arthur, and there asked him a gift that he had promised her when she gave him his shining sword.

That is sooth, said Arthur, a gift I promised you, but I have forgotten the name of my sword that ye gave me. This he said in cunning, for he knew the name well, but that he was not sure the Lady was the same as she from whom he had his sword aforetime.

The name of it, said the lady, is Excalibur, that is as much to say *I-cut-steel*.

Ye say well, said the king, assured that it was she; Ask what ye will and ye shall have it, if it lie in my power to give it you.

I ask the head of the knight that hath won the sword, said the lady; or else the head of the damosel that brought it hither; I take no force though I have both their heads, for he slew my brother, a good knight and a true, and that gentlewoman was causer of my father's death.

Truly, said King Arthur, I may not grant neither of their heads with my worship, therefore ask what ye will else, and I shall fulfill your desire.

I will ask none other thing, said the lady.

When Balin was ready to depart, he saw the Lady of

the Lake, that by her means had slain Balin's mother, and he had sought her three years; and when it was told to him that she asked his head of King Arthur, he went to her straight and said, Evil be you found; ye would have my head, and therefore ye shall lose yours. And with his sword lightly he smote off her head before King Arthur.

Alas, for shame! said Arthur, why have ye done so? ye have shamed me and all my court, for this was a lady that I was beholden to, and hither she came under my safe-conduct; I shall never forgive you that trespass.

Sir, said Balin, me forthinketh of your displeasure, for this same lady was the untruest lady living, and by enchantment and sorcery she hath been the destroyer of many good knights, and she was causer that my mother was burnt, through her falsehood and treachery.

What cause soever ye had, said Arthur, ye should have forborne her in my presence; therefore, think not the contrary, ye shall repent it, for such another despite had I never in my court; therefore withdraw you out of my court in all haste ye may.

Then Balin took up the head of the lady and bare it with him to his hostelry, and there he met with his squire, that was sorry he had displeased King Arthur, and so they rode forth out of that town.

Now, said Balin, we must depart, take thou this head and bear it to my friends, and tell them how I have sped, and tell my friends in Northumberland that my most foe is dead. Also tell them how I am out of prison, and what adventure befell me at the getting of this sword, which came out of Avalon. Alas! said the squire, ye are greatly to blame for to displease King Arthur. As for that, said Balin, I will hie me, in all the haste that I may, to meet with King Rience and destroy him, either else to die therefore; and if it may hap me to win him, then will King Arthur be my good and gracious lord.

Where shall I meet with you? said the squire. In King Arthur's court, said Balin. So his squire and he departed at that time.

Then King Arthur and all the court made great dole

and had shame of the death of the Lady of the Lake. Then the king buried her richly.

## IV

*How Merlin told the adventure of this damosel*

At that time there was a knight, the which was the king's son of Ireland, and his name was Lanceor, the which was an orgulous knight, and counted himself one of the best of the court; and he had great despite at Balin for the achieving of the sword, that any should be accounted more hardy, or more of prowess than himself. And he asked King Arthur if he would give him leave to ride after Balin and to revenge the despite that he had done.

Do your best, said Arthur, I am right wroth with this Balin. I would that he were quit of the despite that he hath done to me and to my court.

Then this Lanceor went to his hostelry to make him ready.

In the meantime came Merlin unto the court of King Arthur, that was a famous magician. And there was told him the adventure of the sword, and the death of the Lady of the Lake.

Now shall I say you, said Merlin; this same damosel that here standeth, that brought the sword unto your court, I shall tell you the cause of her coming: she was the falsest damosel that liveth in the world.

Say not so! said they. She hath a brother, said Merlin, a passing good knight of prowess and a full true man; and this damosel loved another knight that held her to paramour, and this good knight her brother met with the knight that held her to paramour, and slew him by force of his hands. When this false damosel understood this, she went to the Lady Lile of Avalon, and besought her of help, to be avenged on her own brother.

## V

*How Balin was pursued by Sir Lancelot, knight of Ireland, and how he jousted and slew him*

And so this Lady Lile of Avalon took her this sword that she brought with her, and told there should no man pull it out of the sheath but if he be one of the best knights of this realm, and he should be hard and full of prowess, and with that sword he should slay her brother. This was the cause that the damosel came into this court, said Merlin. I know it as well as ye. Would God she had not come into this court, but she came never in fellowship of worship to do good, but always great harm; and that knight that hath achieved the sword shall be destroyed by that sword, for the which will be great damage, for there liveth not a knight of more prowess than he is, and he shall do unto you, my lord Arthur, great honour and kindness; and it is great pity he shall not endure but a while, for of his strength and hardiness I know not his match living.

So the knight of Ireland armed him at all points, and dressed his shield on his shoulder, and mounted upon horseback, and took his spear in his hand, and rode after a great pace, as much as his horse might go; and within a little space on a mountain he had a sight of Balin, and with a loud voice he cried, Abide, knight, for ye shall abide whether ye will or nill, and the shield that is tofore you shall not help.

When Balin heard the noise, he turned his horse fiercely, and said, Fair knight, what will ye with me, will ye joust with me?

Yeah, said the Irish knight, therefore come I after you.

Peradventure, said Balin, it had been better to have holden you at home, for many a man weeneth to put his enemy to a rebuke, and oft it falleth to himself. Of what court be ye sent from? said Balin. I am come from the court of King Arthur, said the knight of Ireland, that come hither for to revenge the despite ye did this day to King Arthur and to his court. Well, said Balin, I see well I must have ado with you, that me forethinketh for to grieve King Arthur, or any of his court; and your quarrel is full simple, said Balin, unto me, for the lady that is dead did me great damage, and else would I have been loathe as any knight that liveth for to slay a lady.

Make you ready, said the knight Lanceor, and dress you unto me, for that one shall abide in the field.

Then they took their spears, and came together as much as their horses might drive, and the Irish knight smote Balin on the shield, that all went shivers off his spear, and Balin hit him through the shield, and the hauberk perished, and so pierced through his body and the horse's croup, and anon turned his horse fiercely, and drew out his sword, and wist not that he had slain him; and then he saw him lie as a dead corpse.

## VI

*How a damosel, which was love to Lanceor, slew herself for love, and how Balin met with his brother Balan*

Then he looked by him, and was ware of a damosel that came riding full fast as the horse might ride, on a fair palfrey. And when she espied that Lanceor was slain, she made sorrow out of measure, and said, O Balin, two bodies thou hast slain and one heart, and two hearts in one body, and two souls thou hast lost! And therewith she took the sword from her love that lay dead, and fell to the ground in a swoon. And when she arose she made great dole out of measure, the which sorrow grieved Balin passingly sore, and he went unto her for to have taken the sword out of her hand, but she held it so fast he might not take it out of her hand unless he should have hurt her, and suddenly she set the pommel to the ground and drove the blade through her body.

When Balin espied her deeds, he was passing heavy in

his heart, and ashamed that so fair a damosel had destroyed herself for the love of his death.

Alas, said Balin, me repenteth sore the death of this knight, for the love of this damosel, for there was much true love betwixt them both, and for sorrow might not longer behold him, but turned his horse and looked toward a great forest, and there he was ware, by the arms, of his brother Balan.

And when they were met they put off their helms and kissed together, and wept for joy and pity. Then Balan said, I little weened to have met with you at this sudden adventure; I am right glad of your deliverance out of your dolorous prisonment, for a man told me, in the Castle of Four Stones, that ye were delivered, and that man had seen you in the court of King Arthur, and therefore I came hither into this country, for here I supposed to find you.

Anon the knight Balin told his brother of his adventure of the sword from out of Avalon, and of the death of the Lady of the Lake thereby, and now King Arthur was displeased with him. Wherefore said Balin, he sent this knight after me, that lieth here dead, and the death of this damosel grieveth me sore.

So doth it me, said Balan, but ye must take the adventure that God will ordain to you.

Truly, said Balin, I am right heavy that my Lord Arthur is displeased with me, for he is the most worshipful knight that reigneth now on earth, and his love will I get or else will I put my life in adventure. For the King Rience lieth at a siege at Castle Terror, and thither will we draw in all haste, to prove our worship and our prowess upon him.

I will well, said Balan, that we do, and we will help each other as brethren ought to do.

And, this said, they rode forth together.

## VII

*How a dwarf reproved Balin for the death of Lanceor, and how King Mark of Cornwall found them, and made a tomb over them*

Now go we hence, said Balin, and well be we met!

The meanwhile as they talked, there came a dwarf from the city of Camelot on horseback, as much as he might, and found the dead bodies, wherefore he made great dole, and pulled out his hair for sorrow, and said, Which of you knights have done this deed?

Whereby asketh thou it? said Balan. For I would wit it, said the dwarf. It was I, said Balin, that slew this knight in my defense, for hither he came to chase me and to challenge me to the joust, wherefore might I not refuse, and either I must slay him or he must slay me; as for this damosel, she slew herself for his love, which repenteth me, and for her sake I shall owe all women the better love.

Alas, said the dwarf, thou hast done great damage unto thyself, for this knight that is here dead was one of the most valiantest men that lived, and trust well, Balin, the kin of this knight will chase you through the world till they have slain you.

As for that, said Balin, I fear not greatly, but I am right heavy that I have displeased my lord King Arthur for the death of this knight.

So as they talked together, there came a king of Cornwall riding, the which hight King Mark. And when he saw these two bodies dead, and understood how they were dead, by the two knights above said, then made the king great sorrow for the true love that was betwixt them, and said, I will not depart till I have on this earth made a tomb, and there he pight his pavilions and sought through all the country to find a tomb, and in a church they found one was fair and rich, and then the king let them put them both in the earth, and put the tomb upon them, and wrote the names of them both on the tomb.

How here lieth Lanceor the king's son of Ireland, that at his own request was slain by the hands of Balin; and how his lady, Colombe, and paramour, slew herself with her love's sword for dole and sorrow.

# Tom o'Bedlam's Song
## *Anonymous*

MAGIC AND the commonplace, realism and wild nightmarish fantasy inhabit the strange world of Tom o'Bedlam. And, in the tension that lives between these two ends of the spectrum of experience rises the intensity and fire that has kept the following poem alive since the days of Shakespeare.

Tom was one of the vagrants or "Abraham-men" who roamed and begged along the roadways of England during the 16th and 17th Centuries. He seems to have been discharged as a harmless incurable from the Abraham ward of the Hospital of St. Mary of Bethlehem in London—or *Bedlam,* as it was called. Such unfortunates were given a badge to wear that entitled them to beg, lest they be taken for dangerous escaped lunatics or gypsies.

Tom appears in Shakespeare's *King Lear,* where the banished son of the Earl of Gloucester disguises himself as an Abraham-man of that name:

"Poor Tom, that eats the swimming frog, the toad, the tadpole, the wall-newt, and the water; that in the fury of his heart, when the foul fiend rages, eats cow-dung for sallet, swallows the old rat and the ditch-dog; drinks the green mantle of the standing pool; who is whipped from tithing to tithing, and stocked, punished, and imprisoned; who hath had three suits to his back, six shirts to his body, horse to ride and weapons to wear..."

Tom's wild, weird lyric cry has appealed to many writers. Fans of John Collier will recognize in the same play the source of his title, *Tom's A-Cold;* Alfred Bester quotes from Tom o'Bedlam's song in the novel *The Stars*

*My Destination;* and Robert Heinlein may have taken the line "The moon's my constant mistress" as source for the title of his Hugo-winning recent novel, *The Moon is a Harsh Mistress*.

Shakespeare may—just *may*—have had even more to do with Tom than put him in a play. More than one important literary figure (Dame Edith Sitwell and Robert Graves among them) has voiced the opinion that "the same hand that fashioned the mad scene in *Lear,* fashioned *Tom o'Bedlam's Song.*"

Perhaps. At any rate, it is a lovely poem, this anonymous English ballad which dates from about Shakespeare's time. Into the madness of the poem comes snatches and echoes of street cries, yet the whole is more than just a patchwork or nonsense-poem. We sense a shaping hand in the mounting level of fantasy, and, in the last mighty stanza, at least, it is a hand of greatness and genius and power . . .

⇜§ ⇝

From the hag, and hungry goblin
   That into rags would rend ye,
And the spirit that stands by the naked man
   In the book of moons, defend ye,
That of your five sound senses
   You never be forsaken,
Nor wander from yourselves with Tom,
   Abroad to beg your bacon.

Of thirty bare years have I
   Twice twenty been enragèd,
And of forty been three times fifteen
   In durance soundly cagèd
On the lordly lofts of Bedlam,
   With stubble soft and dainty,
Brave bracelets strong, sweet whips, ding-dong,
   With wholesome hunger plenty.

With a thought I took for Maudlin,
    And a cruse of cockle pottage,
With a thing thus tall, sky bless you all,
    I befell into this dotage.
I slept not since the Conquest,
    Till then I never wakèd,
Till the roguish boy of love where I lay
    Me found and stripped me naked.

When I short have shorn my sour-face,
    And swigged my horny barrel,
In an oaken inn I pound my skin,
    As a suit of gilt apparel.
The moon's my constant mistress,
    And the lovely owl my morrow,
The flaming drake and the night-crow make
    Me music to my sorrow.

The palsy plagues my pulses,
    When I prig your pigs or pullen,
Your culvers take, or matchless make
    Your chanticleer or sullen.
When I want provent, with Humphry
    I sup, and when benighted,
I repose in Powles* with waking souls,
    Yet never am affrighted.

I know more than Apollo,
    For oft when he lies sleeping,
I see the stars at bloody wars
    In the wounded welkin weeping,
The moon embrace her shepherd,
    And the queen of love her warrior,
While the first doth horn the star of morn,
    And the next the heavenly Farrier.

The gypsy Snap and Pedro
    Are none of Tom's comradoes.
The punk I scorn, and the cutpurse sworn,

---

* *Powles:* probably the churchyard of St. Paul's where homeless beggars were sometimes permitted to shelter from bad weather.

And the roaring boys' bravadoes.
The meek, the white, the gentle,
  Me handle, touch, and spare not;
But those that cross Tom Rhinoceros
  Do what the panther dare not.

With a host of furious fancies
  Whereof I am commander,
With a burning spear and a horse of air
  To the wilderness I wander.
By a knight of ghosts and shadows
  I summoned am to tourney
Ten leagues beyond the wide world's end,
  Methinks it is no journey!

# The Last Giant Of The Elder Age

## from The Kiev Cycle

### Translated by Isabel Florence Hapgood

JUST AS a glorious heroic literature gathered about King Arthur of Britain and his Knights of the Round Table, and about the Emperor Charlemagne of France and his Twelve Peers, so did a splendid cycle of legends come to cluster about the kingly figure of Prince Vladimir of Kiev and the mighty Bogatyrs of his *druzhina,* or personal bodyguard of heroic warriors.

Historians have traced, behind the glittering and fabulous figures of Arthur and Charlemagne, genuine historical personages: so, too, with Vladimir. He was the last of the purely Scandinavian princes of Kiev, and Russian historians venerate him as the father of the Russian Empire. A baptismal date of 988 A.D. has been recorded for him.

The mythological history of his reign is called *The*

*Kiev Cycle*. It is made up of a great body of heroic lays called *byliny* (in the plural; the singular form is *bylina*, and the word is believed derived from *byl* which may be translated as "that which has been," or elder lore).

The *byliny* of ancient Russia are a precious legacy of heroic materials. These anonymous lays were sung or chanted by the old Russian bards, who were often completely illiterate; hence, they existed completely apart from any connection with written literature. A pure oral tradition uncontaminated by "Court epics" is rare and priceless, and Russia's store of *byliny* and the bards that sung them was believed long extinct as a living form until Rybnikov discovered them still flourishing about the remote and inaccessible shores of Lake Onega in the middle of the 19th Century. The news of his incredible discovery created a sensation comparable to that which greeted James Macpherson when he reported the discovery of his Ossianic literature. And, for a time, it met with much the same scepticism that Macpherson eventually faced; luckily, other Russian folklorists penetrated into the same country and found the same traditional bards chanting the same ancient heroic songs, and Rybnikov was triumphantly vindicated.

Folklorists found the *byliny* still being sung by wandering bards to an audience of peasants whenever the countryfolk gathered together—at wayside inns or around campfires; sometimes the bard would be invited into the *izba* or hut of a prominent local. There he would sing all night to a hut crowded with eager listeners who sat on wooden benches, on the bedstead, the table, or wherever they could find room, hungry to hear again the wonderful tales of their beloved Ilya Murometz, "the Old Cossack," and of his heroic brethren of great Kiev in the days of its glory.

Among the great number of *byliny* now recorded, several distinct Cycles may be distinguished. Among the earliest of these—and certainly the largest and most popular—is *The Kiev Cycle*, which concerns the adventures of the heroes of the Court of Kiev under Vladimir I. The bardic historians of his reign have partially confused him with another Russian prince of the same name, Vladimir

Monomakh, who died in 1126; but he is still far more distinct and discernible than is the historical Arthur long since hidden behind the chivalrous Lord of Logres.

Just as with Arthur and Charlemagne, Vladimir himself has few adventures: he is the center of the Cycle, and around him the Bogatyrs and their adventures revolve, as planets circling a sun. (Curiously *apropos* to this metaphor, the bardic chroniclers of the reign of Prince Vladimir habitually call him *Solnyshko*, a sort of Homeric epithet which means "Little Sun.")

According to the mythos of *The Kiev Cycle*, his reign was transitional: before him lay the dim, mysterious Elder Age of the giant heroes; and after him came the age of the merely human warriors, of whom the most famous was the immortal Ilya of Murom, one of the most beloved heroes of Russian folklore.

I had wanted a tale of Ilya Murometz for this collection, but all I could seem to find were fairy-tale versions of his epic adventures, watered down and retold for children's books. Hence I am much indebted to a young lady named Dena Benatan of Pittsburgh, who had read my book *Tolkien: A Look Behind "The Lord of the Rings."* Learning that I was in the throes of putting together this anthology, and wanted a tale of Ilya of Murom to include, she called my attention to an early English prose version of the *byliny*—Hapgood's *Epic Songs of Russia* (1886). I have since found versions more scholarly and far closer to the original, but the Hapgood translation has a verve and flavor to it that more recent versions (such as *Heroic Russian Poetry* by N. Kershaw Chadwick [1964], a line-for-line translation) unfortunately lack.

\*

In the legend that follows, we see the coming of the first of the human heroes and the death of the last of the giant heroes of the Elder Age. Svyatogor was the last of the Elder Heroes, that is, of the pre-historic, purely mythical giants of the cycle preceding the Vladimirian Age. In this tale we see the Elder Giants making way for the younger Bogatyrs much in the same way the Titans did for the Olympians in Greek mythology, or the Jotuns for the Aesir in the Norse myths. There is a certain melancholy that haunts this ancient song and renders its rude music poignant; and we cannot help being moved by the friendship between the human warrior, Ilya, and the last of the ancient giants.

Svyatogor himself is purely mythical, but Ilya of Murom is now considered historical. At least his legend is very ancient: his antiquity is proven by the fact that he is mentioned quite clearly in the Norse *Thidreks Saga* written down in the 13th Century from earlier songs.

A few notes to explain some of the unfamiliar terms used in my version. A "Bogatyr" is more than just a knight or a warrior, the words usually used to translate the untranslatable Russian term. The Bogatyrs were *heroes* in the most sublime sense of the word: warriors of terrific strength, superhuman endurance and courage, like Samson or Herakles or Gilgamesh or Achilles. The term was originally used in reference to the giant warriors of the Elder Age—warriors (in Chadwick's fine phrase) "so richly endowed with superhuman qualities as to be more supernatural than human." The Elder *Bogatyri* are sometimes thought to represent the debris of ancient Slavonic, sometimes even of "primitive" Aryan, mythology. But the term was carried over as a superlative with which to label the human heroes of the Vladimirian Age, wherein Russia was born.

And, incidentally, "Russia" at this period meant, most probably, little more than the valley of the Dnieper.

Hapgood has combined two *byliny* in her version. The first half of her tale incorporates the *bylina* which Chadwick translates under the title of "The Healing of Ilya of Murom"; the second half of her tale comprises the song Chadwick titles "Svyatogor." While the Hapgood version, merging two separate *byliny* into one tale, is thus in error, the two *byliny* fit well together and are, after all, in chronological sequence: hence I have retained her ordering of the text, except that I have indicated the division with a numeral.

And since neither title should be used in regards to the

two *byliny* in this combined form, I have taken the liberty of calling this version by a title of my own . . .

※

In the hamlet of Karacharof, by Murom town, dwelt Ilya the Old Kazák. Thirty years he sat upon a chair, having no use of neither arms nor legs, because of his grandfather's sin.

And when thirty years were past, in summer, at the time of haying, his father and mother went forth to clear the forest-girdled meadows, and left Ilya alone in the cottage. Then there came to him three Kaleki, three wandering holy brethren, and they rapped at his windowsill with their shepherds' crooks, and besought him that he would give them to drink.

"Alas! ye wayfarers, aged men, dear friends!" said Ilya, "fully gladly would I give you to drink: but I cannot rise, and there is none in the cottage with me."

And the men made answer: "Arise, and wash thyself; so shalt thou walk and fetch us drink."

Then he arose and walked; and having filled a cup with kvas, brought it to the aged men. They received it, drank, and gave it again to Ilya, saying:

"Drink now after us, Ilya, son of Ivan." When he had drunk, the old men said: "How is thy strength now, Ilya?"

Ilya answered: "I thank you humbly, ye aged men. I feel a very great strength within me, so that I could even move the earth."

Then the men looked each upon the other, and said: "Give us to drink yet again." And Ilya did so. And when they had drunk, they gave the cup to him the second time, and inquired: "How is it with thee now, Ilya?"

"The strength I feel is very great," said Ilya, "yet but as half the former strength."

"Thus let it be," spoke the men: "for if we give thee

more, mother earth will not bear thee up." And they said: "Go forth now, Ilya."

So Ilya set his cup upon the table, and went forth into the street with all ease; and the aged men said:

"God hath blessed thee, Ilya, with this strength of His. Therefore, defend thou the Christian faith, fight against all infidel hosts, bold warriors and daring heroes, for it is written that death shall not come to thee in battle. Stronger than thee there is none in the white world, save only Volgá, (and he will take thee not by might but by craft), and Svyatogor, and, stronger yet, beloved of damp mother earth, Mikula Selyaninovich, the Villager's Son. Against these three contend thou not. Live not at home,—labour not; but go thou to royal Kiev town." And therewith the men vanished.

Then Ilya went forth to his father, in the clearing, and found him with his wife and labourers reposing from their toil. He grasped their axes and began to hew; and what his father with the labourers could not have done in three days, that Ilya achieved in the space of one hour. Having thus felled a whole field of timber, he drove the axes deep into a stump, whence no man could draw them.

When his father with wife and labourers woke, and beheld the axes, they marvelled, saying: "Who hath done this?" Then came Ilya from the forest, and drew the axes from the stump; and his father gave thanks to God that his son should be so famous a workman.

But Ilya strode far over the open plain; and as he went, he beheld a peasant leading a shaggy brown foal, the first he had seen. What the peasant demanded for the foal, that Ilya paid. For the space of three months, he tied the foal in the stall, feeding it with the finest white Turkish wheat, and watering it from the pure spring. After these months were past, he bound the foal for three nights in the garden, anointing it with three dews. When that was done, he led the foal to the lofty paling, and the good brown began to leap from side to side, and was able to sustain Ilya's vast weight; for he had become a heroic steed. All this Ilya did according to the commands of the aged psalm-singers who had healed him.

Then Ilya saddled his good steed Cloudfall, prostrated himself, and received the farewell blessing of father and mother, and rode forth far over the open plain.

## 2

As he rode, he came to a pavilion of white linen, pitched under a damp oak; and therein was a heroic bed, not small, for the length of the bed was ten fathoms, and the breadth six fathoms. So he bound his good steed to the damp oak, stretched himself upon that heroic bed and fell asleep. And his heroic slumber was very deep; three days and nights he slept. On the third day, good Cloudfall heard a mighty clamour toward the North. Damp mother earth rocked, the dark forests staggered, the rivers overflowed their steep banks. Then the good steed beat upon the earth with his hoof, but could not wake Ilya, and he shouted with human voice:

"Ho there, Ilya of Murom! Thou sleepest there and takest thine ease, and knowest not the ill fortune that hangeth over thee. Here Svyatogor cometh to this his pavilion. Loose me now, in the open plain, and climb thou upon the damp oak."

Then sprang Ilya to his nimble feet, loosed his horse and climbed into the damp oak.

And lo! a hero approached; taller than the standing woods was he, and his head rested upon the flying clouds. Upon his shoulder he bare a casket of crystal, which, when he was come to the oak, he set upon the ground and opened with a golden key. Out of it stepped his heroic wife; in all the white world, no such beauty was ever seen or heard of; lofty was her stature and dainty her walk; her eyes were as those of the clear falcon, her brows of blackest sable, and her white body was beyond compare.

When she was come forth from the crystal casket, she placed a table, laid a fair cloth thereon and set sugar viands; and from the casket, she also drew forty mead for drink. So they feasted and made merry. And when Svyatogor had well eaten, he went into the pavilion and fell asleep.

But his fair heroic wife roamed about the open plain, and so walking, espied Ilya upon the damp oak.

"Come down now, thou good and stately youth," she cried: "descend from that damp oak, else will I waken Hero Svyatogor and make great complaint of thy discourtesy to me."

Ilya could not contend against the woman, and so slipped down from the oak as she had commanded.

And after a space, that fair heroic woman took Ilya and put him in her husband's deep pocket; and roused the hero from his heavy sleep. Then Svyatogor put his wife in the crystal casket again, locked it with his golden key, mounted his good steed, and rode his way to the Holy Mountains.

After a little, his good steed began to stumble, and the hero to beat him upon his stout flanks with a silken whip. Then said the horse in human speech:

"Hitherto I have borne the hero and his heroic wife; but now I bear the heroic woman and two heroes. Is it a marvel that I stumble?"

Thereupon Hero Svyatogor drew Ilya from his deep pocket, and began to question him:—who he was and how he came in the pocket. And Ilya told him all the truth. When he heard it, Svyatogor slew his faithless heroic wife; but with Ilya he exchanged crosses, and called him his younger brother.

And as they talked together, Ilya said: "Full gladly would I see Svyatogor that great hero; but he rideth not now upon damp mother earth, nor appeareth among our company of heroes."

"I am he," quoth Svyatogor. "Gladly would I ride among you, but damp mother earth would not bear me up. And furthermore, I may not ride in Holy Russia, but only on the lofty hills, and steep precipices. Let us now ride among the crags, and come thou to the Holy Mountains with me."

Thus they rode long together, diverting themselves; and Svyatogor taught Ilya all heroic customs and traditions.

On the way, Svyatogor said to Ilya: "When we shall come to my dwelling, and I shall lead thee to my father, heat a bit of iron, but give him not thy hand."

So when they were come to the Holy Mountains, to the palace of white stone, Syvatogor's aged father cried:

"Aï, my dear child! Hast thou been far afield?"

"I have been in Holy Russia, father."

"What hast thou seen and heard there?"

"Nothing have I seen or heard in Holy Russia, but I have brought with me thence a hero." The old man was blind, and so said:

"Bring hither the Russian hero, that I may greet him."

In the meanwhile, Ilya had heated the bit of iron, and when he came to give the old man his hand in greeting, he gave him, in place of it, the iron. And when the old man grasped it in his mighty hands, he said: "Stout are thy hands, Ilya! A most mighty warrior art thou!"

Thereafter, as Svyatogor and his younger brother Ilya journeyed among the Holy Mountains, they found a great coffin in the way; and upon the coffin was this writing: "This coffin shall fit him who is destined to lie in it."

Then Ilya essayed to lie in it, but for him it was both too long and too wide. But when Svyatogor lay in it, it fitted him. Then the hero spoke these words:

"The coffin was destined for me; take the lid now, Ilya, and cover me." Ilya made answer: "I will not take the lid, elder brother, neither will I cover thee. Lo! This is no small jest that thou makest, preparing to entomb thyself."

Then the hero himself took the lid, and covered his coffin with it. But when he would have raised it again, he could not, though he strove and strained mightily; and he spoke to Ilya: "Aï, younger brother! 'Tis plain my fate hath sought me out. I cannot raise the lid; do thou try now to lift it."

Then Ilya strove, but could not. Said Hero Svyatogor:

"Take my great battle sword, and smite athwart the lid."
But Ilya's strength was not enough to lift the sword, and Svyatogor called him:

"Bend down to the rift in the coffin, that I may breathe upon thee with my heroic breath." When Ilya had done this, he felt strength within him, thrice as much as before, lifted the great battle sword, and smote athwart the lid. Sparks flashed from that blow, but where the great brand struck, an iron ridge sprang forth. Again spoke Svyatogor:

"I stifle, younger brother! essay yet one more blow upon the lid, with my huge sword."

Then Ilya smote along the lid, and a ridge of iron sprang forth. Yet again spoke Svyatogor:

"I die, oh, younger brother! Bend down now to the crevice. Yet once again will I breathe upon thee, and give thee all my vast strength."

But Ilya made answer: "My strength sufficeth me, elder brother; had I more, the earth could not bear me."

"Thou has done well, younger brother," said Svyatogor, "in that thou hast not obeyed my last behest. I should have breathed upon thee the breath of death, and thou wouldst have lain dead beside me. But now, farewell. Possess thou my great battle sword, but bind my good heroic steed to my coffin; none save Svyatogor may possess that horse."

Then a dying breath fluttered through the crevice. Ilya took leave of Hero Svyatogor, bound the good heroic steed to the coffin, girt the great battle sword about his waist, and rode forth into the open plain for great Kiev of the Heroes.

And Svyatogor's burning tears flow through the coffin evermore.

Thus passed the last of the giant heroes. And thus a new age began for Holy Russia.

# The Lost Words Of Power

## *from* The Kalevala

## Translated by John Martin Crawford

THE great national epic of Finland, *The Kalevala*, is one of the most remarkable oddities in all literature—a made-to-order masterpiece.

You see, one of the many theories scholars have worked up to account for the immortal *Odyssey* of Homer is that "Homer" did not write it; there were, say a few, merely a haphazard number of heroic poems written about various episodes in the life of Odysseus, which some later anthologist strung together into a connected narrative.

This would sound far sillier than it does, if a distinguished Finnish philologist named Elias Lönnrot (1802–84) had not proved the theory at least possible by duplicating the feat of this hypothetical anthologist. Lönnrot began collecting backwoods folk-ballads as early as 1827, and before long he noticed that these ballads could, with a little bridging and trimming, be fitted together into a narrative sequence. He did just that, and published the complete text of *The Kalevala* in 1849.

## THE LOST WORDS OF POWER

This extraordinary epic became a national treasure almost overnight. Before long, it was hailed as a work of superlative genius and is now a world-famous classic. Part of its unique charm lies in the freshness and originality of its materials, for the Finnish national mythology was very little known outside of Finland until *The Kalevala* burst on the world's consciousness. And then there is the limpid, hypnotic music of *The Kalevala*'s lilting rhythms (the meter is called trochaic tetrameter, and Longfellow was so enchanted with it that he borrowed it for the metrics of his "American epic," the *Song of Hiawatha*, which was published in 1855, only six years after the complete text of Lönnrot's do-it-yourself masterwork).

But above all there is the story. The mighty legends of the warrior heroes of Kalevala, the Land of Heroes, form a titanic fantasy saga of war and quest and unearthly magic. Through the fifty *runos*, or cantos, we watch the Universe created by the divine Ilmatar, and follow the interwoven adventure of a magnificent cast of heroes, villains, magicians and evil beings, such as the young handsome prince of warriors, Lemminkainen, the great Wainamoinen the Warrior Wizard, wise Ilmarinen the Wondersmith who created the enchanted Sampo, the sly old Witch of Pohyola the Shadowy Land, and Kullervo the doomed wanderer in strange places.

In the beginning of the story, the hero Wainamoinen has fallen in love with the Maid of Pohyola. Her mother, the cunning old Witch, demands he perform certain mighty tasks. One of these is to construct an enchanted ship without using his hands or touching it in any way. Wainamoinen, who is a wizard as well as a warrior, almost completes this task, but finds he lacks knowledge of three key Words of Power. Lacking these he cannot finish the magic craft. His quest for the lost Words takes him long and far; he travels through curious and unearthly realms, even the Kingdom of Death, but he cannot find the magic he seeks. At last he hears of the giant sorcerer Wipunen who has slept in a state of half-life, half-death for ages, and who was once master of the Lost Words of Power . . .

Wainamoinen, old and truthful,
Did not learn the words of magic
In Tuoni's gloomy regions,
In the kingdom of Manala.
Thereupon he long debated,
Well considered, long reflected,
Where to find the magic sayings.

Then a shepherd came to meet him
Speaking thus to Wainamoinen:
"Thou canst find of words a hundred,
Find a thousand wisdom-sayings,
In the mouth of wise Wipunen,
In the body of the hero;
To the spot I know the footpath,
To his tomb the magic highway,
Trodden by a host of heroes.
Long the distance thou must travel,
On the sharpened points of needles;
Then a long way thou must journey
On the edges of the broadswords;
Thirdly thou must travel farther
On the edges of the hatchets."

Wainamoinen, old and trustful,
First considered all these journeys,
Traveled then to forge and smithy,
And addressed the metal-worker:

"Ilmarinen, worthy blacksmith,
Make a shoe for me of iron,
Forge me gloves of burnished copper,
Mold a staff of strongest metal,
Lay the steel upon the inside,
Forge within the might of magic.
I am going on a journey

To procure the magic sayings,
Find the lost-words of the Master,
From the mouth of the magician,
From the tongue of wise Wipunen."

Spake the artist, Ilmarinen:
"Long ago died wise Wipunen.
He is gone these many ages,
Lays no more his snares of copper,
Sets no longer traps of iron.
None can learn from him the wisdom,
None can find in him the lost-words."

Wainamoinen, old and hopeful,
Little heeding, not discouraged,
In his metal shoes and armor,
Hastened forward on his journey:
Ran the first day fleetly onward,
On the sharpened points of needles;
Sleepily he strode the second
On the edges of the broadswords;
Swung himself the third day forward
On the edges of the hatchets.

Then Wipunen, wisdom-singer,
Ancient bard and great magician,
With his magic songs lay yonder.
Stretched beside him, lay his sayings;
On his shoulder grew a birch tree;
On his mighty chin an alder;
From his beard grew willow-bushes;
From his mouth a dark green fir-tree,
And an oak tree from his forehead.

Wainamoinen, coming closer,
Drew his sword, lay bare his hatchet
From his magic leathern scabbard.
Fell'd he aspen from the shoulder;
Fell'd the birch-trees from the temples;
From the chin he fell'd the alder,
From the beard, the branching willows,
From the mouth the dark-green fir tree;

Fell'd the oak tree from the forehead.
Next he thrust his staff of iron
Through the mouth of wise Wipunen,
Pried the mighty jaws asunder,
Spoke these words of master-magic:
"Rise, thou master of magicians,
From the sleep of Tuonela,
From thine everlasting slumber!"

Wise Wipunen, ancient singer,
Quickly waking from his sleeping,
Keenly felt the pangs of torture,
From the cruel staff of iron;
Bit with mighty force the metal,
Bit in twain the softer iron;
But when steel flew not asunder,
Open'd wide his mouth in anguish.

Wainamoinen of Wainola,
In his iron shoes and armor,
Careless walking, headlong stumbled,
Fell into the mouth thus opened
Of the Magic Bard, Wipunen.
Wise Wipunen, full of song-charms,
Closed his open mouth and swallowed
Wainamoinen and his magic,
Shoes and staff, and iron armor.
Then, outspoke the wise Wipunen:
"Many things before I've eaten,
Dined on goat, and sheep and reindeer,
Bear, and ox, and wolf, and wild-boar,
But in all my recollection
This must be the sweetest morsel!"

Wainamoinen soon decided
How to live and how to prosper,
How to conquer this condition.
In his belt he wore a poniard,
With a handle hewn from birch-wood,
And this handle soon through magic
Was a boat of large proportions.

In this vessel rowed he swiftly
Through the entrails of the hero,
Rowed through every gland and vessel
Of the wisest of magicians.
But Wipunen, master-singer,
Barely felt the hero's presence,
Gave no heed to Wainamoinen.

Then the artist of Wainola
Straightway set himself to forging,
Set at work to hammer metals.
Of his armor made he smithy,
Of his sleeves contrived the bellows;
Made the air-valve from his fur-coat;
From his stockings, made the muzzle;
Used his knees for sturdy anvil;
Made a hammer of his fore-arm.
Like the storm-wind roared the bellows,
Like the thunder rang the anvil.
For one day, and then a second,
And a third the forging pounded
In the body of Wipunen,
In the sorcerer's abdomen.

Then at last the Old Wipunen,
Spoke these words in wonder, guessing:
"Who art thou of ancient heroes,
Who of all the host of heroes?
Although many I have eaten,
And of men a countless number,
Never was there such as thou art.
Smoke arises from my nostrils,
From my mouth the fire is streaming,
In my throat are iron-clinkers.

"Go, thou monster, hence to wander.
Flee this place thou plague of Northland,
Ere I go to seek thy mother,
Tell the ancient dame thy mischief;
She shall bear thine evil conduct,
Great the burden she shall carry;
Great a mother's pain and anguish,

When her child runs wild and lawless.
    "Why thou camest here, O monster,
Camest here to give me torture?
Art thou Hisi sent from heaven,
Some calamity from Ukko?
Art, perchance, some new creation,
Ordered here to do me evil?
If thou art some evil genius,
Some calamity from Ukko,
Sent to me by my creator,
Then am I resigned to suffer;
God does not forsake the worthy,
Does not ruin those that trust him,
Never are the good forsaken.
    "If by man thou wert created,
If some hero sent thee hither,
I shall learn thy race of evil,
Shall destroy thy wicked tribe-folk.
If some scourge the winds have sent me,
Sent me on the air of spring-tide,
Brought me by the frosts of winter,
Quickly journey whence thou camest,
On the air-path of the heavens,
Perching not upon some aspen,
Resting not upon the birch-tree;
Fly away to copper mountains,
That the copper-winds may nurse thee,
Waves of ether, thy protection.
    "Didst thou come from high Junala,
From the hems of ragged snow-clouds,
Quick ascend beyond the cloud-space,
Quickly journey whence thou camest,
To the snow-clouds, crystal-sprinkled,
To the twinkling stars of heaven;
There thy fire may burn forever;
There may flash thy forked lightnings,
In the Sun's undying furnace.
    "Wert thou sent here by the spring-floods,
Driven here by river-torrents?
Quickly journey whence thou camest,

Quickly hasten to the waters,
To the borders of the rivers,
To the ancient water-mountain,
That the floods again may rock thee,
And thy water-mother nurse thee.

"Didst thou come from Kalma's kingdom,
From the castles of the death-land?
Haste thou back to thine own country,
To the Kalma-halls and castles,
To the fields with envy swollen,
Where contending armies perish.

"Art thou from the Hisi-woodlands,
From ravines in Lempo's forest,
From the thickets of the pine-wood,
From the dwellings of the fir-glen?
Quick retrace thine evil footsteps
To the dwellings of thy master,
To the thickets of thine kindred;
There thou mayest dwell in pleasure,
Till thy house decays about thee,
Till thy walls shall mould and crumble.

"Evil genius thee I banish,
Get thee hence, thou horrid monster,
To the caverns of the white-bear,
To the deep abysm of serpents,
To the vales, and swamps, and fenlands,
To the ever-silent waters,
To the hot-springs of the mountains,
To the dead-seas of the Northland,
To the lifeless lakes and rivers,
To the sacred stream and whirlpool.

"Should thou ask for steeds for saddle,
Shouldst thou need a fleet-foot courser,
I will give thee worthy racers,
I will give thee saddle-horses;
Evil Hisi has a charger,
Crimson mane, and tail, and foretop,
Fire emitting from his nostrils,
As he prances through his pastures;
His hoofs that are of strongest iron

And his legs of steel and copper,
Quickly scale the highest mountains,
Dart like lightning through the valleys,
When a skillful master rides him.

  "Should this steed be insufficient,
I will give thee Lempo's snow-shoes,
Give thee Hisi's shoes of elm-wood,
Give to thee the staff of Piru,
That with these thou mayest journey
Into Hisi's courts and castles,
To the woods and fields of Juntas.

  "Hasten hence, thou thing of evil,
Heinous monster, leave my body
Ere the breaking of the morning,
Ere the Sun awakes from slumber;
Haste away thou plague of Northland,
Haste along the track of moonbeams,
Wander hence, forever wander,
To the darksome fields of Pohya.

  "If at once thou dost not leave me,
I will send the eagle's talons,
Send to thee the beaks of vultures,
To devour thine evil body,
Hurl thy skeleton to Hisi.
Much more quickly cruel Lempo
Left my vitals when commanded,
When I called the aid of Ukko,
Called the help of my creator.
Flee, thou motherless offendant,
Flee, thou fiend of Sariola,
Flee, thou hound without a master,
Ere the morning sun arises,
Ere the Moon withdraws to slumber!"

Wainamoinen, ancient hero,
Spoke at last to old Wipunen;
  "Satisfied am I to linger
In these old and spacious caverns.
Pleasant here my home and dwelling;
For my meat I have thy tissues,

## THE LOST WORDS OF POWER

Have thy heart, and spleen, and liver;
For my drink, the blood of ages.
Goodly home for Wainamoinen.
  "I shall set my forge and bellows
Deeper, deeper in thy vitals;
I shall swing my heavy hammer,
Swing it with a greater power
On thy heart, and lungs, and liver.
I shall never, never leave thee
Till I learn thine incantations,
Learn thy many wisdom-sayings,
Learn the lost-words of the Master.
Never must these words be hidden;
Earth must never lose this wisdom,
Though the wisdom-singers perish."

Old Wipunen, wise magician,
Ancient prophet, filled with power,
Opened then his store of knowledge,
Lifted covers from his cases
Filled with old-time incantations,
Filled with songs of time primeval,
Filled with ancient wit and wisdom.
Sang he then the oldest folk-songs,
Sang of origin of witchcraft,
Sang of earth and its beginnings,
Sang the first of all creations,
Sang the source of good and evil,
Sung alas! by youth no longer.
Sang he orders of enchantment,
How, upon the will of Ukko,
By command of the Creator,
How the air was first divided,
How the water came from ether,
How the earth arose from water,
How from earth came vegetation,
Fish and fowl, and man, and hero.
  Sang again the wise Wipunen,
How the Moon was first created,
How the sun was set in heaven,

Whence were made the rainbow's colors
Whence the ether's crystal pillars,
How the skies with stars were sprinkled.

   Then again sang wise Wipunen,
Sang in miracles of concord,
Sang in magic tones of wisdom.
Never was there heard such singing:
Songs he sang in countless numbers.
Sang he one day, then a second,
Sang a third from dawn till evening,
Sang from evening till the morning.
Listening were the stars of heaven,
And the Moon stood still to listen;
Stop'd the waves upon the sea-deep,
In the bay the tides stopped rising,
Stop'd the rivers in their courses,
Stop'd the waterfall of Rutya,
Even Jordan ceased its flowing
And Wuoksen stopped and listened.

When the ancient Wainamoinen
Well had learned the magic sayings,
Learned the ancient songs and legends,
Learned the words of ancient wisdom,
Learned the lost-words of the Master,
He prepared to leave the body
Of the wisdom-bard, Wipunen;
And he spoke to the enchanter,
"O thou Antero Wipunen,
Open wide thy mouth and wider,
I have found the magic lost-words,
I will leave thee now forever,
Leave thee and thy wondrous singing,
Will return to Kalevala
To Wainola's fields and firesides."

Then Wipunen spake in answer:
"Many are the things I've eaten,
Eaten bear, and elk and reindeer,
Eaten ox, and wolf, and wild-boar,
Eaten man and eaten hero;

But, O never have I eaten
Such a thing as Wainamoinen.
Thou hast found what thou desirest,
Found the three words of the Master;
Go in peace, and ne'er returning,
Take my blessing on thy going."

Thereupon the bard Wipunen
Open'd wide his mouth, and wider,
And the good, old Wainamoinen
Straightway left the wise enchanter,
Left Wipunen's great abdomen.
From the mouth he made his journey
O'er the hills and vales of Northland,
Swift as red-deer of the forest,
Swift as yellow-breasted marten,
To the fires of Wainola,
To the plains of Kalevala
Straightway went he to the smithy
Of his brother, Ilmarinen.

There the iron-artist asked him,
"Hast thou found the long-lost wisdom,
Hast thou heard the secret doctrine,
Has thou learned the master magic,
How to fasten in the ledges,
How the stern should be completed,
How to make the ship's forecastle?"

Wainamoinen thus made answer;
"I have learned of words a hundred,
Learned a thousand incantations,
Hidden deep for many ages;
Learned the words of ancient wisdom,
Found the keys of secret doctrine,
Found the lost-words of the Master."

Wainamoinen, magic-builder,
Straightway journeyed to his vessel,
To the spot of magic labor.
Quickly fastened he the ledges,

Firmly bound the stern together
And completed the forecastle.
Thus the ancient Wainamoinen
Built the boat with magic only,
And with magic launched his vessel,
Using not the hand to touch it,
Using not the foot to move it,
Using not the knee to turn it,
Using nothing to propel it.

Thus the third task was completed,
For the hostess of Pohyola,
Dowry for the Maid of Beauty
Sitting on the arch of heaven,
On the bow of many colors . . .

# Wonderful Things Beyond Cathay

## from The Voyages and Travels of Sir John de Mandeville.

### Edited by Arthur Layard

I FEEL SURE that in some literary Valhalla, perhaps the famous Fiddler's Green itself, where all old sailors go, there is a long low inn by the shore, with spiced hams and strings of onions and peppers dangling from smoke-blackened rafters, and a great fire roaring on a stone grate, and mugs of foaming beer and hot spiced ale and old black bottles of wine in inexhaustible plenty.

There, on cold stormy nights, when the winds howl about the eaves and gusts of icy spray shake the heavy door, a number of old gentlemen sit about the grate, warm and safe and cozy, toasting their toes and swapping yarns and emptying innumerable tankards. In this pleasurable way they pass eternity; nor can I think of a better way.

One of them, tall and bony, with a great proud nose, a white powdered peruke, and a splendid crimson coat with brass buttons, an ivory spyglass stuck in one capacious pocket, is a certain Baron Munchausen.

Next to him, in gorgeous Eastern silks and a glorious tarboosh, is a garrulous Musselman not unknown to the librarians, a certain Sailor who set forth from the port city of Bassorah for seven voyages into literary immortality.

And a third, snug and warm in a huge chair, is a fat, jolly, bewhiskered old English knight from St. Albans, Sir John de Mandeville by name, and he, too, goes not unremembered among the lovers of good books.

There they sit forever, the three old travellers, swapping yarns of Tartary, and Amazonia, the Valley of Diamonds and the Land of Darkness; trading reminiscences of Prester John and the Grand Cham of Cathay, while the fire roars on the grate and the storm whoops and howls beyond the windows; there they sit forever, their voyages done, come to a safe anchorage and a snug harbor at last.

*

Sir John, as he tells us, set out from the town of St. Albans in England on Michaelmas Day of the year 1322 and voyaged to the Domains of the Grand Turk, from thence through Ermony the Less and Ermony the Great, visiting Persia, Araby, Libya, Tartary, Syria, Chaldea, Amazonia, Ethiopia, Golden Ind and Far Cathay.

Returning from his travels, he paused a while in the city of Liège to dictate his memoirs to a local physician. We have a delightful portrait of him in his study at this time, grown somewhat stout, gouty and rheumatic, seated in his great chair dictating to his amanuensis. Once his literary labors were finished, we lose sight of him. But I have no doubt the wonderful old scoundrel set sail once more for one last voyage.

The *Boke of the Voiages and Travailes of Sir John de Mandeville, Kt.*, which that worthy and indefatigable old gentleman set down at the city of Liège in the year of Our Lord 1355, became one of the glories of our language (for all that it was first written in French). It was first published sometime between 1357 and 1371, and it became one of the most beloved and popular books of the 14th Century: a reputation it has continued to enjoy, with only slight diminishment, ever since. Over three hundred manuscript versions are known. Editions exist in English, French, Italian, Spanish, German and Danish, to say nothing of more exotic tongues like Walloon, Dutch, Bohemian and even Irish (and I doubt not they know and love Sir John well in special editions in Tartary, Chaldea and the Country of the Amazons, too, although these translations have thus far escaped the attention of the bibliographers).

Not only did old Sir John write the most tremendously popular travel book of the Middle Ages (no book of *any* considerable age has been so often copied and printed, except perhaps for the Bible and *Tyll Eulenspiegel*), but he enjoys today the dignity and fame of being "the father of English prose" as well. And I trust my readers will join me in grandly ignoring the complaints of sourfaced and grumpish scholars that "no such person" ever existed and that his *Boke of Voiages and Travailes* is a hoax and a forgery. What do they know, the old frumps, who have never dared emerge from their dusty libraries to tread the heaving quarterdeck and raise sail for Golden Ind, and Far Cathay, and the Islands of Prester John?

⊷§ ⁊⊷

This land of Cathay is in Asia the Deep; and after, on this Side, is Asia the More. The Kingdom of Cathay marcheth toward the West with the Kingdom of Thurse, of the which was one of the Kings that came to give Presents to our Lord in Bethlehem.

In Thurse they eat no Flesh, neither drink they any Wine. The Folk of that Country be hardy Warriors, nonetheless.

## Ethille, the River of Coldness

And on this Side is the Kingdom of Comania, wherefrom the Comanians that dwelled in Greece sometime were chased out. This is one of the greatest Kingdoms of the World, but it is not all inhabited. For at one of the Parts there is so great Cold that no Man may dwell there; and in another Part there is so great Heat that no Man may endure it, and also there be so many Flies that no Man may know on what Side he may turn him.

They lie in Tents; and they burn the Dung of Beasts for Default of Wood.

And through that Country runneth the River of Ethille that is one of the greatest Rivers of the World. And it freezeth so strongly every Year, that many times Men have fought upon the Ice with great Hosts, both Parties on Foot, and their Horses quitted for the Time, and what with those on Horse and on Foot, more than 200,000 Persons on each Side.

## The Mount Chotaz, That Is High

And between that River and the great Sea Ocean, that they call the Sea Maure, lie all these Realms. And toward the Head, beneath, in that Realm is the Mount Chotaz, that is the highest Mount of the World, and it is between the Sea Maure and the Sea Caspian. There is a full strait and dangerous Passage to go toward Ind. And therefore King Alexander made there a strong City to guard the Country, that no Man should pass without his Leave.

And the principal City of Comania is clept Sarak, that is on one of the 3 Ways to go into Ind. But by this Way, may not pass any great Multitude of People, but if it be in Winter. And that Passage Men call the Derbent. The tother Way is to go from the City of Turkestan by Persia, and by that Way be many Days' Journey by Desert. And the 3rd Way is that which cometh from Comania and then goes by the great Sea and by the Kingdom of Abchaz.

And ye shall understand that all these Kingdoms be all obeissant to the Grand Cham of Cathay. Wherefore his Power and his Lordship is full great and full mighty.

## The Marvellous Country of Darkness

After that Kingdom, that beginneth toward the East, at the great Mountain that is clept Abzor, is the Kingdom of

Abchaz. The King of Abchaz hath the more Strong country and he always vigorously defendeth his Country against all those that assail him so that no Man may make him in Subjection to any Man.

In that Kingdom of Abchaz is a great Marvel. For a Province of the Country that hath well in Circuit 3 Days' Journeys, that Men call Hanyson, is all covered with Darkness, without any Brightness or Light; so that no Man may see there, nor no Man dare enter into him. And, nevertheless, they of the Country say, that sometimes Men hear Voices of Folk, and Horses neighing, and Cocks crowing. And Men wit well that Men dwell there, but they know not what Men. And they say, that Darkness befell by Miracle of God. For a cursed Emperor of Persia, that was hight Saures, pursued all Christian Men to destroy them and to compel them to make Sacrifice to his Idols, and rode with a great Host, in all that ever he might, to confound the Christian Men, the which left their Goods and would have fled. And when they were in a Palin that was hight Megon, anon this cursed emperor met with them all his Host to have slain them and hewn them in Pieces. And anon the Christian Men kneeled to the Ground, and made their Prayers to God to succour them. And anon a Thick Cloud came and covered the Emperor and all his Host. And so they endure in that Manner that they must not go out any Side; and so shall they evermore abide in Darkness till the Day of Doom, by the Miracle of God.

Also ye shall understand that out of that Land of Darkness goeth out a great River that sheweth well that there be Folk dwelling there by many ready Tokens; but no Man dare enter into it.

## Some Other Lands Thereabout

And after, on this Side, is Turkey, that marcheth with Ermony the Great, and many Provinces, as Brique, Quesiton, Pytan and Gemethe. And in every one of these be good Cities. And also it hath, above toward Ind, the Kingdom of Chaldea, that stretcheth from the Mountains of Chaldea toward the East unto the City of Nineveh that sitteth upon Tigris.

In Chaldea it is a flat Country and few Hills and few Rivers. After is the Kingdom of Mesopotamy, that beginneth, toward the East, at the River Tigris, and it stretcheth toward the West unto a City that is clept Roianz; and in Length it goeth from the Mountains of Ermony unto the Desert of Ind the Less. This is a good Country and a flat. It hath but 2 Mountains in that Country, of the which one is called Symar and the other Lyson. And this Land marcheth with the Kingdom of Chaldea.

Now I have advised you of many Countries on this Side the Kingdom of Cathay, of the which many be obeissant to the Grand Cham.

## Of Gog and Magog Prison'd

Now shall I say to you, following, of Countries and Isles that be beyond the Countries that I have spoke of.

In that same Region be the Mountains of Caspian that Men call Uber in the Country. Between those Mountains the Jews of 10 lineages be enclosed, that Men call Gog and Magog, and they may not go out on any Side. There were enclosed 22 Kings with their People, that dwelled between the Mountains of Scythia. There King Alexander chased them between those Mountains and there he thought to enclose them through Work of his Men. But when he saw that he might not do it, nor bring it to an End, he prayed to the God of Nature that He would perform that he had begun. And albeit so, that he was a Paynim and not worthy to be heard, yet God of His Grace closed the Mountains together, so that they dwell there all fast locked and enclosed with high Mountains all about, save only on one Side, and on that Side is the Sea of Caspian.

Now Men may ask, Since that the Sea is on that one Side, wherefore go they not out on the Sea to that Side, to go whence it liketh them?

But to this Question, I shall answer; That Sea of Caspian goeth out by Land under the Mountains, and runneth by the Desert at one Side of the Country, and after it stretcheth unto the Ends of Persia, and although it be clept a Sea it is no Sea, nor toucheth it to any other Sea, but it is a Lake, the greatest of the World; and though they would put them on to that Sea, they wist never where they should arrive.

And they yield Tribute for that Land to the Queen of Amazonia, the which maketh them to be kept enclosed full dilligently, that they shall not go out on any Side but at the Cost of their Land.

## Of the Land of Serpents

And after, is there then a Land all Desert, where Men may find no Water, neither by Digging nor by any other Thing.

Wherefore Men may not dwell in that Place, so full is it of Dragons, Serpents and other venomous Beasts, that no man dare pass, but if it be in severe Winter. And that strait Passage Men, in that Country, call Clyron. And that is the Passage that the Queen of Amazonia maketh to be kept. And though it happen that some of them by Fortune go out, they know no Manner of Language but Hebrew, so that they cannot speak to the People.

## The Marvellous Land of Bacharia

From that Land go Men toward the Land of Bacharia, where be full evil Folk and full cruel. In that Land be Trees that bear Wool, as though it were of Sheep, whereof they make Clothes and all Things that may be made of Wool.

In that Country be many Hippotaynes that dwell sometime in the Water and sometime on the Land. And they be half Men and half Horse. And they eat Men when they may take them.

And there be Rivers of Waters that be full bitter, 3 times more than is the Water of the Sea.

In that Country be many Griffins, more Plenty than in any other Country. Some Men say that they have the

Body upward as an Eagle, and beneath as a Lion; and truly they say Truth, that they be of that Shape. But one Griffin hath the Body more great and is more strong than 8 Lions, of such Lions as be on this Side, and more great and stronger than an 100 Eagles such as we have amongst us. For one Griffin there will bear, flying to his Nest, a great Horse if he may find him at the Place, or 2 Oxen yoked together as they go to the Plough. For he hath Talons so long and so large and so great upon his Feet, as though they were Horns of great Oxen or of Buffaloes or of Kine, that Men make Cups of them to drink of. And of their Ribs and of the Feathers of their Wings, Men make Bows, full strong to shoot Arrows with.

That is all I know of Bacharia.

## Going Toward Ind the Greater

From thence go Men by many Days' Journey through the Land of Prester John, the great Emperor of Ind. And Men call his Realm the Isle of Pentexoire.

The best City that is in the Isle of Pentexoire is Nyse, that is a full Royal City and a noble, and full rich.

This Prester John hath under him many Kings and many Isles and many Divers Folks of Divers Conditions. And this Land is full good and rich, I ween, as any in the World, but not so rich as is the Realms of the Grand Cham. For the Merchants come not thither so commonly to buy Merchandises, for it is too far to travel to. And on that other Side, in the Isle of Cathay, Men find all manner of Thing that is need-ful to Man—Cloths of Gold, of Silk, and Spicery. And therefore, albeit that Men have greater Cheapness in the Isle of Prester John, nevertheless, Men dread the long Way, and the great Perils in the Sea in those Parts.

## Of Magnet Mountain

For in many Places of the Sea be great Rocks of Stones of the Adamant or Lode-stone that of his own Nature draweth Iron to him. And therefore pass there no Ships that have either Bonds or Nails of Iron within them. And if they do, anon the Rocks of the Adamants draw them, to them, that never they may go thence.

I have myself have seen afar off in that Sea as though it had been a great Isle full of Trees and Bush, full of Thorns and Briars, great Plenty. And the Shipmen told us, that all that was of Ships that were drawn thither by the Adamants, for the Iron that was in them. And from the Rotten-ness, and other Things that were within the Ships, grew such Bush, and Thorns, and Briars and green Grass, and such manner of Things, and from the Masts and the Sail-yards it seemed a great Wood or a Grove. And such Rocks be in many Places thereabout. And therefore dare not the Merchants pass there, but if they know well the Passages, or else that they have good Pilots.

## More of These Merchants

And the Merchants pass by the Kingdom of Persia, and go to a City that is clept Hermes, or Ormuz, for Hermes the Philosopher founded it. And after that they pass an Arm of the Sea, and then go to another City that is clept Golbache. And there be Popinjays or Parroquets, as great Plenty as Men find here of Geese.

Beyond that is a River, more upward to the Deserts, and a great Plain all gravelly, between Mountains. And in that Plain, every Day at the Sun-rising, begin to grow small Trees, and they grow till Mid-day, bearing Fruit; but no Man dare take of that Fruit, for it is a Thing of Faerie.

And after Mid-day, they decrease and enter again into the Earth, so that at the going down of the Sun they appear no more. It is a great Marvel.

In that Desert be many Wild Men, that be hideous to look on; for they be horned, and they speak nought, but they grunt, as like Pigs. And there is also great Plenty of wild Hounds. And there be many Popinjays that they call *Psittakes*. And they speak of their own Nature and say,

*God save you!*, to Men that go through the Deserts, and speak to them as freely as though it were a Man that spoke. They have 5 Toes upon a Foot. And there be also some of another Manner, that have but 3 Toes upon a Foot, and they speak not, or very little.

## Of the Very Great State of Prester John in That Island

His principal Palace is so rich and noble that no Man will believe it but he had seen it of his own Eye. Above the chief Tower of the Palace be 2 round Pommels, or Balls of Gold, and in each of them be 2 Carbuncles great and large, that shine full bright upon the Night. And the principal gates of his Palace be of precious Stone that Men call Sardonyx, and the Border and the Bars be Ivory. And the Windows of the Halls and Chambers be of Crystal. And the Tables whereon Men eat, some be of Emeralds, some of Amethyst, and some of Gold full of precious Stone.

And of the Steps to go up to his Throne, where he sitteth at Meat, one is of Onyx, another is of Crystal, and another of green Jasper, another of Amethyst, another of Sardine, another of Cornelian, and the 7th, that he setteth his Feet upon, is of Chrysolite. And all these Steps be bordered with fine Gold and with tother precious Stone, set with great Orient Pearls.

And albeit that the Carbuncles give Light right well enough, nevertheless, at all Times burneth a Vessel of Crystal full of Balm, to give good Smell and Odour to the Emperor.

This Emperor Prester John taketh always to Wife the Daughter of the Grand Cham; and the Grand Cham also, in the same Wise, the Daughter of Prester John. For these 2 be the greatest Lords under the Firmament.

# Prospero Evokes The Air Spirits

## from The Tempest

### William Shakespeare

THERE are many great and potent Magicians in literature—wizards, thaumaturgists, witches, sorcerers, warlocks, enchanters, archimages and whatnot—and they are a grand lot, every one of them. We all have our personal favorites: you may prefer Aladdin's Uncle, the African Magician, that wily old villain from *The Thousand and One Nights*, or L. Frank Baum's delightful old carnival-hoaxer, the Wonderful Wizard of Oz himself (his real name, by the way, was Oscar Zoroaster Phadrig Isaac Norman Henkel Emmanuel Ambrose Diggs, and he was born in Omaha, Nebraska, the son of a local politician, and was really more of a circus ventriloquist-*cum*-balloonist than a practising Magus).

Or you may prefer Sir Thomas Malory's mighty Merlin (or T. H. White's), or the wicked and cunning Archelaus the Enchanter in the 13th Century Portuguese romance *Amadis of Gaul*, or old Atalante who lived with his flying hippogriff in the Castle of Iron atop an inaccessible peak of the Pyrenees, in Ariosto's Italian extravaganza *Orlando Furioso*. Or, if wonder-working ladies are more to your taste, you can take your pick between Morgana le Fay and the Lady of the Lake, mystic and mysterious Urganda the Unknown or Glinda the Good Witch, whose red castle rises deep in the Quadling Country of Oz, on the very edge of the Deadly Desert.

Most recently, we have been introduced to a whole new crop of appropriately sinister, ambiguous and awesome characters, since the rise of the fantasy novel began with William Morris. I am thinking of people like James Branch Cabell's Miramon Lluagor (in *The Silver Stallion*, 1926), E. R. Eddison's Doctor Vandermast (in *Mistress of Mistresses*, 1935), J. R. R. Tolkien's Gandalf the Grey (in *The Hobbit*, 1937), Fletcher Pratt's Dr. Meliboë (in *The Well of the Unicorn*, 1948), L. Sprague de Camp's Master Ryn (in *The Tritonian Ring*, 1953), or, for that matter, my own character Sharajsha the Great (in *The Wizard of Lemuria*, 1965).

But one of the mightiest of all magicians is Prospero in *The Tempest*. The play is one of Shakespeare's most brilliant: subtle, suave, sophisticated, illuminated with flashes of dazzling poetry, told in a rich, luxuriant language. Perhaps I am particularly fond of it because I once played Prospero in an hour-long adaptation of the play broadcast over the college radio station when I was a student at Columbia. (Incidentally, *The Tempest* is perhaps the very last play written by Shakespeare; modern scholarship dates it to 1613.)

I have chosen Prospero's great speech from Act V, Scene 1—the most powerful single passage in the literature of magic . . .

Ye Elves of hills, brooks, standing lakes and groves,
And ye that on the sands with printless foot
Do chase the ebbing Neptune, and do fly him
When he comes back: you demy-Puppets that
By Moon-shine do the green sour ringlets make,

Whereof the Ewe not bites: and you, whose pastime
Is to make Midnight mushrooms, that rejoice
To hear the solemn Curfew; by whose aid
(Weak Masters though ye be) I have bedimmed
The Noon-tide Sun, call'd forth the mutinous Winds,
And twixt the green Sea and the azur'd vault
Set roaring War. To the dread rattling Thunder
Have I given fire, and rifted Jove's stout Oak
With his own Bolt: the strong-bas'd Promontory
Have I made shake, and by the spurs pluck'd up
The Pine and Cedar. Graves at my command
Have wak'd their sleepers, ope'd, and let 'em forth
By my so potent Art. But this rough Magic
I here abjure: and when I have requir'd
Some heavenly Music (which even now I do)
To work mine end upon their Senses, that
This Airy-charm is for, I'll break my staff,
Bury it certain fathoms in the earth,
And deeper than did ever Plummet sound
I'll drown my book.

# The Lords Of Faerie
## from The Faerie Queen

### Edmund Spenser

THE HISTORY of Faerie has been, thus far, somewhat neglected in this book—which promises, after all, to tell you of "Dragons, *Elves* and Heroes," I hasten to repair this omission.

Mr. William Shakespeare, who contributed our last selection, is of course one of the primary historians of the race of the Elvish kings. His splendid comedy, *A Midsummer Night's Dream*, preserved for all time a precious glimpse into the Court of Faerie and its leading figures, King Oberon and Queen Titania. But one of Shakespeare's contemporaries, the poet Edmund Spenser, devoted his masterpiece to the full history of the Elvish race.

In the summer of 1580, Edmund Spenser went to Ireland as secretary to Lord Grey de Wilton, the Lord Deputy. He undertook the new position with high hopes of advancement, but he was to languish forgotten and neglected in that "savage nation" for the remainder of his brief, unhappy life. However, he made the best of a bad job and buckled down to work on a poetic epic he had begun shortly before. *The Faerie Queene* was the title of this ambitious prospect. He had started work on it while living at Leicester House in London, under the wing of his powerful patron Robert Dudley, Earl of Leicester, one of Queen Elizabeth's favorites. With the encouragement of Leicester, and at the urging of the poet Sir Philip Sidney, Spenser planned his poem to be an English rival to Ariosto's Italian extravaganza, the *Orlando Furioso* (first published in Italian in 1523, it rapidly became one of the most popular poems of its age).

*The Faerie Queene* was originally conceived as a romantic epic in the style and form of Ariosto, but it was intended to far exceed the brilliant Italian poet. Not only was the epic to be a closely interwoven tissue of the adventures of wandering knights, but also a satire on currently important political figures in Elizabethan England, and (at the same time) an allegory of the triumph of virtue over vice. He took Aristotle's list of the Twelve Moral Virtues—Holiness, Temperance, Courtesy, Justice and so on—matched them to twelve Elizabethan courtiers and pitted them allegorically against twelve corresponding vices.

The poem was to be written in twelve books, each book coming to grips with one vice and one virtue. No one knows just how much Spenser actually wrote, but six books and a portion of the seventh survive. Tradition asserts that the rest of the poem, or a portion of the remainder, anyway, was destroyed when Kilcolman Castle burned to the ground during Tyrone's rebellion in 1598. This is as it may be: at any rate, even in fragmentary form, and only slightly more than half of the work surviving as originally conceived, *The Faerie Queene* is very nearly the longest single poem in our language. Thirty five thousand lines is plenty: the imagination boggles at the size the book would have formed if completed.

Spenser's epic has its admirers. Keats, Shelley and Byron enthused over it; in our own time, T. S. Eliot and C. S. Lewis have voiced its praise. I must, however, add a dissenting voice. I find *The Faerie Queene* almost unreadable. The allegory is absurd, mechanical, and detracts from whatever pleasures might be found in the verse. The tangled skein of inter-connecting stories is, for this reader at least, impossible to follow. The poem, to my taste, is botched in the conception. In seeking to outdo Ariosto, Spenser has failed even to make his book as interesting as the masterwork of the great Italian romancer. And in attempting to create a gigantic romance of Elfland and England, Spenser has needlessly burdened himself with all manner of extraneous materials: characters borrowed from Italian *commedia dell'arte*, like Braggadocio—characters stolen straight out of Ariosto, like Britomart the Lady Knight—and characters borrowed from Greek mythology, Welsh legendry, French romances and Greek hagiography. The thing becomes simply bewildering and the reader gets lost. (This reader, at any rate.)

But I am willing to overlook my own dislike of Spenser as merely a personal blind spot. Thus I have selected an extract (from the Second Book, Canto X), in which Spenser reveals the genealogy of the Elvish kings. It is a charming conceit and has some amusing things in it—and it gives us considerable information on the history of Faerie.

Spenser traces the descent of the Elf Emperors from Elfe and Fay, the Elvish version of Adam and Eve. He then gives a capsulized history of the 713 monarchs of Faerie from the first king, Elfin, down to the Princess Tanaquill—the daughter of Oberon and Titania, who reigned after them as Queen Gloriana. In passing, Spenser tosses off some interesting glimpses of Elvish history. For instance, he tells us it was Elfinan the second king who built Cleopolis (elsewhere, as in *Huon*, called Mommur), the capital of Faerie; and King Elfinell's war against the Goblins is mentioned; the founding of another Faerie city, Panthea, is credited to the fifth king, and so on. There is something quite delightful in the matter-of-fact way in which Spenser slips in bits of corraborative detail, as with his reference to:

. . . *Elfar*, who two brethren gyants kild,
The one of which has two heads, th'other three

I have called my selection The Lords of Faerie . . .

\*

### 70

... *Guyon* all this while his booke did read,
  Ne yet has ended: for it was a great
  And ample volume, that doth far excead
  My leasure, so long leaves here to repeat:
  It told, how first *Prometheus* did create
  A man, of many partes from beasts derived,
  And then stole fire from heaven, to animate
  His worke, for which he was by *Jove* deprived
Of life him selfe, and hart-strings of an Aegle rived.

### 71

That man so made, he called *Elfe*, to weet
  Quick, the first authour of all Elfin kind:
  Who wandring through the world with wearie feet,
  Did in the gardins of *Adonis* find
  A goodly creature, whom he deemed in mind
  To be no earthly wight, but either Spright,
  Or Angell, th'authour of all woman kind;
  Therefore a *Fay* he her according hight,
Of whom all *Faeryes* spring, and fetch their lignage right.

### 72

Of these a mightie people shortly grew,
  And puissaunt kings, which all the world warrayd,
  And to them selves all Nations did subdew:
  The first and eldest, which that sceptre swayd,
  Was *Elfin*; him all *India* obayd,
  And all that now *America* men call:
  Next him was noble *Elfinan*, who layd

*Cleopolis* foundation first of all:
But *Elfiline* enclosd it with a golden wall.

### 73

His sonne was *Elfinell*, who overcame
   The wicked *Gobbelines* in bloudy field:
   But *Elfant* was of most renowmed fame,
   Who all of Christall did *Panthea* build:
   Then *Elfar*, who two brethren gyants kild,
   The one of which had two heads, th'other three:
   Then *Elfinor*, who was in Magick skild;
   He built by art upon the glassy See
A bridge of bras, whose sound heavens thunder seem'd to bee.

### 74

He left three sonnes, the which in order raynd,
   And all their Ofspring, in their dew descents,
   Even seven hundred Princes, which maintaynd
   With mightie deedes their sundry governments;
   That were too long their infinite contents
   Here to record, ne much materiall:
   Yet should they be most famous moniments,
   And brave ensample, both of martiall,
And civill rule to kings and states imperiall.

### 75

After all these *Elficleos* did rayne,
   The wise *Elficleos* in great Majestie,
   Who mightily that sceptre did sustayne,
   And with rich spoiles and famous victorie,
   Did high advaunce the crowne of *Faery:*
   He left two sonnes, of which faire *Elferon*
   The eldest brother did untimely dy;
   Whose emptie place the mightie *Oberon*
Doubly supplide, in spousall, and dominion.

### 76

Great was his power and glorie over all,
   Which him before, that sacred seate did fill,
   That yet remaines his wide memoriall:
   He dying left the fairest *Tanaquill*,
   Him to succeede therein, by his last will:
   Fairer and nobler liveth none this howre,
   Ne like in grace, ne like in learned skill;
   Therefore they *Glorian* call that glorious flowre,
Long mayst thou *Glorian* live, in glory and great powre.

# Tales of the Wisdom of the Ancients

## from The Gesta Romanorum.

### Translated by Charles Swan and Revised by Wynnard Hooper

DURING THE Dark Ages there arose, among people of the Latin race, a strange and curious body of folklore and folk-tales called *The Gesta Romanorum*, or *The Deeds of the Romans*. No one can say who wrote it, or when, but scholars accept the close of the 13th Century as the probable date of its composition.

*The Gesta Romanorum* (the title is very wide of the mark, for tales of European, Oriental and Greek origin are included therein) swiftly became the most popular story-book of the age. The tales and anecdotes come, some of them, from fragments of Classical literature, such as Pliny and the other historians, biographers and encyclopaedists; others can be traced to Medieval legends, tales of the Saints and traveller's fictions of the Mandeville variety. A fantastic slumgullion of odds and ends, curiosities and curios, are commingled in the *Gesta*. Scraps of folk-history about King Alexander and Julius

Caesar, bits of knightly legend and fairy-tale, distorted glimpses of half-forgotten Greek myths, Medieval romances of Guy of Warwick and others of similar kidney, stories gleaned from the monkish chronicles, from Gervase of Tilbury and Geoffrey of Monmouth and comparable sources—all these, stewed up together, are passed off as annals of ancient Rome.

In the pages of this Fabulous History, you will find giants and dwarves, dragons and knights, fairies and Olympian gods, popes and pagans, Emperors and Saints, basilisks, Moorish wizards, Egyptian alchemists, Roman heroes—and the Master Vergilius, the Sorcerer of Rome, for somehow the Roman epic poet Virgil was gradually transmogrified into a wonder-working magician by the inventive minds of the Middle Ages.

The book abounds in delightful things: a tale of the Emperor Theodosius that borrows from the story of *King Lear;* stories taken out of Chaucer and turned into patchwork prose; incredible and heroic anecdotes of the imaginary deeds of such historical monarchs as Marcus Aurelius and Tiberius; and no less incredible and fantastic stories about whole dynasties of emperors who do not appear in history at all—as Gauterus, Philominus, Anselm, Averrhoes (!), Bononius and others.

In the English version of the text, established by the Reverend Charles Swan and Wynnard Hooper, both of Cambridge, in the edition of 1876, there are some 181 different stories, many of them only a paragraph or two in length. From this enormous wealth of material I have selected five good stories for your amusement. Beyond breaking up the old-fashioned solidity of the text into more frequent paragraphing, and interpolating "said the Emperor" and "the necromancer said" into otherwise most confusing passages of dialogue, I have tried not to tamper with the actual prose, which is clumsy and turgid and naïve, but not without a certain charm all its own. And to my selection I have given a new title.

## Tale LVII

*Of Vergilius the Sorcerer of Rome, the Speaking Statue, and the Wisdom of Focus the Carpenter*

WHEN TITUS was Emperor of Rome, he made a decree that the natal day of his first-born son should be held sacred; and that whosoever violated it by performing any kind of labor should be put to death.

This edict being promulgated, he summoned that learned man, Master Vergilius, to his presence, and said: "Good friend, I have established a certain law, but as offenses may frequently be committed without being discovered by the ministers of my justice, I desire you to frame some curious piece of Art Magic which may reveal to me every transgressor of the law."

Vergilius replied: "Sire, your will shall be accomplished." He straightway constructed a magical statue, and caused it to be erected in the midst of the city of Rome. By virtue of the secret powers with which it was invested, it communicated to the Emperor whatever offenses were committed in secret on that day. And thus, by the accusation of the statue, an infinite number of persons were convicted.

Now, there was a certain carpenter called Focus, who pursued his occupation every day alike. Once, as he lay in bed, his thoughts turned upon the accusations of the statue, and the multitudes which it had caused to perish. The next morning he clothed himself and proceeded to the statue, which he addressed in the following manner:

"O statue! statue! because of thy informations, many of our citizens have been apprehended and slain. I vow to my God that, if thou accusest me, I will break thy head."

Having so said, he returned home.

About the first hour, the Emperor, as he was wont, despatched sundry messengers to the statue, to inquire if the edict had been strictly complied with. After they had arrived, and delivered the Emperor's pleasure, the statue exclaimed: "Friends, look up; what see ye written upon mine forehead?"

They looked, and beheld three sentences which ran thus: *"Times are altered. Men grow worse. He who speaks truth will have his head broken."*

"Go," said the statue, "declare to his Majesty what you have seen and read." The messengers obeyed, and detailed the circumstances as they had happened.

The Emperor, therefore, commanded his guard to arm, and march to the place on which the statue was erected; and he further ordered that, if any one presumed to molest it, they should bind him hand and foot, and drag him into his presence.

The soldiers approached the statue and said, "Our Emperor wills you to declare who have broken the law, and who they were that threatened you."

The statue made answer: "Seize Focus the carpenter! Every day he violates the law and, moreover, menaces me."

Immediately Focus was apprehended and conducted to the Emperor, who said, "Friend, what do I hear of thee? Why dost thou break my law?"

"My lord," answered Focus, "I cannot keep it! for I am obliged to obtain every day eight pennies, which, without incessant labor, I have not the means of acquiring."

"And why eight pennies?" inquired the Emperor.

"Every day through the year," returned the carpenter, "I am bound to repay two pennies which I borrowed in my youth; two I lend; two I lose; and two I spend."

"You must make this more clear," said the Emperor.

"My lord," he replied, "listen to me. I am bound, each day, to repay two pennies to my father; for, when I was a boy, my father expended upon me daily the like sum. Now he is poor and needs my assistance, and therefore I return what I borrowed formerly. Two other pennies I lend to my son, who is pursuing his studies; in order that if, by any chance, I should fall into poverty, he may restore the loan, just as I have done to his grandfather. Again, I lose two pennies every day to my wife; for she is contradictious, wilful, and passionate. Now, because of this disposition, I account whatsoever is given to her entirely lost. Lastly, two other pennies I expend upon myself in meat and drink. I cannot do with less; nor can I obtain them without unremitting labor. You now know the truth; and I pray you, give a righteous judgment."

"Friend," said the Emperor, "thou hast answered well. Go, and labor earnestly in thy calling."

Soon after this the Emperor died, and Focus the carpenter, on account of his singular wisdom, was elected in his stead, by the unanimous choice of the whole nation.

He governed as wisely as he had lived; and at his death, his picture, bearing on the head eight pennies, was reposited among the effigies of the deceased Emperors that it should ever remind those who came after to labor dilligently in their vocation, repay the debts incurred in their youth, and make wise and ample provision for old age.

## Tale CII

*How a Wicked Necromancer Would Have Done to Death a Certain Noble Knight, But for the Cleverness of a Goodly Sage*

Also in the reign of Titus there lived a certain noble and devout knight, who had a beautiful wife; but she dishonored herself, and persisted in every vice and folly. The knight, therefore, was very sorrowful, and resolved to undertake a journey to the Holy Land to pray for the assistance of Heaven.

In this determination, he bade farewell to his faithless wife and left his home. No sooner had he embarked than the lady sent for a certain skillful Necromancer whom she loved, so that he might dwell with her openly in licentious riot and luxurious display.

It happened that, as they lay in bed, the lady observed: "If you would do one thing for me, I might become your wife."

"What is it," replied the Necromancer, "that will please you, and which I can perform for you?"

"My husband has gone into the Holy Land, and loves me little; now, if by your Art Magic you could destroy him, all that I possess could become yours."

"I acquiesce," said the clerk, "but on condition that you marry me." To this the faithless lady bound herself with vows, and thus the Necromancer set about to devise and fashion an image under the similitude and name of the knight her husband, and fixed it before him upon the wall.

In the meanwhile, as the knight was passing through the main street of Rome, a wise and goodly Sage met him in the way, and, observing him narrowly, said unto the knight: "My friend, I have a secret to communicate."

"Well, master, what would you please to say?"

"This day you are one of death's children, unless you follow my advice: your wife is a harlot, and contrives your death."

The knight, hearing what was said of his spouse, put confidence in the speaker, and said: "Good master, save my life, and I will amply recompense you."

"Willingly," answered the other, "if you will do as I shall tell you."

The knight promised, and the master took him to a bath, undressed him, and desired him to bathe. Then putting into his hand a polished mirror, said: "Look attentively upon this, and you will see wonders."

He did so, and the meanwhile the master read to him from a book. "What see you?" he asked.

"I see," said the knight, "a certain clerk in my house, with an image of wax which resembles me most marvelous, and which he hath fastened against the wall."

"Look again," continued the Sage; "what do you perceive now?"

"He takes a bow," replied the knight, "and places in it a sharp arrow; and now he aims it at the effigy of myself!"

"As you love your life," admonished the goodly Sage, "the moment you discern the arrow flying to its mark, place yourself deep in the bath, and remain there until I tell you to come out."

As soon, therefore, as the arrow quitted the string, he plunged his body deep into the water. This done, the master said, "Raise your head and look again into the mirror. What do you perceive now?"

"The effigy is not struck, and the arrow is sticking by its side. The clerk appears much concerned."

"Look into the mirror but once more," advised the master, "and observe what he does."

"He now goes nearer to the image, and refixes the arrow in the string in order to strike it."

"As you value your life, do as before."

Again the knight plunged his body into the water as soon as he saw by the mirror that the clerk was bending the bow; and then, at the command of the master, resuming his inspection of the mirror, said—

"The clerk makes great lamentation, and says to my wife, 'If the third time I do not strike the effigy, I shall lose my life.' Now he approaches so near that I think he cannot miss it."

"Take care," said the master, "as soon as you see him bend the bow, immerse your body as I before told you."

The knight watched attentively, and as soon as he saw the clerk drag back the bow to shoot, plunged below the surface of the water.

"Rise quickly, and look yet again into the mirror."

When he had done so, he began to laugh.

"My friend," said the master, "why do you laugh?"

"I observe," answered the knight, "very distinctly, that the clerk has missed the effigy, and that the arrow, rebounding, has entered his own bowels and destroyed his life. My wife makes a hole under my bed and has buried therein the body."

"Rise, then; dress yourself, and pray to God," said the Sage.

The knight returned sincere thanks for his life to Heaven, and, having performed his pilgrimage, journeyed toward his own home. His wife met and received him with much apparent pleasure. He dissembled for a few days, and then sending for her parents, said to them—

"My dear friends, hear why I have desired your presence. This woman, your daughter and my wife, has committed foul adultery; and, what is worse, designed me to murder me."

The lady denied the accusation with an oath. The knight then began to relate the whole story of the clerk's actions and end. "And," he continued, "if you do not credit this, come and see where the clerk is buried."

He then led them into the bed-chamber, and dragged the body from its hiding-place. The judge was called, and sentenced the lady to be burnt, and her ashes to be scattered in the air.

The knight soon afterwards espoused a beautiful and faithful virgin, by whom he had many children, and with whom he finished his days in peace.

## Tale CIII

*How the Emperor Domitian Purchased Three Wise Maxims of a Merchant, and How He Found Great Profit Thereby*

Domitian was a very wise and just prince, and suffered no offender to escape the punishments of his law.

It happened that as he once sat at table, a certain merchant knocked at the gate. The porter opened it, and asked what he pleased to want.

"I have brought some useful things for sale," answered the merchant. The porter introduced him and he very humbly made obeisance to the Emperor.

"My friend," said the Emperor, "what merchandise have to you to dispose of?"

"Three maxims of especial wisdom and excellence, my lord," answered the merchant, bowing low.

"And how much will you take for your maxims?" inquired the worthy Domitian.

"A thousand florins."

"And so," said the king, "if they are of no use to me, I lose my money?"

"My lord," answered the merchant, "if the maxims do not stand you in stead, I will return the money."

"Very well," said the Emperor, "let us hear your maxims."

"The first, my lord, is this—'*Whatever you do, do wisely, and think of the consequences.*'"

"Very wise," the Emperor commended.

"The second is—'*Never leave the highway for the byway.*'"

"Ah," said the Emperor. "And the third of these good sayings?"

"Thirdly,—'*Never stay all night as a guest in that house where you find the master an old man, and the wife a young woman.*' These three maxims," said the merchant, finishing, "if you attend to them, will be extremely serviceable."

The Emperor, being of the same opinion, ordered him to be paid his thousand florins; and so pleased was he with the wisdom of the first of the three wise maxims thus purchased, that he commanded it to be inscribed in his court, in his bedchamber, and in every place where he was accustomed to walk—and even upon the tablecloths used within the palace.

Now, the rigid justice of the Emperor occasioned a conspiracy among a number of his disaffected subjects; and, finding a means of accomplishing their purposes somewhat difficult, they engaged a barber, by large promises, to cut the Emperor's throat as he did shave him.

When the Emperor, therefore, was to be shaved, the barber lathered his beard and began to operate upon it after the fashions of his craft; but, steeling himself for the act of treachery and murder, he cast his eyes upon the towel, which he had fastened round the royal neck, he perceived, woven thereon, the maxim—'*Whatever you do, do wisely, and think of the consequences.*'

The inscription startled the tonsor, and he said to himself: "I am to-day hired to destroy this man; if I do it, my end will be ignominious; I shall be condemned to the most shameful death. Therefore, whatsoever I do, it is good to consider the end, as this writing testifies."

These cogitations disturbed the worthy barber so much that his hand trembled, and the razor fell to the ground. The Emperor, seeing this, inquired the cause of his perturbation.

"O my lord," said the barber, "have mercy upon me: I was hired this day to destroy you; but accidentally, or rather by the will of God, I read the inscription on the towel, *Whatever you do, do wisely, and think of the consequences.*' Whereby, considering that, of a surety, the consequence would be my own miserable destruction, my hand trembled so much, that I lost all command over it."

"Well," thought the Emperor, "this first maxim hath assuredly saved my life: in a good hour was it purchased!—My friend," said he to the trembling tonsor, "on condition that you be faithful hereafter, I pardon you."

The noblemen, who had conspired against the Emperor, finding that their project had failed, consulted with one another what they were to do next. "On such and such a day," said one, "he journeys to a certain city; we will hide ourselves in a bypath, through which he will pass, and fall upon him and so kill him."

This counsel met with an general approval among the conspirators. The king, as had been expected, prepared to set forth on his journey to a nearby city; and riding on till he came to the bypath, his knights said unto him: "My lord, it will be better for you to go this way, than to pass along the broad road; for this byway is considerably nearer."

The king pondered the matter within himself. "The second maxim," thought he, "admonishes me never to forsake the highway for the byway. I will adhere to that maxim."

Then turning to his soldiers: "I shall not quit the public road; but you, if it please ye, may proceed by that path, and prepare for my approach."

Accordingly a number of them went; and the ambush, imagining that the king rode in their company, fell upon them and put the greater part to the sword. When the news reached the king, he secretly exclaimed: "My second maxim hath also saved my life!"

Seeing, therefore, that by this piece of cunning they were unable to slay their lord, the conspirators again took counsel, and said amongst themselves, "On a certain day he will lodge in a particular house, where all the nobles lodge, because there is no other fit for his reception. Let us then agree with the master of that house and his wife, for a sum of money, and then kill the Emperor as he lies in bed."

This was agreed to. But when the Emperor had come into the city, and had been lodged in the house to which the conspirators referred, he commanded his host to be called into his presence. Observing that he was an old man, the Emperor said: "Have you not a wife?"

"Yes, my lord."

"I wish to see her."

The lady came; and when it appeared that she was very young—not eighteen years of age—the king said hastily to his chamberlain, "Away, prepare me a bed in another house. I will remain here no longer."

"My lord," replied he, "be it as you please. But they have made everything ready for you: were it not better to lie where you are, for in the whole city there is not so commodious a place."

"I tell you," answered the Emperor, "I will sleep elsewhere." The chamberlain, therefore, removed; and the king went privately to another residence, saying to the soldiers about him, "Remain here, if you like; but join me early in the morning."

Now, while they slept, the old man and his wife arose, being bribed to kill the king in his sleep, and put to death all the soldiers who had remained.

In the morning the king arose and found his soldiers slain. "Oh," cried he, "if I had continued here, I should have been destroyed. So the third maxim hath also preserved me."

But the old man and his wife, with the whole of their family, were crucified, in punishment for their falsity and treachery.

The Emperor retained the three maxims in memory during life, and ended his days in peace.

## Tale CLXII

*Of a Certain Mountain Whereupon Was a Palace of the Demons, and of the Several Terrible Things Which Thereabouts Occurred*

In the days of Otto the Roman Emperor, there was in Catalonia a very high mountain whose ascent was extremely arduous, and, except in one place, inaccessible.

On the summit of this mountain there was an unfathomable lake of black water. Here also stood, as it is reported in Gervase of Tilbury, a palace of demons, with a large gate continually closed. But the palace itself, as well as its inhabitants, existed in invisibility.

If any one cast a stone or other hard substance into this lake, the demons exhibited their anger with furious storms. In one part of the mountain was perpetual snow and ice; here there was abundance of crystal, and the sun never was seen. At its foot flowed a river, whose sands were of gold; and the precious metal thus obtained was denominated by the vulgar its *cloak*.

The mountain itself, and the parts adjacent, furnished silver; and its unexhaustible fertility was not the least surprising of its peculiarities.

Not far from hence lived a certain farmer, who one day being much occupied with domestic matters, and troubled exceedingly by the incessant squalling of his little girl, at length, after the manner of people when angry, wished his infant to the devil.

This incautious desire was scarcely uttered ere the girl was seized by an invisible hand and carried off!

Seven years afterwards, a person journeying at the foot of the terrible mountain near the farmer's dwelling, distinguished a man hurrying along at a prodigious rate, and uttering in the most doleful tones: "Alas! for me, wretched man! what shall I do to get rid of this huge load?"

The traveller stopped to inquire the occasion of this lamenting; and he was told that, for the space of seven years past, he had been committed to the custody of the demons upon that mountain, who daily made use of him as a chariot, in consequence of an unwary exclamation to that effect.

The traveller, startled at an assertion so extraordinary, and more than a little incredulous, was informed that his neighbor had suffered in a similar degree; for that, having hastily committed his daughter to their power, the demons had instantly borne her off. He added that the demons, weary of instructing the girl, would willingly restore her, provided the father presented himself on the mountain and there received her.

The auditor, thunder-struck at this communication, doubted whether he should conceal things so incredible, or relate what he had heard. He determined at last to declare the girl's situation to her father; and hastening, accordingly, found him still bewailing the lengthened absence of his daughter.

Ascertaining the cause, he went on to state what he had heard from the man whom the devils used as a chariot. "Therefore," said he, "I recommend you, attesting the Divine name, to a demand of these devils the restitution of your daughter."

Amazed at what was imparted to him, the father deliberated upon the best method of proceeding and finally pursued the counsel of the traveller.

Ascending the mountain, he passed forward to the lake, and adjured the demons to restore the girl whom his folly had committed to their unholy clutches.

Suddenly a violent blast swept by him, and a girl of lofty stature stood in his presence. Her eyes were wild and wandering, and her bones and sinews were scarcely covered with skin. Her horrible countenance discovered no sign of sensibility; and, ignorant of all language, she scarcely could be acknowledged for a human being. The father, wondering at her strange appearance, and doubtful whether she should be taken to his own home or not, posted to the bishop of Girona, and, with a sorrowful aspect, detailed what had befallen him; at the same time requesting his advice.

The bishop, as a religious man, and one intrusted with a charge of so much importance, narrated every circumstance respecting the girl to his diocese. He warned them against rashly committing their fortunes to the power of demons, and showed that our adversary the devil, as a raging lion, goeth about seeking whom he may devour; that he will slay those who are given to him, and hold them in eternal bonds, and torment and afflict those devoted to him for a time.

The man who was used by the devils as a chariot, remained a long time in this miserable situation; but his subsequent faith and discretion emancipated him. He stated that near the above-mentioned place there was an extensive subterranean palace, whose entrance was by a single gate, enveloped in the thickest darkness. Through this portal the devils, who had been on evil embassies to the various parts of the world, returned, and communicated to their fellows what they had done.

No one could tell of what the palace was constructed, save for themselves, and those who passed under their yoke to eternal damnation. From all which, my beloved reader, we may gather the dangers we are exposed to, and how cautious we should be of invoking the devil to our assistance, or of committing any member of our families to his power with a loose or incautious word. Let us guard our hearts, and beware that he catch not up the sinful soul, and plunge it into the lake of everlasting misery; where there is snow and ice unthawed—crystal, that reflects the awakened and agonized conscience, perpetually burning with immortal fire!

## Tale CLXXV

### Of the Wonderful Things to be Found in the Far Places of the World

Pliny telleth there be certain men who have their heads of dogs; who bark when they converse, and clothe themselves in the skins of animals. Also in India there are men who possess a single eye, which is situate in the forehead. They live upon the flesh of animals.

In Africa there are women without heads, having eyes and mouths in their breasts. And in the East, over against the terrestrial Paradise, are people who never eat, and whose mouth is so small that what they drink is conveyed into the belly by means of a hollow reed. They live upon the odor of apples and flowers, and a bad smell destroys them.

There are, also, men without a nose, but otherwise with the faces of Christian men complete; and whatsoever they see they think good. Such are the foolish of the world.—And there are some whose nose and lower lip is so long, that it covers all the face, while they sleep.

In Scythia are men with ears that completely envelop their whole body. And some men there are also who walk like cattle, and these honor neither God nor His saints.—There are likewise people who are horned, having short noses and the feet of a goat.

In Aethiopia are men with but one leg, whose velocity nevertheless is such, that they run down the swiftest animal. And in India are pygmies two cubits long; they ride upon goats for horses and make war against cranes.

In India there are also men who possess six hands. They are without clothes, but are extremely hairy, and dwell in rivers. There, too, are men who have six fingers on each hand, and six toes on each foot.

Certain women there are bearded to the breast; but their heads are totally bare.

In Aethiopia there are men with four eyes each. They turn one eye to God, to live well; another to the world, to flee from it; a third to the devil, to resist him; and the last to the flesh, to chastise it.—In Europe are very *beautiful* men, but they have a crane's head, and neck, and beak. They make good judges, because a judge ought to have long necks and beaks in order that *what the heart thinks may be long before it reach the mouth.*

If all judges were thus we should have fewer injudicious awards.

# The Magical Palace of Darkness
### from Palmerin of England

## Francisco De Moraes

THE imaginary-world fantasy arose in the myths and epics of the Near East. The wanderings of Gilgamesh the Sumerian hero and the voyages and adventures of Odysseus the Greek mariner are basically akin (in fact, some authorities have tried to prove traces of direct influence or borrowing on the part of "Homer"); and the later Greek epic poets derive wholly from the Homeric poems, as do the yet later Roman epics, for the supreme masterpiece of Roman epic literature, the *Aeneid* of Virgil, is closely modeled on the Homeric original, and all later Roman poets who attempted the epic imitate either Homer or Virgil, or both.

But with the collapse of Classical literature, the young emerging nations of Europe began codifying and writing down their own epic myths. To a considerable extent, these poems—such as the French *chansons de geste*—display, if anything, an ignorance of the Homeric poems. The revival of Classical literature had to await the coming of the Renaissance, but the European national epics arose before that Rebirth of Knowledge. And with the

## THE MAGICAL PALACE OF DARKNESS

rediscovery of Homer and the other masters of the epic, the first flush of enthusiasm wore off and the native epics declined: it was almost as if, with the towering masterpieces of the ancient poets before them, the naïve Medieval poets lost faith in their own powers.

Sometime in the 13th or 14th Century the prose romance assumed prominence. The foremost of these, in terms of excellence, and very nearly the earliest in point of time, was the great *Amadis of Gaul*. Literary tradition ascribes its authorship to a noble Portuguese named Vasco de Lobeira who lived during the reign of that Ferdinand of Portugal who died in 1385; but modern scholars tend to dispute this, and ascribe the mighty *Amadis* to a certain Galician knight named João de Lobeira who was at the Portuguese court more than a century earlier, between 1258 and 1285. And whether the work was originally composed in the Portuguese language or not is still open to dispute, for the book survives only in a Spanish version dating from around 1500. *Amadis* was a colossal success—a Medieval best-seller, whose astounding fertility of invention and richness of narrative prompted the writing of something like a dozen sequels or continuations by other hands. And this in turn gave rise to a enormous literature of imitations with such delicious tles as *Palmerin of England, Tirante the White, Parthe opex of the Wood, Belianus of Greece* and *Felixmarte Hyrcania*.

As romance followed romance, each author tried to outdo the competition by piling marvel upon marvel and hyperbole upon hyperbole, until the entire genre decayed into a frenzied seeking after effect. It did not need the inspired lampooning of Cervantes in *Don Quixote* to bring an end to the movement: the heart had long since gone out of the romance by 1605, when the first part of *Quixote* was published.

In my recent book, *Tolkien*, I devoted almost the whole of Chapter 12 to *Amadis of Gaul* and described its style and content in great detail. Hence, for a sample from the Medieval romance for this anthology, I will turn to another example of the genre, to *Palmerin of England*.

*Palmerin* was a fine early example of the whole school;

although not as famous as the great *Amadis*, it was highly popular and much praised. In *Quixote*, for example, Cervantes singles out three of the innumerable romances for particular praise. In Part I, Chapter IV, the curate and the barber are purging Don Quixote's library of unwholesome influences; they destroy most of the old romances he has collected and which have driven him mad; but they spare from the flames three romances—*Tirante* for its "quaintness," *Amadis* because it was the first and foremost of them all, and *Palmerin of England* for its intrinsic merits (and because Cervantes mistakenly fancied its author to have been a King of Portugal).

*Palmeirim de Inglaterra* was written in 1544 by one Francisco de Moraes. The *Britannica* remarks on its "imaginative luxuriance and purity of style," and comments that these elements caused Cervantes to compare it to the works of Homer. De Moraes (*c.* 1500–72) was treasurer to the household of King John III and visited Paris in the suite of de Noronha, the Portuguese ambassador, around 1540. He seems to have written his famous romance of chivalry in French (perhaps while in Paris) and he dedicated it to the Infanta D. Maria, daughter of King Manoel. Although written in 1544, the book was not published until much later: the earliest known Portuguese edition has been dated to 1567. It is a very superior example of the prose romance, with a clearly drawn and vigorous plot, well-conceived characters and a style so admirable that it has been considered a classic of Portuguese literature almost from the date of first publication.

It was also immensely popular. This is proven by the fact that it has continued in print for at least two and a half centuries. I was fortunate enough to purchase a volume of the English translation. It is a most peculiar little book, measuring three and a half inches by six, smaller even than one of today's paperbacks, but over an inch thick. Bound in brown calf, it was published by Longman, Hurst, Rees, and Orme, in Paternoster Row, London, in 1807.

From it I have selected the following extract from Volume III of the romance. Palmerin, a wandering English

THE MAGICAL PALACE OF DARKNESS 163

knight, has come into Greece and is seeking to rescue the Princess Lionarda from dire enchantments and captivity in Thrace ...

## Chapter 95

*Of What Befell Palmerin in the Adventure of the Enchantment of Lionarda, Princess of Thrace*

THE LORDS of the kingdom of Thrace led Palmerin to a hill, from whence they showed him the place where Lionarda remained enchanted. Now as the day was clear, at the foot of the hill he beheld in a pleasant valley some brave and stately towers among the green trees, a goodly sight to behold; for not only was the valley wherein they were edified as fresh and delightful a place as nature could make, but also the edifices and palaces displayed such numerous pinnacles and sumptuous varandas of marble, so white and lofty, that they seemed to touch the sky; with other surpassing devices and inventions, so worthy of admiration that he thought them to be framed by the celestial powers rather than by any earthly creatures.

Well was Palmerin pleased to see a thing so pleasant; and though at that time his spirit was as it were dead with the longing remembrances which tormented it, yet the beauty of the place stirred in him a certain lively joy, and he thought how fair a lot would be his who should enjoy it, together with Lionarda; a lot which, however fair, he wished not for himself, nothing sufficing for him, but only the hope he had of his services and merits with Polinarda. After he had stayed awhile, beholding the manner of the valley, and thinking of the dangers which had been menaced, holding them in little, seeing that the place rather promised to delight the senses than to dismay the heart, he began to think lightly of the enterprise, which in truth a wise man ought not to have done, because that divers times the doubtfullest things have the pleasantest issue; and that which seemeth most pleasant at the beginning, doth prove to be the sharpest danger in the ending. But as in Palmerin this contempt of the danger arose from his surpassing hardihood, and from the many dangers which he had happily gone through, and this seemed to threaten none, he is the less worthy of blame.

*

One of the knights that kept him company then advanced from among the others; he was a man of great authority, for his grey hairs, and the quality of his person, and the experience of things which many years had shewn him. Sir Knight, said he to Palmerin, to whom fortune hath always been so great a friend, that in no danger or distress hath she ever played you false, not for this, your accustomed prosperity, should you cease to fear dangers, which to appearance may seem little; for she who in great things hath been willing to forward you, may peradventure in lesser ones forsake you, for the greater proof of her power: moreover, nothing should be judged of by its first appearance, seeing from such judgement errors arise for which afterwards there is no remedy. This I say, because the adventure which you are about to essay seemeth in its beginning more made for contentment than to be feared. But I would have you know, that this contentment is to be gained by danger, and perchance when you find yourself in it, you will find it greater than you thought for.

*

Sir, answered Palmerin, your counsel, shewing so great good will, deserves a guerdon which I cannot now bestow; and indeed your words are full of truth. I am right thankful that you have given me so good a lesson to bear in mind hereafter; God grant that this may have the end which we all desire, and if I speed to my wish, I will not be unmindful of your friendly warning. This promise, presented with so great humanity, inflamed a sudden envy in the hearts of some there present, who for the hope they had to see him king, began to enter into more praises than any true or faithful subject would offer. For they began to persuade him, that no adventure, how dangerous soever it proved, might astonish his person: but he declining from such praise as was the daily gift and work of flatterers, set spurs to his horse and rode down the hill.

*

An example surely worthy of great praise to all princes and rulers living on the earth, that they should not incline and lean to such, who only study with sweet words, flattering tales, and false reports, to rest and bring them asleep in so vile an exercise. Which painted faces if they would surpass, their subjects, friends, and servants, should be equally regarded, their renown plentifully increased, and accordingly honoured; yea, the virtuous rightfully should be richly rewarded, and the vicious rightfully for ever reproached; then would not th‾ plain dealer be governed by such as have been note⌐ but the good should be openly discerned from the e⌐ and all enjoy one hope for a continual quiet: but to ⌐ matter. As soon as Palmerin pricked forward, the light began to darken, the air to be marvellously troubled, and misty, so that the lords of Thrace lost sight of him, and could not even see one another; and there was loud thundering, and great earthquakes, and other fearful signs, so they were overcome with such fear, that some fell before their horses, being astounded; others lost their stirrups and clung to the horses' necks, and thus they made their way to the city, tearing their cloaks in the thickets, neither remembering the road nor any thing else. But as the signs that day were different from what they had been at any former time when this adventure had been essayed, the city itself was overspread with so thick and black a cloud, and filled with sounds so dolorous and dismayful, that no one had either judgment so free, or heart so strong, as to be exempt from the fear which these terrors occasioned.

*

Selviam, whom Palmerin had ordered to say upon the hill, seeing his master as he deemed in such danger, forgot all fear, and being guided by the love with which he served him, spurred his horse to follow him. But as the nature of the enchantment was, that no one could enter the forbidden ground, except by great prowess and force of arms, he found himself suddenly in the city, without knowing how he came there, in company with the rest, and at such time as the cloud was beginning to disperse: Palmerin, meantime, remembering the words of the old knight, perceived the error of his first opinion; for he knew not whither he went in that thick darkness, nor could he resist an inward pain, which seemed as if it would have rent his heart; whereat he greatly marvelled, thinking that nothing but his own passion could have touched him there. And now, certain invisible bodies appproached him, and by force plucked him from the saddle, and threw him down; and though to defend himself he drew his sword, and struck on all sides, he found that his blows did no harm, for they were smitten against the air. Then he thought to mount on horseback again, but his labour was in vain; it was not possible for him to find his horse, which was far enough away, and presently, not only his sword was taken from him, but likewise all his armour was caught away on a sudden; whereat he began to stand in some fear, as knowing that strength hath need of arms to execute its purpose. Finding himself thus disarmed, and weary with striving to seize these bodies which were without souls, he sate himself down, not knowing what to do, and holding that the adventure was impossible to be achieved, for he could see none with whom to fight; and even if he had seen any, he was spoiled of all implement of offence or defence. The darkness became every minute more and more; he could neither go forward nor return; wherefore he said to himself, Certes, there are more adventures in

# THE MAGICAL PALACE OF DARKNESS

the world than men suspect; and let not him who is without mishap wish to enter into them, for he who fears it least will find it, and they who have longest avoided it cannot escape at last.

## Chapter 96

### Of What Farther Befell Palmerin in This Adventure

The history saith that Palmerin remained some time sitting upon the ground, deliberating with himself what he should do; and seeing that in these cases there was no room for counsels, he rose without any determination, committing himself to the difficulties which fortune might ordain, and careless what might happen, even if it were the end of his life, which he was resolved to sell as dearly as he could, believing that he who does what he can when dying, satisfies with his life what he owes to honour. Still it troubled him to see himself without arms, fearing that for lack of them he could not fulfil his intention. But what most dismayed him was, to feel his soul so depressed within him, that his limbs seemed to be almost deprived of their wonted virtue. And now there came from the hill above, a mighty and terrible thundering, that he expected the earth would have opened under him. With this he heard fearful hollow voices, and when the rolling sounds reached him, then was he snatched up a mighty height, and presently let fall, so that he thought himself descending to the abyss. These fears, however, he underwent as one who expected worse; what he most grieved at being that they were of such a nature that resistance could not be made. At this time the darkness began to clear away, when he found himself to be in the midst of a little island, enclosed round about with a water so black and deep, that it seemed as if it came from the centre of the earth. In the midst of this islet, Palmerin espied an old withered tree, and underneath it stood a knight armed in his own lost armour, with his sword likewise in his hand, who said unto him, Now, O thou valiant knight, I would fain see what thy courage will avail, or by what means thou canst defend thyself from the wrath of my hands, which with the edge of thy own sword will mangle thy flesh and bones, whereon the wide beasts of the country shall feed: so that thy renown, famed over all the whole earth, shall here take full end, where none can approach to bear witness of thy death.

*

Of a truth, he who should say that Palmerin was at this time free from the fears which such a danger might well bring upon him, might say what he pleased; for his heart, though it were always accompanied with all virtue and all courage, at that hour was not so, in that he was destitute of any thing for his defence in this extremity; and seeing that he had to defend himself with nothing but the limbs which nature had given him, against an armed enemy, who, according to his proportions and semblance, was no little to be feared, committing himself to the will of fortune, though things of honour ought not to be committed to her, yet being in such a state that there was no other remedy, he approached the knight, who with all fierceness advanced to meet him with his lifted sword. A dark cloud suddenly overshadowed them; but in the cloud, though he saw him not, Palmerin seized him in his arms, and the other thrust his sword into his breast up to the hilt, he feeling such pain as if he had indeed received so deadly a thrust; and though against such a fear no courage could suffice, yet was his such that it never forsook him, and he grappled with that phantom, till by fine force at length he overthrew; then meaning to cut off his head, at the instant when he drew the sword out of his own body, the cloud dispersed, and he found himself with it in his hand, and his armour under the tree, but the knight was gone.

*

Amazed at these things, but seeing that what was at first so fearful proved at last to be fantastic and vain, he

## THE MAGICAL PALACE OF DARKNESS

began to recover confidence, and donned his armour, wherewith he felt his strength increased, and a lively hope of more wonders, being now disposed to be delighted with them. Presently the day cleared, and he could see every thing as far as the eye could reach, and then on the other side beyond the island, in the midst of a green field and among goodly trees, he saw the edifices which he had seen from the hill; but there was no way of crossing to them, because of that great water which hath been spoken of, except by swimming; and this he feared to attempt, having no skill therein. Moreover, the bank on both sides was so steep that its height appeared immeasurable. Now seeing that he had this precipice to descend, and neither knowing how he could get up on the opposite side, nor how he could get to it, for the weight of his armour would drown him, he was so confounded, that neither was his courage sufficient to induce him to attempt it, nor his understanding to console him. There seemed to be no remedy, and for his more dismay, on the other side of the water he espied a company of monstrous and misshapen beasts, who seemed to be waiting there to devour him; and as if they were quarrelling who should be the first to fall on him, they began a furious battle, some helping others, so that it looked like a challenge and pitched battle, party against party. This Palmerin judged to be one of the most notable things that ever he had seen: for while the battle continued many of them spoiled and killed one another, howling the while so loudly, that it was heard in the city as though they were in the midst of it, so that the fear there was greatly increased, for they thought that Palmerin was surely in some great danger. He who resented the most fear was Selviam, grieving that he was not present with his lord, to go through the same dangers, with that true love of a faithful servant, which masters for the most part understand so well, and so ill requite. The fury of this battle was so great, that at last all who were engaged in it lay dead upon the field.

\*

Their grievous fight being thus ended, Palmerin went about the island, to see where he might have passage to the other side. At last, in one part where the waters made a resting-place, he espied a boat, having four oars in it, which were handled and governed by four beasts of marvellous bigness, each one tied with a mighty chain, and at the poop sate a mighty lion, all imbrued in blood, as though he were master of the passage, who fed himself with nothing else but the flesh of his passengers.

*

While Palmerin was beholding this fearful boat, he espied a man on the farther side, crying to the beasts to carry him over with them; whereat he was much amazed, as thinking no man to be so foolish as to hazard himself in so perilous a river with such boatmen, and under such a pilot. The boat put off to take him in, and the man was no sooner entered, but the lion seized him in his paws, and with his mighty claws straightway rent him in pieces, and devoured him, giving part to his companions the rowers; for this was their ordinary food. Any one may conceive in what state was Palmerin's heart when he beheld all this, for he saw no way to pass but the terror of death was both before and behind him; but seeing there was no remedy, for if he remained in the islet he must needs die for want of food, so as a last resolution, he concluded to put himself to the rigour of the beasts, and shift with them by strength of arms; for he saw himself wholly destitute of any other hope. Hereupon he looked how he might descend, but there was no other way except by a rock which reached down to the water side, and which was so slippery and steep, that there was nothing on which he could lay hold, or stay himself; and he thought that he must needs be dashed to pieces before he could reach the bottom. This made him demur a little; and as this extreme danger was so greatly to be dreaded, he addressed himself to the remedy which he always reserved for the worst perils, that is, to the remembrance of his lady, with which he was accustomed to surmount all, how great and terrible soever they might be. And having invoked her, he felt his fear gone, and without further dread or delay let himself slide down the rock; but as all those dangers were in truth no otherwise dangerous than in appearance, he attained the river-side without any harm: the lion and his fellows pushed off from the opposite shore to receive him into the boat; and he perceiving this, drew his sword, and with shield advanced, made ready for the adventure. But for this adventure such readiness, which is elsewhere so profitable, was nothing needed, for all were but phantasms and unreal shapes; and as soon as the prow was run ashore, and he had leapt in, he saw none to attack, for forthwith that strange pilot and his boatmen were gone, he knew not how, and he found himself alone in the boat: then taking the oars, he rowed himself to the farther side; but when he had crost the river, the opposite bank was so steep and overhanging, that he could by no possible means climb up; so that he was again utterly at a loss how to proceed. Being thus confounded, presently he saw an old and broken basket lowered down to him from the top of the rock, by a rope which was so weak and slender, that he thought the mere weight of the basket would have broken it. When Palmerin perceived that there was no other means of ascending that great height, once more trusting in the remembrance of her whom he served, he thought to lay aside his arms, that he might be less heavy; and disarming himself, he was about to get into the basket with nothing but his sword. But as many times the heart feels within itself foreboding doubts of what is to come, a fear came upon him which made him put them on again, thinking they might still be necessary. Then, trusting to fortune and abiding the chance, he got into the basket, and without seeing any one to hoist him, was raised into the air, but with so slow and swaying a motion, that the delay doubled his fear. And now when he was at a great height, he saw that the basket began to break, and the cord give way with the weight, and untwist itself, so that at last nothing but a single thread was left, which was almost invisibly small.

*

Certes, though he had already suffered many fears, this was the worst of all, for he saw himself in the last extremity, being suspended in heaven by a single hair. This made him again betake himself to his lady for help, as the only one in whom he trusted in such need; and as it is by faith alone that we must stand or fall, so this faith which he had in his lady was of such avail, that, overcoming the slowness of the enchantment in one moment it brought him up, and landed him above in the field where the battle of the beasts had been, of which he could now see no sign, neither of the water below. The disappearance of these things which had caused him such fear, giving him now a new joy, which dissipated all his sorrows, as joy when it is unexpected is ever wont to do.

## Chapter 97

### How the Enchantment of Lionarda was Ended

The day now was now spent, and the moon, which was then full and in her strength, having no clouds to oppose or obscure her, began to rise in the East with a splendour which seemed almost unnaturally bright. The nightingales and other birds with which that land abounded began to welcome the night with such variety of songs and rejoicing, that Palmerin forgot all his past troubles. And laying himself down under a tree, intending to listen to them, fatigue so overpowered him, that he fell asleep, not having eaten all that day, food indeed being little needed by him: for though without it nature cannot be sustained, yet, when the spirits are roused by difficulties, the very occasion administers strength to the limbs, provided it be not over long; for of long want nature is incapable, and thereby in course becomes weak and broken down and finally perishes. Palmerin past as peaceful a night as he had painful a day. When the dawn appeared, the birds awoke him with a song so joyous to hear, and so delightful to muse upon, that he wished the day had tarried longer, to have let him longer enjoy so sweet contentment. But as these follow their appointed order, it was not long before they forsook him, bright day-light, and their custom of seeking food, making them disperse.

*

Palmerin rose, and looking around the field, well pleased at its beauty, beheld towards the East the towers and edifices which he had seen from the hill yesterday, surrounded with the same goodly trees; and though in this there was no show of danger, what he had already witnessed taught him still to apprehend it; on the other hand, the same experience taught him to have little fear. He had not advanced far towards them, before he espied his horse tied to a tree, saddled and bridled, and in such case as when he left him; at which he little marvelled, being now accustomed to the wonders of this land. So mounting upon him, he rode a little further, where he met with two knights, who were of great stature, and clad in the brightest and richest armour that he had ever seen; and they, without any words, couched their spears against him. He encountered the first full upon his shield, and the knight presently vanished away: the second burst his lance upon him. Palmerin veered round to requite him with a blow of his sword, but he vanished in like manner as the other.

*

Then Palmerin looking about, espied some men about to draw up a bridge, which was the passage over a moat of one of the towers: at this he clapt spurs to his horse, and galloped thither apace, so that he crossed the bridge before that they could raise it up, and before they could fasten the gate he forced his way with them into a court, which was surrounded with fair apartments. But though the manner of this was worthy to be admired, two giants who came out with huge maces in their hands did not give him leisure for this. This danger was more welcome to Palmerin than the others which he had past; so leaping from his horse, he advanced on foot to attack them with his wonted courage. The battle was soon finished, for all that they were designed to do was in appearance, and as soon as he touched them they dissolved into air, of which they were made. Then seeing that all the dangers which had threatened him were illusions, he determined all which might yet present themselves to him as nothing more.

\*

And now looking to see how he might ascend into the building, he perceived a little gate under some arches, and from thence a flight of steps ascended so steep, that it was a labour to climb them, so narrow that it was with difficulty a man could get up between the walls, and so long, that the top of them was out of sight. Palmerin, desirous to see the end of his labours, adventured to go up, and when he was a little way up the walls about him began to shake vehemently, so that sometimes he thought the vaulted roof would fall in and crush him; at other times he was so squeezed between the sides that he could not move. Long it was before he could gain the top, but then the shaking ceased, and he found himself in a long open gallery, which was of marvellous workmanship. At the end thereof there was a great door, made fast with three great locks and bolts of iron, and before the door lay a mighty serpent, whose horrible bigness not only filled up the door-way, but likewise a great part of the gallery; the countenance of this serpent was such that the very sight of it struck fear to the heart; and his eye above all was so watchful, that it seemed hopeless to attempt aught against him by

## THE MAGICAL PALACE OF DARKNESS

slight, if it could not be obtained by force. About his neck, upon a string, were hanged the keys that should open the three locks. Then Palmerin perceived that whoever would enter must use these keys; and seeing the porter was so unsociable that he would give them to no one, and that to take them from him against his will would be a hopeless endeavour, he stood awhile in doubt what he should do; but calling to mind the illusions of this place, he determined to attack him, and advanced to strike. The serpent rose in anger, glowing with fire, and breathing out flames from his mouth. But the danger quickened Palmerin's courage, and seeing himself so engaged, he thrust his sword into one of the huge nostrils. At this the serpent snorted out such volumes of smoke as blackened the whole air, and fled out of the gallery with terrible roarings, which seemed to shake the very earth.

*

The people seeing him fly over the city, and how fearful a monster he was, well judged that Palmerin had been in some dread danger, and though they were in great trouble for him, it was far greater pain to Selviam, who, though he was free from bodily dangers, felt in his soul those of his master.

*

When Palmerin saw himself delivered from this danger, and the smoke had dispersed, he found the keys on the ground, wherewith he opened the locks, and entered into so fair a hall, and so marvellously wrought, that neither those in the island which he had won from Eutropa, nor the abode of Daliarte in the Dark Valley, might compare with this.

*

Entering then into other apartments, for there was none

to oppose him, he saw that they were all of the same cunning workmanship, which made him highly account the rare knowledge of the king of Thrace, by whom such a work had been devised. Now, as the serpent was the last of these vain perils, nothing more hindered him from approaching the true danger, which was the sight of Lionarda, from which no human wisdom could secure him. So proceeding from one apartment to another, at last he heard the voices of women in one of the rooms, who as soon as they perceived him, being terrified at such a novelty as the sight of an armed man, fled from the apartment, leaping from some verandas into a garden. Palmerin followed them into this garden, which seemed to him yet more worthy of admiration than all which he had seen within. He had not proceeded far, when, under the shade of some thick and green laurels, round about a fountain of rare and more marvellous fashion than he had ever beheld, he saw some damsels seated, so fair that they seemed worthy to be in so fair a place; and amongst them was Lionarda, who in form and feature was more beautiful than the rest, beyond comparison. They, when they saw him approach, rose up to receive him, knowing that by him they were released for that enchantment. Lionarda welcomed him with that graceful courtesy which nature had imparted to her. Sir Knight, said she, though certes the obligation which of so great a debt as you have laid me under, cannot be discharged with words, yet I beseech you accept now the wish I have to requite you, in satisfaction for your deeds; and hereafter, if time shall give me room to requite you better, standing with mine honour, then shall you see the desire I have to recompense you what is due.

\*

Lady, he replied, abundant recompense for any achievement, how great soever, is this sight, and this beauty, for one who should have a heart free enough to let him understand so great a happiness. The things of this place are all so wonderful that the present put the past out of remembrance;—I intreat you tell me, if I have any greater danger to pass, than this which you present before me, for if there be I shall despair to accomplish it. The hope of such great things ought to be reserved for a greater heart than mine. Now, though Lionarda of a truth was so fair that fairer might not be, what she felt at these words sent up so modest a colour into her countenance as made her appear yet fairer, for they seemed to have in them the meaning which might well be suspected. She replied, I know not, Sir Knight, what danger you sustain at this present; all the dangers of this place were ended at such time as you came into this garden. But then to break off their talk, there came in the lords and governors of the city, who seeing the serpent fly over the city, which they knew to be the end of the enchantment, came with full speed riding to the castle, where coming into the garden, they humbled themselves on their knees before the Princess Lionarda, offering likewise to kiss the hand of Palmerin as their king; but he, whose resolution was otherwise, would not suffer this, but received them with equal courtesy. It was not long before a letter arrived, sent by Queen Carmelia, for the princess. She was received into the city, with all the feasts and rejoicing which the people could devise, in so short a time. Palmerin was amazed, as he returned, not to find that water which he had crost: for though he knew the other things to have been only visionary, this he thought had certainly been real. As soon as they reached the palace, Lionarda was received by her grand-mother Carmelia, with as much joy as a thing so long desired, deserved.

\*

Palmerin was lodged in the same apartment as before, where Selviam disarmed him, being full joyful to have his lord again, returned from so many dangers with such honour.

# Rustum Against the City of Demons

## from The Shah Namah of Firdausi

### Lin Carter

THE Great King of Persia, Chosroes *Anushirvan,* or The Blesséd, was a mighty man of war, a prince of monarchs, the Splendor of the Age. He went down in history as the great peace-maker who ended for all time the age-old struggle between the empires of Rome and Persia, and concluded an Eternal Peace with the Emperor Justinian which was to stand forever as an example of concord between mighty nations.

It lasted exactly nine years.

If Chosroes the Blesséd is remembered for anything constructive (he spent the next thirty-nine years in almost continuous warfare, usually against the Roman Empire, and died in the middle of haggling over truce terms with Tiberius II), it is for a literary project begun in his reign which was to set the all-time record as the largest literary task ever attempted, and the longest in the making, except for the Bible. For under the aegis of Blesséd Chosroes an attempt was made to collect all the tales and legends of the great monarchs and heroes of antiquity into one titanic chronicle-saga that would form a complete mythological history of Persia from the Creation of the Universe on down to whatever comparable milestone (say, for instance, the glorious reign of peace-making Chosroes) was deemed a major turning-point in cosmic history.

This colossal task long outlived the Great King under whose reign it began. It petered out for a time until revived in the last years of the Sassanid Dynasty, the compiled material being revised and added to by a team of learned and scholarly *mobeds*. Other scholars and poets puttered away over this immense body of mythic and heroic materials for a century or two, but what was needed was for one single literary genius to draw these diverse texts together into coherent focus with the hand of a master-craftsman.

This man did not appear until a good four hundred years after King Chosroes. His name was Abu'l Kasim Mansur. He was born in the city of Tus about 941 A.D., during the reign of Sultan Mahmoud, about the same time the Danes were invading England. Many things had happened to Persia in three hundred years (including the Moslem Conquest), and the task had grown that much lengthier. The poet Mansur (who wrote under a *takhallus*, a sort of literary pen-name) was hired by the Sultan to do the job; the Sultan promised to pay him one thousand pieces of gold for every thousand verses, or one gold piece per verse, which is quite a good fee, as author's royalties go. Which may explain why Mansur sat down and spent the next thirty-five years writing one of the longest poems ever written, an epic consisting of some sixty thousand verses.

Mansur wrote under the name of Firdausi, a Persian word meaning "Paradise." I hope Firdausi made it to Allah's heaven, for he certainly got gypped in this world. He made the big mistake of not collecting his money as he went along, you see, preferring to wait until the end before presenting the bill. This meant he labored for thirty-five years in direst poverty, looking forward to a rich old age. But when the last verse was completed and the tome was delivered, Mahmoud not only beat him down on the price, but grudgingly paid him off in *silver*, not in gold!

It is, the Sultan soon discovered, unwise to make mock of men of literary genius. For Firdausi promptly sat down and wrote one of the most merciless and savage satires ever penned. It made Mahmoud the laughing-stock of the Moslem world, and of course Firdausi never got his sixty thousand pieces of gold.

However, he left behind him one of the world's most magnificent books, a stupendous and staggering chronicle covering aeons of time, teeming with demons and dragons and enchanters, rose-colored horses, flying thrones, talking birds, seven-winged angels, magic crowns, giant warriors, century-old heroes, enchanted cities; a crowded panorama of surging wars, battles, invasions, rebellions, mighty quests, magical love-scenes, stark drama, and even tragedy. It is called *The Shah Namah,* the Book of the Kings, and although based on the work and research of scholars and poets over four hundred years, it is the work of one supreme literary artist, who won enduring fame although he never got paid for the job.

*The Shah Namah* is the national epic of Persia just as the *Odyssey* is the national epic of Greece and the *Aeneid* the national epic of Rome. It became a classic, the center of a national literature, in Firdausi's own lifetime; today it is a world classic, although it has never achieved the kind of popularity it deserves in the English-speaking world. I became so annoyed at the inadequacies of the standard English versions that I attempted one myself, although I am (Allah knows!) no Persian scholar. Forgive my immodesty if I frankly prefer my own version to another's.

For this anthology, I have selected the tale of Shah Kaikooz and the Enchanted City. This Kaikooz, according to the mythological history of the Persians, was the twelfth King of Persia from the Creation, and a descendant of Jamshid. (Readers familiar with the *Rubaiyat* of Omar Khayyam will recognize many names herein, such as Zal and Rustum, Jamshid and so on.)

Incidentally, it is heartening to learn that the mythological history of Persia is still believed in as historical truth. The Parsee sect of India, descended from those devout Persians who fled there to escape forcible conversion to Islam under the Moslems, still accept the ancient legendary chronicle and its mythological king-list. *The Shah Namah* lists the generations from Kahmurath, the Persian Adam and the first king of the world, through Siyamak, Hushang, Tahmurath, Jamshid, Zohak, Feridoon, Manuchehar, Nauder, Jotemash and Garshasp, and Kaikobad, to Kaikooz. The Parsees list: Gayomard, Hoshang, Tehmurasp, Jamsheed, Zohak, Farduin, Miocher, Nodar, a foreign usurper called Afrasiab, Jotemash and Gershasp as the mythological or Pishdadian Dynasty, followed by the nine kings of the "historical" or Kyanian Dynasty, of which the first two are Kae-kobad and Kae-Kaus.

It's nice to know that, in India at least, people still believe in heroes. And doubtless they still tell the ancient tale of Rustum and the City of Demons ...

## The Crowning of Kaikooz

THERE was great rejoicing among the Persians when their new Shah was crowned. The kingdom had passed through dangerous and difficult times, when powerful enemies like the Prince of the Turanians, leagued with wicked magicians, had gone up against the Persians in war. But now that splendid hero, Zal, mightiest of the warriors of the world, had broken the strength of the Turanians; the old Shah, Kaikobad, had gone into Paradise; and young Prince Kaikooz ascended to the Throne of Thrones as the twelfth Shah of the Persians, and all his people cheered his name.

But the Demons of the Mountain, who watch ever for the chance to destroy the happiness of mankind and who only take pleasure in evil deeds, were not pleased. They were angry that the heroes of Persia had won peace. The Dark Princes gathered in council to conspire against the new monarch of the Persians. They met within their hollow mountain in mighty halls of black marble filled with bitter smoke and lit with strange fires.

Some were horned and hairy. Others were clad in glittering scales like mighty serpents, with a single fierce eye glaring from the center of their brows. A few had cruel beaks and black clawed wings like terrible birds.

The most powerful of them all was Ibleez the Evil. He was throned on a globe of fire and wore a wreath of woven serpents for his crown.

"We must pull down this Kaikooz, my brothers," he said, in a voice that rang like iron trumpets through the gloomy hall lit with flashes of subterranean fire. "If we do not, then Persia will become great among the nations and Mankind, whose doom we have plotted since the beginning of time, will enter a new golden age of peace."

"How shall we break the Persian, O Ibleez?" asked one of the lesser demons whose body was covered with bristling spines and who had hooves of brass.

On his throne of fire, Ibleez mused thoughtfully. "This Kaikooz is young and vain and foolish. He is all puffed up with pride in his own importance. We could strike at him through his vanity, and tempt him to some rash act which will bring only humiliation and despair to him and to the Persians."

Another of the evil spirits spoke up. It was the one known among men as Suffid the White, for that he was of the color of pale ashes and had great eyes that blazed like spheres of colorless fire.

"But what of Zal the Mighty, O Ibleez? He is the bravest of warriors and the wisest of men, and he is sprung of that race of Giants who has opposed our evils in battle since first the world was made. Will not he see the danger and persuade the Shah against rash and thoughtless actions?"

The Lord of Evil laughed, a cold jangle of sound like breaking glass.

"Nay, for this Kaikooz is the least cautious of kings, and this I know for I have read that which is written on the tablets of his heart and I know him well. When his pride and vanity urge him, he forgets to listen to the wisest of his counselors, even the noble Zal."

## RUSTUM AGAINST THE CITY OF DEMONS

The White Demon breathed blue fire and bared glistening talons.

"But Zal is one of the Great Heroes, a child of the giants of old. Will he not, then, use his mighty valor and unconquerable strength to save Kaikooz from the perils into which his pride and rashness will immerse him?"

Ibleez fondled a monster crouching like a dog at the foot of his Fire Throne, and he fed it one of the serpents plucked writhing from his crown.

"Nay. Mighty indeed was Zal the White-Haired in the fullness of his youth! But is he not old now and long past the days of his greatness? Seven kings of the Persians hath he served, father to son, and his years weigh heavily upon him and we need fear his great strength nor valor nor the wisdom of his counsels any longer. Now, my brothers, here is the scheme I have devised for the undoing of rash Kaikooz and all his peoples . . ."

\*

That night Kaikooz walked alone in the gardens of his palace. The roses were in bloom by still pools of black water and silver moonbeams bathed the flowering trees and velvet lawns in a fulgour of pallid glory. As he strolled the garden paths, which were strewn with crushed rubies and crunched richly beneath the tread of his gilded sandals, the new-made Shah listened to the song of the bulbuls and looked upon the peace of the star-bright evening.

He remembered the pomp and splendor of the day, how the brilliant crown of diamonds had been set upon his brows and how he had ascended the Jewel Throne of the richest kingdom of all the earth. Before him in that high place had sat Kahmurath the First King of the World, whose son Siyamak was slain in battle against the Demons; and his grandson Hushang the Dragon-killer who rode in war against the giants mounted on his magic twelve-legged horse; and Tahmurath the Mighty who subjugated the Demons of the Mountain in his day and rode their King like a winged steed halfway between heaven and earth; and Jamshid the Wise who knew the language of birds and wild beasts; and evil Zohak from whose shoulders grew black serpents; and Feridoon who overthrew and trampled down the vile Usurper, and his son Manuchehar; and Nauder who fell in battle against the legions of Turan, and his sons Jotemash and Garshasp after him; and the wise and good Kaikobad, whose throne had now passed unto him, Kaikooz, as the Twelfth King of the World.

And the heart of Kaikooz swelled with thought of his own power and greatness, for the Evil One had read well the passions that flamed in his breast and had not erred in calling him a vain and empty-headed King.

It was in this mood that the Shah came upon what seemed to be a young man in the robes of a wandering troubadour. The youth sat on a bench of carven alabaster by the edge of the lotus pools, and he was playing upon a zither.

So sweet was the music of his playing, and so haunting the song the youth sang, that Kaikooz lingered to listen, and it did not occur to him to wonder how this stranger was come into the garden of crushed rubies where only the kings of Persia may walk.

The minstrel sang a dreamy tune: of a fair and goldbright city of enchanted loveliness that lay far and far away beyond the mountains of the north. It was a superb city of brilliant palaces whose tower-tops brushed against the lowest stars, and it was the heart and center of a land of magical beings, a kingdom thronged with a thousand marvels, where young men never need grow old.

> *O the way to my country is ever north till
>     you pass the Mouth of Hell,
> Past the Limbo of Dreams and the desolate Land
>     where Shadows dwell.
> And when you have reached the Fount of Wonder,
>     you ford the waters wan
> To the Land of Elves and the Land of Fairies,
>     Enchanted Masinderan.*

## RUSTUM AGAINST THE CITY OF DEMONS

The youth sang on and from time to time he stole a sly, sidewise glance at the king, who stood like one in a dream. And when the song was over, the Shah blinked his eyes once or twice like one who has just awakened from a gorgeous vision, and he asked the minstrel-lad if the song were true or only a song: was there such a place in all the world like enchanted Masinderan?

"Aye, O Shah! And the enchanted City of Marvel is even as I described it in my song," the youth replied.

"Can any place on earth be half so fair as the city of which you sing?" Again the youth replied, yes. He told the Shah that Masinderan was the very garden of spring, where winter never comes nor harsh winds blow: "There the air is sweet and fragrant with ten thousand flowers, for it is spring forever in Masinderan, and snow is only a legend that foolish poets speak of," he said. "The Nightingale sings in every bush, pouring his soft melodious song into the calm of twilight. There each streamlet is born of the dew that falls from the roses, and beautiful maidens wander in that blissful garden and are young and fair forever. True are my words, O Shah: he who hath never seen Masinderan hath never known happiness."

They spoke long of the marvels of the enchanted city, and at length the Shah inquired, "What fortunate man is Shah over Masinderan the Fair?"

"Alas, a wicked and unfortunate man," the minstrel made reply. "Once the City of Marvels was tributary to thy throne, O Kaikooz, in the days of thy forefathers. But a wicked monarch rose to power over the Golden Land, and now no more do caravans bear over the mountains the tribute of ten thousand jewels to lay at thy feet!"

And at that the face of Kaikooz hardened with wrath. And he turned from the garden and strode back into the palace, and in his heart burned only the desire to come into Masinderan and to punish the wicked Shah who had usurped the glory that was his by lawful and ancient descent from the ancestral kings of old.

When the Shah was gone from sight, the Demon

threw off his disguise and stood eleven feet tall in his own true likeness, which was that of a scarlet thing with webbed vans like some tremendous bat, and the fanged and snarling visage of a green-furred wolf.

With a mighty bound, the Demon soared into the air. His scarlet wings roared like kettle-drums as he flew around the palace of the Shah seven times, laughing in hideous mockery. (They heard him within the palace, and asked if there was not thunder in the hills.)

"Wise are thy schemes. O Ibleez!" the Demon crowed. "Behold, the Shah of all the Persians drank magic from the spell of my song and rides forth to conquer the Golden Land—and all the Demons of the Mountain wait in ambush to take him captive. Woe unto thee, O Persia, for thy king is a fool and not even the wisdom of Zal canst save thee from the wiles of Ibleez now!"

And he flew away to the edge of the earth, while behind in the palace of kings, Kaikooz sent forth his heralds to summon the lords and nobles of Persia for a war against the City of Marvel.

## The Anger of Zal

Now this Zal whereof you have heard much was old and full of years and long ago had he retired from the life of court to rule over the Province of Nimruz. And this night as he lay asleep, the Angel of Protection, who each night flies nine times around the earth to guard the children of men from harm, appeared to Zal in a dream and warned him of the rashness of the Shah.

Whereupon Zal rose up and called for his steed and his warriors, and set forth out of Nimruz into the City of the Kings, so that he might give counsel and warning to the king.

He came unto Kaikooz in the midst of his preparations. The elephants were lined in a row like moving mountains, with wooden castles borne upon their broad backs, and the tents of the mighty warrior-lords of Persia were set each in his place. There was a tent draped in black, and a banner set before it that was broidered with an elephant; and this was the standard of Tus the son of Nowzar, a great lord. And beyond, aged Zal could see a crimson pavilion with a gold flag set before it that bore the image of a lion; and this was the standard of Gudarz the Brave, who led his eighty sons to battle, and all were mighty men of war. And beyond them all stood the tent hung with leopard skins and surrounded with elephants of war; there was a throne of jeweled gold within it, sparkling in the morning sun, and there was a banner of purple set before it that was broidered with the faces of the sun and the moon, and priests of Ormazd went about the pavilion bearing aloft a great standard covered with diamonds. And Zal knew this standard and he bowed low before it, for this was the famous leather apron of Kavah the Blacksmith, the lowly one who raised the Persians to revolt against the unjust and sorcerous Zohak and to whelm him down utterly, and to set in his place the rightful monarch, Feridoon.

This leather apron, now sewn all over with a thousand jewels, was the Kaviana, the Sacred Standard of Persia. And this was the tent of Shah Kaikooz.

Zal went in and bowed him low before the Shah, and told him of his dream. But the Shah was filled with preparations of war and had no time to hearken unto the wise old man, although the lord Gudarz and the lord Tus and many another of the Princes of Persia begged Kaikooz to listen unto the wise words of Zal.

"Zal is old and has forgotten the smell of war," said Kaikooz.

Zal heard, but swallowed the king's words, and pled anew that the journey was long, the way was hard and beset with a thousand perils, and no man knew aught of the City of Marvel, for none had ever heard tell of it before.

"All the more reason for me to go up against it in war," answered Kaikooz, "for if I attempt a deed that no man hath ever dreamed of doing, all the more glory shall be mine when the deed is achieved. But if Zal the son of Sahm hath grown cowardly and fears war in his eld, let him depart unto his province, for we have young warriors aplenty!"

At these words the wrath of Zal grew fierce and he rose up in his might, and all the warriors of Persia paled and shrank back to see the old lion stirred to anger. For this Zal was of the lineage of the giants and he was taller than any of the children of the earth, save only for his son, Rustum. His snowy hair flowed over the breadth of his mighty shoulders like a frozen cataract, and his beard descended to his waist, and amidst the hoary locks, his eyes blazed forth like balls of lightning.

"Go, then, to thy wars, O king," he growled; "but ask no aid from me when trouble befalls thee!"

And Zal strode from the camp of war, although the seven and seventy lords of Persia sought to stay him and begged with him to disuade the Shah from this futile and perilous expedition.

And thus it came to pass the Shah Kaikooz departed into the mountains of the north with a mighty host of warriors, to set red war against the depraved and treacherous Shah of the City of Marvel. As for Zal, he rode out of the capitol and returned unto his Province of Nimruz, and his wrath against the king was hot within his breast, and he swore to lift no hand to aid the Shah in deed or word.

And seven days after this, there came riding out of the mountains of the north a warrior of the king's host much travel-stained and weary. His mail was rent as by great fierce claws, his spired helm was shorn awry, and his blade was blunted. He rode into the courtyard of Zal's palace and cast himself down in the dust before the mighty warrior, saying:

"Behold, O Zal, the king thy lord is embattled against the Demons of the Mountain, and beseeches thine aid!"

And Zal said: "How has this thing come to pass? Not since the days of Shah Tamurath the Mighty, during whose reign was the war against the White Mountain concluded, have demons been seen in the land!"

The messenger replied: "How these things came to be, knoweth not I. But as the host of Persia approached

## RUSTUM AGAINST THE CITY OF DEMONS

the outskirts of the City of Marvel, there came a black darkness as of deepest night down upon us, so that a man might not see his neighbor. And from this black cloud rained down great hailstones that might not be believed, such were their girth. And lightning flamed, striking fire from the earth, and all the host was thrown into a confusion of turmoil and feared to go forward; hence did the Shah Kaikooz dispatch me to return to ask aid of thee and all thy warriors."

The heart of Zal was disturbed at these words, but still was he heavy with wrath at the slighting and unjust words of the foolish king. Hence he replied:

"I have sworn I shall not lift my hand to aid the king in this enterprise." And he would say no more.

And seven days after this there came out of the mountains of the north a second messenger, and in worse state than the first; for his raiment was all but torn from his body, and he was weak from exhaustion and terror. He staggered from his weary steed, and fell in the earth before the feet of Zal, crying out:

"Behold, O Zal, the king thy lord is carried off in the grip of a monster out of the midst of his warriors, and beseeches thine aid!"

And Zal said: "How has this thing come to pass? Not since the day of Shah Nauder, during whose reign was the war against the Turanians, hath a king of Persia been seized from the midst of his warriors!"

The messenger replied: "How these things came to be, knoweth not I. But as the host of Persia lay embattled amidst the cloud of black darkness, swept by buffets of hailstone and blasts of lightning, there came a White Demon out of the skies who fell on Kaikooz and plucked him forth into the air, carrying him off; hence did the Shah Kaikooz cry out that I should return to beg the aid of thee and all thy warriors."

The heart of Zal was very greatly troubled at this dire news, and he yearned to set his iron strength against the White Demon and to wrest the Shah from his grasp; yet still was there great wrath in his heart. Hence he replied:

"I have sworn I shall not lift my hand to aid the king in this enterprise." And he would say no more.

And seven days after this there came out of the mountains of the north a third messenger, and in a worse state than was the second; for he was naked and the flesh all but torn from his bones with terrible wounds, so that he fainted from loss of blood and was like to die. He fell from his horse before the feet of Zal, whispering as with his dying breath:

"Behold, O Zal, the king thy lord is imprisoned in a cavern beneath the Seven Mountains, held captive by the Demons who have blinded him so that he dwelleth forever in perpetual darkness, bemoaning his sad estate, and he doth beseech thine aid!"

And Zal said: "How has this thing come to pass! Not since the day of Shah Zohak the Usurper, hath a king of Persia been enslaved to the vile host of Ibleez!"

The messenger replied: "How these things come to be, knoweth not I. But the White Demon who bore away Shah Kaikooz amidst the whirling darkness hath sealed him far beneath the mountains, where he lieth guarded by a dragon. And the lords of Persia commanded that I should return to beg the aid of thee and all thy warriors."

Now Zal was deeply sorrowed to hear of the unhappy fate of the Shah, and he knew that all the realm would be thrown into confusion at this word, yet still was he minded of his oath. Hence he replied:

"I have sworn I shall not lift my hand to aid the king in this enterprise." And he would say no more.

And there came unto him thereafter no further messengers.

## The Arming of Rustum

Now this Zal was father to a son whose name was Rustum, born of his union with Rudabeh the daughter of Mihrab the King of the land of Zabolestan. And although but a youth, Rustum was mighty of stature and a warrior of great renown. And when word reached the

## RUSTUM AGAINST THE CITY OF DEMONS

land of Zabolestan of the perils into which the Shah of all the Persians had fallen because of his pride, rashness and vanity, and of the dilemma of Zal who had sworn to withhold his aid and was greatly troubled that he should break this holy oath, the son of Zal rose up and came into the Province of Nimruz where his father dwelt and cast himself down in the dust before Zal, saying:

"O father, let me take up this task and strive to set free the lord our king; for thine oath bindeth only thyself, and not the others of thy house; therefore, I pray you, give me permission to go up against this City of Demons."

And the heart of Zal was filled with joy at the word, and he lay his hand on the head of Rustum and blest him, saying:

"Choose from all the herds in my land of Nimruz the steed that can bear thee, and take from my hand this mighty mace which thine ancestors have born in battle before the Shahs of Persia." And he gave him a great mace of iron whose shaft was as long as a man is high, and whose head was a heavy sphere of metal, horned like the bull. Rustum knew that this was the famous bull-horned mace that had of old been fashioned by that same Kavah the Blacksmith who had saved all the kingdom from the hand of Zohak in elder time, and he humbly thanked his father for entrusting into his hand the mighty weapon of the giant-born heroes.

Then Rustum went out into the fields, but nowhere could he find a steed strong enough to bear up under his weight, for Rustum was the mightiest man on earth and greater even than his father Zal. Long and far he searched, and at last he came into a field wherein grazed horses of kingly and noble mien and of far greater girth than any he had heretofore seen.

And amongst these he perceived a powerful mare far stronger than the rest, who went followed by a colt. This colt caught the eye of Rustum for he was of a peculiar hue, even of the color of roses; and he had the mighty chest and shoulders of a lion. The moment Rustum espied the colt he knew he had found his steed: but finding and riding are not the same. For as he cast out his noose and ensnared the young colt, the furious mare reared up halfway to heaven and struck at him with glittering hooves, slashing and biting and stamping as if to crush the head of any who dared lay a hand on her colt.

Rustum could have slain the mare with his mace, but he lay it by and instead gave voice to his mighty battle-cry, which in after-time was to strike terror into entire armies of the foe. So great was this cry that the mare sank half stunned to the ground beneath the frightful sound, and he turned to make captive the colt. But although his noose was about its neck, the rose-colored horse was by no means yet tamed, and it sped away at a furious pace. Rustum must either run behind it or let go of the noose he held in his hand, so off they raced, the hero and the great horse, and the greater half of the Province of Nimruz they traversed ere at length the horse grew weary and lay panting under his hand. And when at last this was accomplished, and the horse lay tamed under his hand, the heart of Rustum swelled with joy, and he could say:

"Now am I well-armed with the mace of Kavah and I go forward mounted with a horse after mine own heart to join the warriors of the world!"

And he named the colt Rakush, for his speed: for the name meaneth "the Lightning-Swift." And together they set forth to venture into the land of enchanted Masinderan where the Shah Kaikooz lay in bondage, bemoaning his fate that he had not hearkened to the wise counsels of Zal.

## The Courage of Rakush

There be two roads that lead into the lands about the City of Marvel. One road is long but easy, and withouten peril or danger. And the second is short and swift, but it passeth through the debatable lands where the Demons hold sway.

Down the short way went Rustum on his rose-colored steed, the great bull-horned mace of the heroes clenched in his fist. All that day they rode and saw naught to affright them and lay that night beside the road, where Rustum slept with the mace at his side while Rakush grazed the green grass.

Forth from the underbrush came a huge lion which sprang upon Rakush to devour him, but the horse turned on the savage beast and fought it, trampling the snarling lion to death under glittering hooves, and then went on grazing.

The next day they rode on through the debatable land and crossed a vast desert where the sun shone so fierce and hot it seemed as if they rode over sands made of molten lead; but Rakush made no demur and sped forward although the heat was nigh to melt his steel-shod hooves. That night they lay on the edge of a green forest and again Rustum slept while Rakush grazed the flowering mead. And there came forth out of the wood a vast and fearsome dragon, unwinding itself from the trees, coil by glistening coil, and it slithered towards the hero where he slept, the great mace near his hand, and would have devoured him.

But the brave steed of Rustum espied the writhing length of the dragon and sprang between its slavering jaws and the slumbering body of his master, and fought the dragon with slashing hooves and biting jaws, holding the monster at bay until the hero roused from his slumbers and seized up the mace and turned to face the dragon. And they did battle side by side, the horse and the hero, until at length the bull-horned mace crushed the dragon's skull and besplattered the verdant grass with its reeking brains.

And Rustum stroked the mane of his rose-colored steed and rejoiced greatly, saying: "Was ever such a horse in all the annals of the world! I pray Ormuzd that my own strength and courage prove equal to thee, O Rakush!"

And they went forward by day and came into the mountains where the Demons had rule, and Rustum bore away with him seven drops of the blood of the slain dragon in a crystal phial.

## The Whelming of Suffid

At length and after many trials and perils, they came into the Seven Mountains to the mouth of the cavern wherein was the Shah Kaikooz imprisoned. It lay at the end of a narrow cleft or valley. As he made his way therethrough, Rustum saw before him the mouth of a black cavern. Dismounting, he girded his loins in a leopard skin and bound the hair back from his brows, and went to the mouth of the cavern. He saw therein a monstrous white form that lay slumbering, and he roused it with his great battle-cry that shook the Seven Mountains to the peaks thereof. The thunderous cry awoke the White Demon (for it was he) and he issued forth from the entrance in the form of a gigantic dragon, which said:

"Art thou so weary of life that thou wouldst invade the very fortress of the Demon Kings? Tell me thy name, I beseech you, that I may not destroy a nameless thing."

And Rustum answered, saying: "Rustum am I, the son of Zal and grandson of Sahm, sent by my father to avenge thy treatment of the king of Persia!"

And he smote the Demon alongside the head a fearsome blow with the bull-horned mace of the Giant-heroes. With a roar that shook the earth, the Demon, still in the form and likeness of a dragon, seized up a boulder as huge as a millstone and hurled it straightway at the hero. But he smote it in mid-passage through the air with his mace, shattering it to a thousand fragments which fell harmlessly about him.

Then he sprang forward and leapt astride the dragon's back, clamping his powerful legs about the barrel of the monster, clouting it atop the head with his mace until the horns of its crest were all shattered. In vain the dragon twisted and turned, seeking to bathe Rustum in the torment of its fiery breath, but Rustum smote it first on one scaly cheek and then the other, so that it could not turn its head and burn him with its breath.

And then the Demon transformed itself into a mighty

lion and in the transformation Rustum was thrown clear of the back of the monster and sprawled in the rocky floor of the gorge as the lion with a roar of wrath that shook the very clouds launched itself to spring upon him. He rose to his feet and closed with the gigantic lion in a fierce embrace. And they wrastled there in the narrow cleft, falling first upon this side and then upon the other, grinding boulders to dust as they fell crashing upon them. The Demon in the likeness and form of a lion sought to sink its terrible fangs in the hero's throat and tear off his head, but Rustum smote at it with his mighty mace, dealing it great buffets that smashed the fangs that lined its slavering jaws, so that it could not seize nor rend his flesh.

At last the Demon transformed itself again, and this time into its rightful form and shape, which was of a giant thing seven times man-size, the color of pale ashes, with great moony eyes that blazed like spheres of pallid fire.

It reached down and caught up Rustum in one great hand and like to have squeezed the life from his body. Then it raised him high in the air so as to dash his lifeless form to the rocks below. And gasping for breath, and dizzied, and nigh to falling in a swound for weariness, Rustum knew that he was near the utmost end of his strength, and had within his lion-like thews the strength for but one blow more. So, summoning all his powers, and calling upon the might of holy Ormuzd, he smote the Demon a terrific blow with the bull-headed mace of the Giant-heroes.

So great was the blow that the skull of the Demon was crushed and cloven to the jaw, and the horns of the mace were deep buried in the brain of the Demon. And that blow was the undoing and the whelming of Suffid the White, and it crushed the life out of him and he fell down dead, still clutching the hero against his breast.

And Rustum came to his feet again victorious, for all that it seemed the very life was almost dashed out of his body from the pummeling he had taken, and he ached as if every bone was broken in his body; and he stood for a time, leaning on the shaft of the mace, breathing deeply.

Then he be-thought him of the dragon's blood he had taken in the phial of crystal; and he anointed his wounds with the fiery green ichor that had fallen from the dragon, and Lo! his wounds closed without pain and strength flowed back into him as boundless as the sea.

Greatly heartened that the reign of Suffid the White Demon was undone, he cut out the heart of the Demon and stuffed it in his pouch; and then he went forward alone into the blackness of the cavern to set free Shah Kaikooz and his lords, and he healed the blindness of the king with the last drop of dragon's-blood within the phial, having used up six of the seven drops in closing his wounds and renewing his strength.

And they rode forward into the City of Marvel and drove the Demons forth, and set free the folk thereof that had long gone under the cruel tyranny of Ibleez. And thus were the schemes of the Lord of Evil whelmed and trampled down, and thus was Kaikooz restored to the bosom of his people, and thus was Rustum the son of Zal acclaimed as one of the great ones of the earth, and he lived for three hundred years a mighty warrior famous in renown and loved by all men, and when at last the angels bore him up into the Paradise of Ormuzd they assured him that his name would live upon the lips of the children of men thrice ten thousand years. May it be thus forever!

# "Childe Roland to the Dark Tower Came"

## Robert Browning

THERE IS a poem by Robert Browning that I have never been able to get out of my mind. In its strangeness and its ambiguity, it is haunting; it nags and frets at the back of the mind.

Browning appends a note to the poem, calling attention to his source: a single puzzling, meaningless line uttered by a madman in *King Lear:*

> Childe Rowland to the dark tower came,
> His word was still "Fie, foh, and fum,
> I smell the blood of a British man."

That scrap of verse appears in Act III, Scene 4. The babblings of mad Edgar . . . but the line, it seems, haunted Browning as the poem he built out of that nagging ghost has haunted me!

I know, in all of literature, of only a few poems more deeply and strangely disturbing, poems which hint indirectly and dimly at a dark and terrible knowledge just beyond the borders of speech itself. Few poems are more saturated with the uneasy shadows of melancholy and foreboding, and few more somber and disquieting, than this enigmatic heroic lay of a doomed quest. An eerie glamour of dark enchantment is cast over both the song and its knightly hero, and the poem could easily be singing of the grim marches of Tolkien's Mordor—"Bog, clay and rubble, sand and stark black dearth."

I commend to your uneasy nights and shadow-haunted days this, the most magical ballad of all poetry . . .

※ ❧ ☙ ※

My first thought was, he lied in every word,
That hoary cripple, with malicious eye
Askance to watch the working of his lie
On mine, and mouth scarce able to afford
Suppression of the glee that pursed and scored
Its edge at one more victim gained thereby.

What else should he be set for, with his staff?
What, save to waylay with his lies, ensnare
All travellers who might find him posted there,
And ask the road? I guessed what skull-like laugh
Would break, what crutch 'gin write my epitaph
For pastime in the dusty thoroughfare,

If at his counsel I should turn aside
Into that ominous tract which, all agree,
Hides the Dark Tower. Yet acquiescingly
I did turn as he pointed; neither pride
Nor hope rekindling at the end descried,
So much as gladness that some end might be.

For, what with my whole world-wide wandering,
What with my search drawn out through years, my hope
Dwindled into a ghost not fit to cope
With that obstreperous joy success would bring,—
I hardly tried now to rebuke the spring
My heart made, finding failure in its scope.

As when a sick man very near to death
Seems dead indeed, and feels begin and end
The tears, and takes the farewell of each friend,

## "CHILDE ROLAND TO THE DARK TOWER CAME"

And hears one bid the other go, draw breath
Freelier outside ("since all is o'er," he saith,
"And the blow fallen no grieving can amend;")

While some discuss if near the other graves
Be room enough for this, and when a day
Suits best for carrying the corpse away,
With care about the banners, scarves and staves,—
And still the man hears all, and only craves
He may not shame such tender love and stay.

Thus, I had so long suffered in this quest,
Heard failure prophesied so oft, been writ
So many times among "The Band"—to wit,
The knights who to the Dark Tower's search addrest
Their steps—that just to fail as they, seemed best,
And all the doubt was now—should I be fit.

So, quiet as despair, I turned from him,
That hateful cripple, out of his highway
Into the path he pointed. All the day
Had been a dreary one at best, and dim
Was settling to its close, yet shot one grim
Red leer to see the plain catch its estray.

For mark! no sooner was I fairly found
Pledged to the plain, after a pace or two,
Than, pausing to throw backwards a last view
O'er the safe road, 'twas gone: grey plain all round:
Nothing but plain to the horizon's bound.
I might go on; nought else remained to do.

So, on I went. I think I never saw
Such starved ignoble nature; nothing throve:
For flowers—as well expect a cedar grove!
But cockle, spurge, according to their law
Might propagate their kind, with none to awe,
You'd think; a burr had been a treasure-trove.

No! penury, inertness and grimace,
In some strange sort, were the land's portion. "See
Or shut your eyes," said Nature peevishly,

"It nothing skills: I cannot help my case:
'Tis the Last Judgment's fire must cure this place,
Calcine its clods and set my prisoners free."

\*

A sudden little river crossed my path
As unexpected as a serpent comes.
No sluggish tide congenial to the glooms—
This, as it frothed by, might have been a bath
For the fiend's glowing hoof—to see the wrath
Of its black eddy bespate with flakes and spumes.

So petty yet so spiteful! all along,
Low scrubby alders kneeled down over it;
Drenched willows flung them headlong in a fit
Of mute despair, a suicidal throng:
The river which had done them all the wrong,
Whate'er that was, rolled by, deterred no whit.

Which, while I forded,—good saints, how I feared
To set my foot upon a dead man's cheek,
Each step, or feel the spear I thrust to seek
For hollows, tangled in his hair or beard!
—It may have been a water-rat I speared,
But, ugh! it sounded like a baby's shriek.

Glad was I when I reached the other bank.
Now for a better country. Vain presage!
Who were the strugglers, what war did they wage
Whose savage trample thus could pad the dank
Soil to a plash? toads in a poisoned tank,
Or wild-cats in a red-hot iron cage—

The fight must so have seemed in that fell cirque.
What penned them there, with all the plain to choose?
No foot-print leading to that horrid mews,
None out of it. Mad brewage set to work
Their brains, no doubt, like galley-slaves the Turk
Pits for his pastime, Christians against Jews.

And more than that—a furlong on—why, there!
What bad use was that engine for, that wheel,
Or brake, not wheel—that harrow fit to reel

## "CHILDE ROLAND TO THE DARK TOWER CAME"

Men's bodies out like silk? with all the air
Of Tophet's tool, on earth left unaware,
Or brought to sharpen its rusty teeth of steel.

Then came a bit of stubbed ground, once a wood,
Next a march, it would seem, and now mere earth
Desperate and done with; (so a fool finds mirth,
Makes a thing and then mars it, till his mood
Changes and off he goes!) within a rood—
Bog, clay and rubble, sand and stark black dearth.

Now blotches rankling, coloured gay and grim,
Now patches where some leanness of the soil's
Broke into moss or substances like boils;
Then came some palsied oak, a cleft in him
Like a distorted mouth that splits its rim
Gaping at death, and dies while it recoils.

And just as far as ever from the end!
Nought in the distance but the evening, nought
To point my footsteps further! At the thought,
A great black bird, Apollyon's bosom-friend,
Sailed past, nor beat his wide wing dragon-penned
That brushed my cap—perchance the guide I sought.

For, looking up, aware I somehow grew,
'Spite of the dusk, the plain had given place
All round to mountains—with such name to grace
Mere ugly heights and heaps now stolen in view.
How thus they had surprised me,—solve it, you!
How to get from them was no clearer case.

Yet half I seemed to recognise some trick
Of mischief happened to me, God knows when—
In a bad dream perhaps. Here ended, then,
Progress this way. When, in the very nick
Of giving up, one time more, came a click
As when a trap shuts—you're inside the den!

Burningly it came on me all at once,
This was the place! those two hills on the right,
Crouched like two bulls locked horn in horn in fight;

While to the left, a tall scalped mountain . . . Dunce,
Fool, to be dozing at the very nonce,
After a life spent training for the sight!

What in the midst lay but the Tower itself?
The round squat turret, blind as the fool's heart,
Built of brown stone, without a counterpart
In the whole world. The tempest's mocking elf
Points to the shipman thus the unseen shelf
He strikes on, only when the timbers start.

Not see? because of night perhaps?—Why, day
Came back again for that! before it left,
The dying sunset kindled through a cleft:
The hills, like giants at a hunting, lay,
Chin upon hand, to see the game at bay,—
"Now stab and end the creature—to the heft!"

Not hear? when noise was everywhere! it tolled
Increasing like a bell. Names in my ears,
Of all the lost adventurers my peers,—
How such a one was strong, and such was bold,
And such was fortunate, yet each of old
Lost, lost! one moment knelled the woe of years.

There they stood, ranged along the hillsides, met
To view the last of me, a living frame
For one more picture! in a sheet of flame
I saw them and I knew them all. And yet
Dauntless the slug-horn to my lips I set,
And blew, *"Childe Roland to the Dark Tower came."*

# The Princess of
# Babylon

## Voltaire

MOST PEOPLE who will tell you, yes, of course, they read Voltaire years ago, really mean (if you pin them down to it) that they once read *Candide*. Well, I read *Candide* many years ago too, and thought it was pretty dreary. But the *real* Voltaire lies in the shorter and less well-known romances. I came to them very late, I must confess. In fact, I first encountered the shorter romances only ten years ago, on July 28, 1959 to be exact—and the fact that I know the precise date may indicate something of the impact these enchanting tales had on me.

I picked up the book and leafed through it to the beginning of a tale called "The White Bull," and I read:

The princess Amasidia, daughter of Amasis, King of Tanis in Egypt, took a walk with her ladies. Mambres, ancient magician and eunuch of the Pharaohs, was beside her . . . the princess was twenty-four years old; the magician, about thirteen hundred . . .

My antennae started to tingle—if you are a lifelong lover of good books, you develop these antennae: they tingle when you are in close proximity to the Real Stuff, and mine were tingling like mad.

Then I turned to the opening of the next story, "Zadig," and read:

> There lived at Babylon, in the reign of King Moabdar, a young man named Zadig. Though rich and young, he had learned to moderate his passions. He had learned, in the first book of Zoroaster, that self-love is a football swelled with wind, from which, when pierced, the most terrible tempests issue forth . . .

My antennae were signalling a four-alarm fire, but I was too busy devouring the story to pay any more attention.

*

Voltaire was a satirist given to political lampoons and to the concocting of witty and sharp-edged fables wherewith to puncture the pompous and the puffed-up. Now the trouble with most such writers who have an itch to sell you their Message is that they are dour and deadly-serious folk and their tales, no matter how clever and inventive, have a sour center and a core of bitterness. (Take Swift, for example: *Gulliver* could have been as delightful as *Gargantua* if Swift had been having as much fun as Rabelais, but he was too much in earnest to relax, unbend and enjoy what he was doing.)

Voltaire was something else. He saw mankind with clear, shrewd eyes, and he saw every blemish and flaw sharply. But behind his iconoclasm and in back of each lampoon was a warm love and affection for stupid, superstitious, self-deceived man, and not a brain of impatience or bad humor. He was having too much fun laughing at the droll and hilarious pretensions of humanity to loathe the species as much as Swift did. Hence he is much more fun to read.

"Voltaire" is a pen-name. He was born François Marie Arouet in Paris on November 21, 1694. He came from good Poitevin stock, and his people seem to have been solid, stuffy, middle-class and fairly prosperous. His father was a notary and wanted him to study law, but he had become infected with an enthusiasm for the theatre while in school and, at seventeen, decided to devote his life to letters. After the usual battle between a son who refuses to consider any profession but literature and a father who refuses to consider literature a profession at all, he was packed off to read for the bar. He loafed along, pretending to read law, fell in with bohemian theatrical people, and was lost to the legal profession for good.

His first works were scandalous (and also libellous) poems. He followed these with some searing political lampoons against the regent, Orléans, which got him sent into exile—not bad, for a young writer only twenty-two! —came back, wrote some more and ended up in the jolly old Bastille. At this point he abandoned both the attempt to write lampoons and the name he was born with. When he got out of jail, he was now "Voltaire," with the manuscript of his first verse tragedy under his arm. (The *Encyclopaedia Britannica,* in its usual bumbling way, says "Voltaire" is probably an anagram for "Arouet le jeune," or "Arouet l. j." In a pig's eye, it is! Where did the *v* and the *i* come from?)

As far as I can see, Voltaire seems to have believed his serious dramas were his important work. He couldn't have been more wrong. Some of them (like *Mérope* and *Zaïre*) display technical virtuosity and polish and a sense of style, but most of them (like *Pucelle* and *Oedipe*) are tiresome, laborious and smell of the lamp. He had this disastrous tendency to either pick titanic historical subjects of vast complexity and importance, like *Pucelle*, which is about Joan of Arc—and to turn out a play composed mainly of static tableaus and pageants, devoid of humor or human interest—or to take on such heavyweights as Sophocles, by attempting to write something as good as *Oedipus Rex*. He so desperately wanted to be another Corneille, but, alas, he was "only" a Voltaire . . .

The romances he seems to have tossed off in his lighter moments. He certainly does not seem to have taken them very seriously, and for perhaps that very reason they are vastly more charming and beguiling than the plays. For his scenery, he took the ancient world, laying his tales in Babylon and Egypt. Not very much was known about antiquity in his day—archeology was not yet born—but the imprecision of his settings and his lushly romantic picture of life in ancient times has a naïveté and a freshness that add greatly to the reader's pleasure.

In tales like "The Princess of Babylon" and "Zadig" and "The White Bull," Voltaire was still giving the Establishment a kick in the pants, as in his early lampoons. But instead of being sourly serious about it, he was having fun, and that makes all the difference in the world. He knocked everything about him that seemed knock-worthy: greedy money-lenders, stuffy society people, corruption at Court, money-mad merchants, selfish and venal politicians, the pomposity and superstition-mongering of the church. And he did his knocking with great aplomb, verve and gusto. Since we still have such people among us, even after two centuries, his tales are just as trenchant and meaningful today as when he wrote them.

A free-thinker, an eccentric, a good-humored satirist, Voltaire was a gadfly to his era, just like Socrates long before him, or Mencken and Cabell in our own century. He was continually getting in hot water because of his iconoclastic humor, but it didn't bother him much. Throughout his long life (he died in 1778 at eighty-four) he displayed the most amazing talent for getting into trouble. And he seems to have loved every moment of it.

He became one of the most famous writers of his century, and most of the celebrities of his time were among his friends, including Richelieu, Frederick of Prussia, Madame de Pompadour, and that prince of charlatans, Cagliostro. He travelled quite a bit—Brussels, The Hague, Germany, and even England, where he lived for three years, hobnobbing with Pope, the Walpoles, Congreve and the Duchess of Marlborough.

Voltaire spent his old age at Ferney on the shore of Lake Geneva. There he wrote voluminously, including a gigantic correspondence with everyone in Europe, including kings. He was host to the most celebrated men in Europe, who made frequent pilgrimages to visit him. He died old and happy, surrounded by friends and enemies, one of the most famous men of his century.

He wrote just about everything, from historical works to epic poems, from plays and novels to a dictionary of philosophy. The tale I have selected for you is, to my taste, the most delicious fantasy he ever wrote, and one of the world's most beguiling and entertaining tales . . .

≈§ ¿≈

# I
## Royal Contest for the Hand of Formosanta

THE AGED Belus, king of Babylon, thought himself the first man upon earth, for all his courtiers told him so, and his historians proved it. We know that his palace and his park, situated at a few parasangs from Babylon, extended between the Euphrates and the Tigris, which washed those enchanted banks. His vast house, three thousand feet in front, almost reached the clouds. The platform was surrounded with a balustrade of white marble, fifty feet high, which supported colossal statues of all the kings and great men of the empire. This platform, composed of two rows of bricks, covered with a thick surface of lead from one extremity to the other, bore twelve feet of earth; and upon the earth were raised groves of olive, orange, citron, palm, cocoa, and cinnamon trees, and stock gillyflowers, which formed alleys that the rays of the sun could not penetrate.

The waters of the Euphrates running, by the assistance of pumps, in a hundred canals, formed cascades of six thousand feet in length in the park, and a hundred thousand *jets d'eau*, whose height was scarce perceptible. They afterward flowed into the Euphrates, from whence they came. The gardens of Semiramis, which astonished Asia several ages after, were only a feeble imitation of these ancient prodigies; for in the time of Semiramis, every thing began to degenerate amongst men and women.

But what was more admirable in Babylon, and

eclipsed every thing else, was the only daughter of the king, named Formosanta. It was from her pictures and statues, that in succeeding times Praxiteles sculptured his Aphrodita, and the Venus of Medicis. Heavens! what a difference between the original and the copies! so that king Belus was prouder of his daughter than of his kingdom. She was eighteen years old. It was necessary she should have a husband worthy of her; but where was he to be found? An ancient oracle had ordained that Formosanta could not belong to any but him who could bend the bow of Nimrod.

This Nimrod, "a mighty hunter before the Lord," had left a bow seventeen Babylonian feet in length, made of ebony, harder than the iron of mount Caucasus, which is wrought in the forges of Derbent; and no mortal since Nimrod could bend this astonishing bow.

It was again said, "that the arm which should bend this bow would kill the most terrible and ferocious lion that should be let loose in the Circus of Babylon." This was not all. The bender of the bow, and the conqueror of the lion, should overthrow all his rivals; but he was above all things to be very sagacious, the most magnificent and most virtuous of men, and possess the greatest curiosity in the whole universe.

Three kings appeared, who were bold enough to claim Formosanta. Pharaoh of Egypt, the Shah of India, and the great Khan of the Scythians. Belus appointed the day and place of combat, which was to be at the extremity of his park, in the vast expanse surrounded by the joint waters of the Euphrates and the Tigris. Round the lists a marble amphitheatre was erected, which might contain five hundred thousand spectators. Opposite the amphitheatre was placed the king's throne. He was to appear with Formosanta, accompanied by the whole court; and on the right and left between the throne and the amphitheatre, there were other thrones and seats for the three kings, and for all the other sovereigns who were desirous to be present at this august ceremony.

The king of Egypt arrived the first, mounted upon the bull Apis, and holding in his hand the cithern of Isis. He was followed by two thousand priests, clad in linen vestments whiter than snow, two thousand eunuchs, two thousand magicians, and two thousand warriors.

The king of India came soon after in a car drawn by twelve elephants. He had a train still more numerous and more brilliant than Pharaoh of Egypt.

The last who appeared was the king of the Scythians. He had none with him but chosen warriors, armed with bows and arrows. He was mounted upon a superb tiger, which he had tamed, and which was as tall as any of the finest Persian horses. The majestic and important mien of this king effaced the appearance of his rivals; his naked arms, as nervous as they were white, seemed already to bend the bow of Nimrod.

These three lovers immediately prostrated themselves before Belus and Formosanta. The king of Egypt presented the princess with two of the finest crocodiles of the Nile, two sea horses, two zebras, two Egyptian rats, and two mummies, with the books of the great Hermes, which he judged to be the scarcest things upon earth.

The king of India offered her a hundred elephants, each bearing a wooden gilt tower, and laid at her feet the *vedam*, written by the hand of Xaca himself.

The king of the Scythians, who could neither write nor read, presented a hundred warlike horses with black fox skin housings.

The princess appeared with a downcast look before her lovers, and reclined herself with such a grace as was at once modest and noble.

Belus ordered the kings to be conducted to the thrones that were prepared for them. "Would I had three daughters," said he to them, "I should make six people this day happy!" He then made the competitors cast lots which should try Nimrod's bow first. Their names inscribed were put into a golden casque. That of the Egyptian king came out first, then the name of the king of India appeared. The king of Scythia, viewing the bow and his rivals, did not complain at being the third.

Whilst these brilliant trials were preparing, twenty thousand pages and twenty thousand youthful maidens distributed, without any disorder, refreshments to the spectators between the rows of seats. Every one acknowledged that the gods had instituted kings for no other cause than every day to give festivals, upon condition they should be diversified—that life is too short for any other purpose—that lawsuits, intrigues, wars, the altercations of theologists, which consume human life, are horrible and absurd—that man is born only for happiness —that he would not passionately and incessantly pursue pleasure, were he not designed for it—that the essence of human nature is to enjoy ourselves, and all the rest is folly. This excellent moral was never controverted but by facts.

Whilst preparations were making for determining the fate of Formosanta, a young stranger, mounted upon a unicorn, accompanied by his valet, mounted on a like animal, and bearing upon his hand a large bird, appeared at the barrier. The guards were surprised to observe in this equipage, a figure that had an air of divinity. He had, as hath been since related, the face of Adonis upon the body of Hercules; it was majesty accompanied by the graces. His black eye-brows and flowing fair tresses wore a mixture of beauty unknown at Babylon, and charmed all observers. The whole amphitheatre rose up, the better to view the stranger. All the ladies of the court viewed him with looks of astonishment. Formosanta herself, who had hitherto kept her eyes fixed upon the ground, raised them and blushed. The three kings turned pale. The spectators, in comparing Formosanta with the stranger, cried out, "There is no other in the world, but this young man, who can be so handsome as the princess."

The ushers, struck with astonishment, asked him if he was a king? The stranger replied that he had not that honor, but that he had come from a distant country, excited by curiosity, to see if there were any king worthy of Formosanta. He was introduced into the first row of the amphitheatre, with his valet, his two unicorns, and his bird. He saluted, with great respect, Belus, his daughter, the three kings, and all the assembly. He then took his seat, not without blushing. His two unicorns lay down at his feet; his bird perched upon his shoulder; and his valet, who carried a little bag, placed himself by his side.

The trials began. The bow of Nimrod was taken out of its golden case. The first master of the ceremonies, followed by fifty pages, and preceded by twenty trumptets, presented it to the king of Egypt, who made his priests bless it; and supporting it upon the head of the bull Apis, he did not question his gaining this first victory. He dismounted, and came into the middle of the circus. He tries, exerts all his strength, and makes such ridiculous contortions, that the whole amphitheatre reechoes with laughter, and Formosanta herself could not help smiling.

His high almoner approached him:

"Let your majesty give up this idle honor, which depends entirely upon the nerves and muscles. You will triumph in every thing else. You will conquer the lion, as you are possessed of the favor of Osiris. The princess of Babylon is to belong to the prince who is most sagacious, and you have solved enigmas. She is to wed the most virtuous: you are such, as you have been educated by the priests of Egypt. The most generous is to marry her, and you have presented her with two of the handsomest crocodiles, and two of the finest rats in all the Delta. You are possessed of the bull Apis, and the books of Hermes, which are the scarcest things in the universe. No one can hope to dispute Formosanta with you."

"You are in the right," said the king of Egypt, and resumed his throne.

The bow was then put in the hands of the king of India. It blistered his hands for a fortnight; but he consoled himself in presuming that the Scythian king would not be more fortunate than himself.

The Scythian handled the bow in his turn. He united skill with strength. The bow seemed to have some elasticity in his hands. He bent it a little, but he could not bring it near a curve. The spectators, who had been prejudiced in his favor by his agreeable aspect, lamented his ill success, and concluded that the beautiful princess would never be married.

The unknown youth leaped into the arena and addressing himself to the king of Scythia said:

"Your majesty need not be surprised at not having entirely succeeded. These ebony bows are made in my country. There is a peculiar method in using them. Your merit is greater in having bent it, than if I were to curve it."

He then took an arrow and, placing it upon the string, bent the bow of Nimrod, and shot the arrow beyond the gates. A million hands at once applauded the prodigy. Babylon re-echoed with acclamations; and all the ladies agreed it was fortunate for so handsome a youth to be so strong.

He then took out of his pocket a small ivory tablet, wrote upon it with a golden pencil, fixed the tablet to the bow, and then presented it to the princess with such a grace as charmed every spectator. He then modestly returned to his place between his bird and his valet. All Babylon was in astonishment; the three kings were confounded; whilst the stranger did not seem to pay the least attention to what had happened.

Formosanta was still more surprised to read upon the ivory tablet, tied to the bow, these lines, written in the best Chaldean:

L'arc de Nemrod est celui de la guerre;
L'arc de l'amour est celui du bonheur;
Vous le portez. Par vous ce Dieu vainqueur
Est devenu le maître de la terre.
Trois Rois puissants, trois rivaux aujourd'hui,
Osent prétendre à l'honneur de vous plaire.
Je ne sais pas qui votre cœur préfère,
Mais l'univers sera jaloux de lui.

[The bow of Nimrod is that of war;
The bow of love is that of happiness—
Which you possess. Through you this conquering God
Has become master of the earth.
Three powerful kings—three rivals now

Dare aspire to the honor of pleasing you.
I know not whom your heart may prefer,
But the universe will be jealous of him.]

This little madrigal did not displease the princess; but it was criticised by some of the lords of the ancient court, who said that, in former times, Belus would have been compared to the sun, and Formosanta to the moon; his neck to a tower, and her breast to a bushel of wheat. They said the stranger had no sort of imagination, and that he had lost sight of the rules of true poetry, but all the ladies thought the verses very gallant. They were astonished that a man who handled a bow so well should have so much wit. The lady of honor to the princess said to her:

"Madam, what great talents are here entirely lost? What benefit will this young man derive from his wit, and his skill with Nimrod's bow?"

"Being admired!" said Formosanta.

"Ah!" said the lady, "one more madrigal, and he might well be beloved."

The king of Babylon, having consulted his sages, declared that though none of these kings could bend the bow of Nimrod, yet, nevertheless, his daughter was to be married, and that she should belong to him who could conquer the great lion, which was purposely kept in training in his great menagerie.

The king of Egypt, upon whose education all the wisdom of Egypt had been exhausted, judged it very ridiculous to expose a king to the ferocity of wild beasts in order to be married. He acknowledged that he considered the possession of Formosanta of inestimable value; but he believed that if the lion should strangle him, he could never wed this fair Babylonian. The king of India held similar views to the king of Egypt. They both concluded that the king of Babylon was laughing at them, and that they should send for armies to punish him—that they had many subjects who would think themselves highly honored to die in the service of their masters, without it costing them a single hair of their sacred heads—that they could easily dethrone the king of Babylon, and then they would draw lots for the fair Formosanta.

This agreement being made, the two kings sent each an express into his respective country, with orders to assemble three hundred thousand men to carry off Formosanta.

However, the king of Scythia descended alone into the arena, scimitar in hand. He was not distractedly enamored with Formosanta's charms. Glory till then had been his only passion, and it had led him to Babylon. He was willing to show that if the kings of India and Egypt were so prudent as not to tilt with lions, he was courageous enough not to decline the combat, and he would repair the honor of diadems. His uncommon valor would not even allow him to avail himself of the assistance of his tiger. He advanced singly, slightly armed with a shell casque ornamented with gold, and shaded with three horses' tails as white as snow.

One of the most enormous and ferocious lions that fed upon the Antilibanian mountains was let loose upon him. His tremendous paws appeared capable of tearing the three kings to pieces at once, and his gullet to devour them. The two proud champions fled with the utmost precipitancy and in the most rapid manner to each other. The courageous Scythian plunged his sword into the lion's mouth; but the point, meeting with one of those thick teeth that nothing can penetrate, was broken; and the monster of the woods, more furious from his wound, had already impressed his fearful claws into the monarch's sides.

The unknown youth, touched with the peril of so brave a prince, leaped into the arena swift as lightning, and cut off the lion's head with as much dexterity as we have lately seen, in our carousals, youthful knights knock off the heads of black images.

Then drawing out a small box, he presented it to the Scythian king, saying to him:

"Your majesty will here find the genuine dittany, which grows in my country. Your glorious wounds will be healed in a moment. Accident alone prevented your triumph over the lion. Your valor is not the less to be admired."

The Scythian king, animated more with gratitude than jealousy, thanked his benefactor; and, after having tenderly embraced him, returned to his seat to apply the dittany to his wounds.

The stranger gave the lion's head to his valet, who, having washed it at the great fountain which was beneath the amphitheatre, and drained all the blood, took an iron instrument out of his little bag, with which having drawn the lion's forty teeth, he supplied their place with forty diamonds of equal size.

His master, with his usual modesty, returned to his place; he gave the lion's head to his bird:—"Beauteous bird," said he, "carry this small homage, and lay it at the feet of Formosanta."

The bird winged its way with the dreadful triumph in one of its talons, and presented it to the princess; bending with humility his neck, and crouching before her. The sparkling diamonds dazzled the eyes of every beholder. Such magnificence was unknown even in superb Babylon. The emerald, the topaz, the sapphire, and the pyrope, were as yet considered as the most precious ornaments. Belus and the whole court were struck with admiration. The bird which presented this present surprised them still more. It was of the size of an eagle, but its eyes were as soft and tender as those of the eagle are fierce and threatening. Its bill was rose color, and seemed somewhat to resemble Formosanta's handsome mouth. Its neck represented all the colors of Iris, but still more striking and brilliant. Gold, in a thousand shades, glittered upon its plumage. Its feet resembled a mixture of silver and purple. And the tails of those beautiful birds, which have since drawn Juno's car, did not equal the splendor of this incomparable bird.

The attention, curiosity, astonishment, and ecstasy of the whole court were divided between the jewels and the bird. It had perched upon the balustrade between Belus and his daughter Formosanta. She petted it, caressed it, and kissed it. It seemed to receive her attentions with a mixture of pleasure and respect. When the princess gave the bird a kiss, it returned the embrace, and then looked upon her with languishing eyes. She gave it biscuits and pistachios, which it received in its purple-silvered claw, and carried to its bill with inexpressible grace.

Belus, who had attentively considered the diamonds, concluded that scarce any one of his provinces could repay so valuable a present. He ordered that more magnificent gifts should be prepared for the stranger than those destined for the three monarchs. "This young man," said he, "is doubtless son to the emperor of China; or of that part of the world called Europe, which I have heard spoken of; or of Africa, which is said to be in the vicinity of the kingdom of Egypt."

He immediately sent his first equerry to compliment the stranger, and ask him whether he was himself the sovereign, or son to the sovereign of one of those empires; and why, being possessed of such surprising treasures, he had come with nothing but his valet and a little bag?

Whilst the equerry advanced toward the amphitheatre to execute his commission, another valet arrived upon an unicorn. This valet, addressing himself to the young man, said: "Ormar, your father is approaching the end of his life: I am come to acquaint you with it."

The stranger raised his eyes to heaven, whilst tears streamed from them, and answered only by saying, "*Let us depart.*"

The equerry, after having paid Belus's compliments to the conqueror of the lion, to the giver of the forty diamonds, and to the master of the beautiful bird, asked the valet, "Of what kingdom was the father of this young hero sovereign?"

The valet replied:

"His father is an old shepherd, who is much beloved in his district."

During this conversation, the stranger had already mounted his unicorn. He said to the equerry:

"My lord, vouchsafe to prostrate me at the feet of King Belus and his daughter. I must entreat her to take particular care of the bird I leave with her, as it is a nonpareil like herself."

In uttering these last words he set off, and flew like lightning. The two valets followed him, and in an instant he was out of sight.

Formosanta could not refrain from shrieking. The bird, turning toward the amphitheatre where his master had been seated, seemed greatly afflicted to find him gone; then viewing steadfastly the princess, and gently rubbing her beautiful hand with his bill, he seemed to devote himself to her service.

Belus, more astonished than ever, hearing that this very extraordinary young man was the son of a shepherd, could not believe it. He dispatched messengers after him; but they soon returned with the information, that the three unicorns, upon which these men were mounted, could not be overtaken; and that, according to the rate they went, they must go a hundred leagues a day.

Every one reasoned upon this strange adventure, and wearied themselves with conjectures. How can the son of a shepherd make a present of forty large diamonds? How comes it that he is mounted upon an unicorn? This bewildered them, and Formosanta, whilst she caressed her bird, was sunk into a profound reverie.

## II

### The King of Babylon Convenes His Council and Consults the Oracle

Princess Aldea, Formosanta's cousin-german, who was very well shaped, and almost as handsome as the king's daughter, said to her:

"Cousin, I know not whether this demi-god be the son of a shepherd, but methinks he has fulfilled all the conditions stipulated for your marriage. He has bent Nimrod's bow; he has conquered the lion; he has a good share of sense, having written for you extempore a very pretty madrigal. After having presented you with forty large diamonds, you cannot deny that he is the most generous of men. In his bird he possessed the most curious thing upon earth. His virtue cannot be equaled, since he departed without hesitation as soon as he learned his father was ill, though he might have remained and enjoyed the pleasure of your society. The oracle is fulfilled in every particular, except that wherein he is to overcome his rivals. But he has done more; he has saved the life of the only competitor he had to fear; and when the object is to surpass the other two, I believe you cannot doubt but that he will easily succeed."

"All that you say is very true," replied Formosanta: "but is it possible that the greatest of men, and perhaps the most amiable too, should be the son of a shepherd?"

The lady of honor, joining in the conversation, said that the title of shepherd was frequently given to kings —that they were called shepherds because they attended very closely to their flocks—that this was doubtless a piece of ill-timed pleasantry in his valet—that this young hero had not come so badly equipped, but to show how much his personal merit alone was above the fastidious parade of kings. The princess made no answer, but in giving her bird a thousand tender kisses.

A great festival was nevertheless prepared for the three kings, and for all the princes who had come to the feast. The king's daughter and niece were to do the honors. The king distributed presents worthy the magnificence of Babylon. Belus, during the time the repast was being served, assembled his council to discuss the marriage of the beautiful Formosanta, and this is the way he delivered himself as a great politician:

"I am old: I know not what is best to do with my daughter, or upon whom to bestow her. He who deserves her is nothing but a mean shepherd. The kings of India and Egypt are cowards. The king of the Scythians would be very agreeable to me, but he has not performed any one of the conditions imposed. I will again consult the oracle. In the meantime, deliberate among you, and we will conclude agreeably to what the oracle says; for a king should follow nothing but the dictates of the immortal gods."

He then repaired to the temple: the oracle answered in few words according to custom: *Thy daughter shall not be married until she hath traversed the globe.* In astonishment, Belus returned to the council, and related this answer.

All the ministers had a profound respect for oracles. They therefore all agreed, or at least appeared to agree, that they were the foundation of religion—that reason should be mute before them—that it was by their means that kings reigned over their people—that without oracles there would be neither virtue nor repose upon earth.

At length, after having testified the most profound veneration for them, they almost all concluded that this oracle was impertinent, and should not be obeyed—that nothing could be more indecent for a young woman, and particularly the daughter of the great king of Babylon, than to run about, without any particular destination—that this was the most certain method to prevent her being married, or else engage her in a clandestine, shameful, and ridiculous union—that, in a word, this oracle had not common sense.

The youngest of the ministers, named Onadase, who had more sense than the rest, said that the oracle doubtless meant some pilgrimage of devotion, and offered to be the princess's guide. The council approved of his opinion, but every one was for being her equerry. The king determined that the princess might go three hundred parasangs upon the road to Arabia, to the temple whose saint had the reputation of procuring young women happy marriages, and that the dean of the council should accompany her. After this determination they went to supper.

## III
## *Royal Festival Given in Honor of the Kingly Visitors. The Bird Converses Eloquently with Formosanta*

In the centre of the gardens, between two cascades, an oval saloon three hundred feet in diameter was erected, whose azure roof, intersected with golden stars, represented all the constellations and planets, each in its proper station; and this ceiling turned about, as well as the canopy, by machines as invisible as those which direct the celestial spheres. A hundred thousand flambeaux, inclosed in rich crystal cylinders, illuminated the gardens and the dining-hall. A buffet, with steps, contained twenty thousand vases and golden dishes; and opposite the buffet, upon other steps, were seated a great number of musicians. Two other amphitheatres were decked out; the one with the fruits of each season, the other with crystal decanters, that sparkled with the choicest wines.

The guests took their seats round a table divided into compartments that resembled flowers and fruits, all in precious stones. The beautiful Formosanta was placed between the kings of India and Egypt—the amiable Aldea next the king of Scythia. There were about thirty princes, and each was seated next one of the handsomest ladies of the court. The king of Babylon, who was in the middle, opposite his daughter, seemed divided between the chagrin of being yet unable to effect her marriage, and the pleasure of still beholding her. Formosanta asked leave to place her bird upon the table next her; the king approved of it.

The music, which continued during the repast, furnished every prince with an opportunity of conversing with his female neighbor. The festival was as agreeable as it was magnificent. A ragout was served before Formosanta, which her father was very fond of. The princess said it should be carried to his majesty. The bird immediately took hold of it, and carried it in a miraculous manner to the king. Never was any thing more astonishing witnessed. Belus caressed it as much as his daughter had done. The bird afterward took its flight to return to her. It displayed, in flying, so fine a tail, and its extended wings set forth such a variety of brilliant colors —the gold of its plumage made such a dazzling eclat, that all eyes were fixed upon it. All the musicians were struck motionless, and their instruments afforded harmony no longer. None ate, no one spoke, nothing but a buzzing of admiration was to be heard. The princess of Babylon kissed it during the whole supper, without considering whether there were any kings in the world. Those of India and Egypt felt their spite and indignation rekindle with double force, and they resolved speedily to set their three hundred thousand men in motion to obtain revenge.

As for the king of Scythia, he was engaged in entertaining the beautiful Aldea. His haughty soul despising, without malice, Formosanta's inattention, had conceived for her more indifference than resentment. "She is handsome," said he, "I acknowledge; but she appears to me one of those women who are entirely taken up with their own beauty, and who fancy that mankind are greatly obliged to them when they deign to appear in public. I should prefer an ugly complaisant woman, that exhibited some amiability, to that beautiful statue. You have, madam, as many charms as she possesses, and you, at least, condescend to converse with strangers. I acknowledge to you with the sincerity of a Scythian, that I prefer you to your cousin."

He was, however, mistaken in regard to the character of Formosanta. She was not so disdainful as she appeared. But his compliments were very well received by the princess Aldea. Their conversation became very interesting. They were well contented, and already certain of one another before they left the table. After supper the guests walked in the groves. The king of Scythia and

Aldea did not fail to seek for a place of retreat. Aldea, who was sincerity itself thus declared herself to the prince:

"I do not hate my cousin, though she be handsomer than myself, and is destined for the throne of Babylon. The honor of pleasing you may very well stand in the stead of charms. I prefer Scythia with you, to the crown of Babylon without you. But this crown belongs to me by right, if there be any right in the world; for I am of the elder branch of the Nimrod family, and Formosanta is only of the younger. Her grandfather dethroned mine, and put him to death."

"Such, then, are the rights of inheritance in the royal house of Babylon!" said the Scythian. "What was your grandfather's name?"

"He was called Aldea, like me. My father bore the same name. He was banished to the extremity of the empire with my mother, and Belus, after their death, having nothing to fear from me, was willing to bring me up with his daughter. But he has resolved that I shall never marry."

"I will avenge the cause of your grandfather—of your father—and also your own cause," said the king of Scythia. "I am responsible for your being married. I will carry you off the day after to-morrow by daybreak—for we must dine to-morrow with the king of Babylon—and I will return and support your rights with three hundred thousand men."

"I agree to it," said the beauteous Aldea: and, after having mutually pledged their words of honor, they separated.

The incomparable Formosanta, before retiring to rest, had ordered a small orange tree, in a silver case, to be placed by the side of her bed, that her bird might perch upon it. Her curtains had long been drawn, but she was not in the least disposed to sleep. Her heart was agitated, and her imagination excited. The charming stranger was ever in her thoughts. She fancied she saw him shooting an arrow with Nimrod's bow. She contemplated him in the act of cutting off the lion's head. She repeated his madrigal. At length, she saw him retiring from the crowd upon his unicorn. Tears, sighs, and lamentations overwhelmed her at this reflection. At intervals, she cried out: "Shall I then never see him more? Will he never return?"

"He will surely return," replied the bird from the top of the orange tree. "Can one have seen you once, and not desire to see you again?"

"Heavens! eternal powers! my bird speaks the purest Chaldean." In uttering these words she drew back the curtain, put out her hand to him, and knelt upon her bed, saying:

"Art thou a god descended upon earth? Art thou the great Oromasdes concealed under this beautiful plumage? If thou are, restore me this charming young man."

"I am nothing but a winged animal," replied the bird; "but I was born at the time when all animals still spoke; when birds, serpents, asses, horses, and griffins conversed familiarly with man. I would not speak before company, lest your ladies of honor should have taken me for a sorcerer. I would not discover myself to any but you."

Formosanta was speechless, bewildered, and intoxicated with so many wonders. Desirous of putting a hundred questions to him at once, she at length asked him how old he was.

"Only twenty-seven thousand nine hundred years and six months. I date my age from the little revolution of the equinoxes, and which is accomplished in about twenty-eight thousand of your years. There are revolutions of a much greater extent, so are there beings much older than me. It is twenty-two thousand years since I learnt Chaldean in one of my travels. I have always had a very great taste for the Chaldean language, but my brethren, the other animals, have renounced speaking in your climate."

"And why so, my divine bird?"

"Alas! because men have accustomed themselves to eat us, instead of conversing and instructing themselves with us. Barbarians! should they not have been convinced, that having the same organs with them, the same sentiments, the same wants, the same desires, we have also what is called a soul, the same as themselves—that we are their brothers, and that none should be dressed and eaten but the wicked? We are so far your brothers, that the Supreme Being, the Omnipotent and Eternal Being, having made a compact with men, expressly comprehended us in the treaty. He forbade you to nourish yourselves with our blood, and we to suck yours.

"The fables of your ancient Locman, translated into so many languages, will be a testimony eternally subsisting of the happy commerce you formerly carried on with us. They all begin with these words: 'In the time when beasts spoke.' It is true, there are many families among you who keep up an incessant conversation with their dogs; but the dogs have resolved not to answer, since they have been compelled by whipping to go a hunting, and become accomplices in the murder of our ancient and common friends, stags, deers, hares, and partridges.

"You still have some ancient poems in which horses speak, and your coachmen daily address them in words; but in so barbarous a manner, and in uttering such infamous expressions, that horses, though formerly entertaining so great a kindness for you, now detest you.

"The country which is the residence of your charming stranger, the most perfect of men, is the only one in which your species has continued to love ours, and to converse with us; and this is the only country in the world where men are just."

"And where is the country of my dear incognito? What is the name of his empire? For I will no more believe he is a shepherd than that you are a bat."

"His country is that of the Gangarids, a wise, virtuous, and invincible people, who inhabit the eastern shore of the Ganges. The name of my friend is Amazan. He is no king; and I know not whether he would so humble himself as to be one. He has too great a love for his fellow countrymen. He is a shepherd like them. But do not imagine that those shepherds resemble yours; who, covered with rags and tatters, watch their sheep, who are better clad than themselves; who groan under the burden of poverty, and who pay to an extortioner half the miserable stipend of wages which they receive from their masters. The Gangaridian shepherds are all born equal, and own the innumerable herds which cover their vast fields and subsist on the abundant verdure. These flocks are never killed. It is a horrid crime, in that favored country, to kill and eat a fellow creature. Their wool is finer and more brilliant than the finest silk, and constitutes the greatest traffic of the East. Besides, the land of the Gangarids produces all that can flatter the desires of man. Those large diamonds that Amazan had the honor of presenting you with, are from a mine that belongs to him. An unicorn, on which you saw him mounted, is the usual animal the Gangarids ride upon. It is the finest, the proudest, most terrible, and at the same time most gentle animal that ornaments the earth. A hundred Gangarids with as many unicorns would be sufficient to disperse innumerable armies. Two centuries ago, a king of India was mad enough to attempt to conquer this nation. He appeared, followed by ten thousand elephants and a million of warriors. The unicorns pierced the elephants, just as I have seen upon your table beads pierced in golden brochets. The warriors fell under the sabres of the Gangarids like crops of rice mowed by the people of the East. The king was taken prisoner, with upwards of six thousand men. He was bathed in the salutary water of the Ganges, and followed the regimen of the country, which consists only of vegetables, of which nature hath there been amazingly liberal to nourish every breathing creature. Men who are fed with carnivorous aliments, and drenched with spirituous liquors, have a sharp adust blood, which turns their brains a hundred different ways. Their chief rage is a fury to spill their brothers' blood, and, laying waste fertile plains, to reign over churchyards. Six full months were taken up in curing the king of India of his disorder. When the physicians judged that his pulse had become natural, they certified this to the council of the Gangarids. The council then followed the advice of the unicorns and humanely sent back the king of India, his silly court, and impotent warriors, to their own country. This lesson made them wise, and from that time the Indians respected the Gangarids; as ignorant men, willing to be instructed, revere the philosophers they cannot equal."

"Apropos, my dear bird," said the princess to him, "do the Gangarids profess any religion? Have they one?"

"Yes, we meet to return thanks to God on the days of the full moon; the men in a great temple made of cedar, and the women in another, to prevent their devotion being diverted. All the birds assemble in a grove, and the quadrupeds on a fine down. We thank God for all the benefits he had bestowed upon us. We have in particular some parrots *that preach wonderfully well*.

"Such is the country of my dear Amazan; there I reside. My friendship for him is as great as the love with which he has inspired you. If you will credit me, we will set out together, and you shall pay him a visit."

"Really, my dear bird, this is a very pretty invitation of yours," replied the princess smiling, and who flamed with desire to undertake the journey, but did not dare say so.

"I serve my friend," said the bird; "and, after the happiness of loving you, the greatest pleasure is to assist you."

Formosanta was quite fascinated. She fancied herself transported from earth. All she had seen that day, all she then saw, all she heard, and particularly what she felt in her heart, so ravished her as far to surpass what those fortunate Mussulmans now feel, who, disencumbered from their terrestrial ties, find themselves in the ninth heaven in the arms of their Houris, surrounded and penetrated with glory and celestial felicity.

## IV
### The Beautiful Bird Is Killed by the King of Egypt.
### Formosanta Begins a Journey.
### Aldea Elopes with the King of Scythia

Formosanta passed the whole night in speaking of Amazan. She no longer called him any thing but her shepherd; and from this time it was that the names of shepherd and lover were indiscriminately used throughout every nation.

Sometimes she asked the bird whether Amazan had had any other mistresses. It answered, "No," and she was at the summit of felicity. Sometimes she asked how he passed his life; and she, with transport, learned that it was employed in doing good, in cultivating arts, in penetrating into the secrets of nature, and improving himself. She at times wanted to know if the soul of her lover was of the same nature as that of her bird; how it happened that it had lived twenty thousand years, when her lover was not above eighteen or nineteen. She put a hundred such questions, to which the bird replied with such discretion as excited her curiosity. At length sleep closed her eyes, and yielded up Formosanta to the sweet delusion of dreams sent by the gods, which sometimes surpass reality itself, and which all the philosophy of the Chaldeans can scarce explain.

Formosanta did not awaken till very late. The day was far advanced when the king, her father, entered her chamber. The bird received his majesty with respectful politeness, went before him, fluttered his wings, stretched his neck. And then replaced himself upon his orange tree. The king seated himself upon his daughter's bed, whose dreams had made her still more beautiful. His large beard approached her lovely face, and after having embraced her, he spoke to her in these words:

"My dear daughter, you could not yesterday find a

husband agreeable to my wishes; you nevertheless must marry; the prosperity of my empire requires it. I have consulted the oracle, which you know never errs, and which directs all my conduct. His commands are, that you should traverse the globe. You must therefore begin your journey."

"Ah! doubtless to the Gangarids," said the princess; and in uttering these words, which escaped her, she was sensible of her indiscretion. The king, who was utterly ignorant of geography, asked her what she meant by the Gangarids. She easily diverted the question. The king told her she must go on a pilgrimage, that he had appointed the persons who were to attend her—the dean of the counsellors of state, the high almoner, a lady of honor, a physician, an apothecary, her bird, and all necessary domestics.

Formosanta, who had never been out of her father's palace, and who, till the arrival of the three kings and Amazan, had led a very insipid life, according to the *etiquette* of rank and the parade of pleasure, was charmed at setting out upon a pilgrimage. "Who knows," said she, whispering to her heart, "if the gods may not inspire Amazan with the like desire of going to the same chapel, and I may have the happiness of again seeing the pilgrim?" She affectionately thanked her father, saying she had always entertained a secret devotion for the saint she was going to visit.

Belus gave an excellent dinner to his guests, who were all men. They formed a very ill assorted company—kings, ministers, princes, pontiffs—all jealous of each other; all weighing their words, and equally embarrassed with their neighbors and themselves. The repast was very gloomy, though they drank pretty freely. The princesses remained in their apartments, each meditating upon her respective journey. They dined at their little cover. Formosanta afterward walked in the gardens with her dear bird, which, to amuse her, flew from tree to tree, displaying his superb tail and divine plumage.

The king of Egypt, who was heated with wine, not to say drunk, asked one of his pages for a bow and arrow.

The prince was, in truth, the most unskillful archer in his whole kingdom. When he shot at a mark, the place of the greatest safety was generally the spot he aimed at. But the beautiful bird, flying as swiftly as the arrow, seemed to court it, and fell bleeding in the arms of Formosanta. The Egyptian, bursting into a foolish laugh, retired to his place. The princess rent the skies with her moans, melted into tears, tore her hair, and beat her breast. The dying bird said to her, in a low voice: "Burn me, and fail not to carry my ashes to the east of the ancient city of Aden or Eden, and expose them to the sun upon a little pile of cloves and cinnamon." After having uttered these words it expired. Formosanta was for a long time in a swoon, and revived again only to burst into sighs and groans. Her father, partaking of her grief, and imprecating the king of Egypt, did not doubt but this accident foretold some fatal event. He immediately went to consult the oracle, which replied: *A mixture of everything—life and death, infidelity and constancy, loss and gain, calamities and good fortune.* Neither he nor his council could comprehend any meaning in this reply; but, at length, he was satisfied with having fulfilled the duties of devotion.

His daughter was bathed in tears, whilst he consulted the oracle. She paid the funeral obsequies to the bird, which it had directed, and resolved to carry its remains into Arabia at the risk of her life. It was burned in incombustible flax, with the orange tree on which it used to perch. She gathered up the ashes in a little golden vase, set with rubies, and the diamonds taken from the lion's mouth. Oh! that she could, instead of fulfilling this melancholy duty, have burned alive the detestable king of Egypt! This was her sole wish. She, in spite, put to death the two crocodiles, his two sea horses, his two zebras, his two rats, and had his two mummies thrown into the Euphrates. Had she possessed his bull Apis, she would not have spared him.

The king of Egypt, enraged at this affront, set out immediately to forward his three hundred thousand men. The king of India, seeing his ally depart, set off also on the same day, with a firm intention of joining his three hundred thousand Indians to the Egyptian army. The king of Scythia decamped in the night with the princess Aldea, fully resolved to fight for her at the head of three hundred thousand Scythians, and to restore to her the inheritance of Babylon, which was her right, as she had descended from the elder branch of the Nimrod family.

As for the beautiful Formosanta, she set out at three in the morning with her caravan of pilgrims, flattering herself that she might go into Arabia, and execute the last will of her bird; and that the justice of the gods would restore her the dear Amazan, without whom life had become insupportable.

When the king of Babylon awoke, he found all the company gone.

"How mighty festivals terminate," said he; "and what a surprising vacuum they leave when the hurry is over."

But he was transported with a rage truly royal, when he found that the princess Aldea had been carried off. He ordered all his ministers to be called up, and the council to be convened. Whilst they were dressing, he failed not to consult the oracle; but the only answer he could obtain was in these words, so celebrated since throughout the universe: *When girls are not provided for in marriage by their relatives, they marry themselves.*

Orders were immediately issued to march three hundred thousand men against the king of Scythia. Thus was the torch of a most dreadful war lighted up, which was caused by the amusements of the finest festival ever given upon earth. Asia was upon the point of being overrun by four armies of three hundred thousand men each. It is plain that the war of Troy, which astonished the world some ages after, was mere child's play in comparison to this: but it should also be considered, that in the Trojans' quarrel, the object was nothing more than a very immoral old woman, who had contrived to be twice run away with; whereas, in this case, the cause was tripartite—two girls and a bird.

The king of India went to meet his army upon the

large fine road which then led straight to Babylon, at Cachemir. The king of Scythia flew with Aldea by the fine road which led to Mount Imaus. Owing to bad government, all these fine roads have disappeared in the lapse of time. The king of Egypt had marched to the west, along the coast of the little Mediterranean sea, which the ignorant Hebrews have since called the Great Sea.

As to the charming Formosanta, she pursued the road to Bassora, planted with lofty palm trees, which furnished a perpetual shade, and fruit at all seasons. The temple in which she was to perform her devotions, was in Bassora itself. The saint to whom this temple had been dedicated was somewhat in the style of him who was afterward adored at Lampascus, and was generally successful in procuring husbands for young ladies. Indeed, he was the holiest saint in all Asia.

Formosanta had no sort of inclination for the saint of Bassora. She only invoked her dear Gangaridian shepherd, her charming Amazan. She proposed embarking at Bassora, and landing in Arabia Felix, to perform what her deceased bird had commanded.

At the third stage, scarce had she entered into a fine inn, where her harbingers had made all the necessary preparations for her, when she learned that the king of Egypt had arrived there also. Informed by his emissaries of the princess's route, he immediately altered his course, followed by a numerous escort. Having alighted, he placed sentinels at all the doors; then repaired to the beautiful Formosanta's apartment, when he addressed her by saying:

"Miss, you are the lady I was in quest of. You paid me very little attention when I was at Babylon. It is just to punish scornful capricious women. You will, if you please, be kind enough to sup with me to-night; and I shall behave to you according as I am satisfied with you."

Formosanta saw very well that she was not the strongest. She judged that good sense consisted in knowing how to conform to one's situation. She resolved to get rid of the king of Egypt by an innocent stratagem. She looked at him through the corners of her eyes (which in after ages has been called ogling), and then she spoke to him, with a modesty, grace, and sweetness, a confusion, and a thousand other charms which would have made the wisest man a fool and deceived the most discerning:

"I acknowledge, sir, I always appeared with a downcast look, when you did the king, my father, the honor of visiting him. I had some apprehensions for my heart. I dreaded my too great simplicity. I trembled lest my father and your rivals should observe the preference I gave you, and which you so highly deserved. I can now declare my sentiments. I swear by the bull Apis, which after you is the thing I respect the most in the world, that your proposals have enchanted me. I have already supped with you at my father's, and I will sup with you again, without his being of the party. All that I request of you is that your high almoner should drink with us. He appeared to me at Babylon to be an excellent guest. I have some Chiras wine remarkably good. I will make you both taste it. I consider you as the greatest of kings, and the most amiable of men."

This discourse turned the king of Egypt's head. He agreed to have the almoner's company.

"I have another favor to ask of you," said the princess, "which is to allow me to speak to my apothecary. Women have always some little ails that require attention, such as vapors in the head, palpitations of the heart, colics, and the like, which often require some assistance. In a word, I at present stand in need of my apothecary and I hope you will not refuse me this slight testimony of confidence."

"Miss," replied the king of Egypt, "I know life too well to refuse you so just a demand. I will order the apothecary to attend you whilst supper is preparing. I imagine you must be somewhat fatigued by the journey; you will also have occasion for a chambermaid; you may order her you like best to attend you. I will afterward wait your commands and convenience."

He then retired, and the apothecary and the chambermaid, named Irla, entered. The princess had an entire confidence in her. She ordered her to bring six bottles of Chiras wine for supper, and to make all the sentinels, who had her officers under arrest, drink the same. Then she recommended her apothecary to infuse in all the bottles certain pharmaceutic drugs, which make those who take them sleep twenty-four hours, and with which he was always provided. She was implicitly obeyed. The king returned with his high almoner in about half an hour's time. The conversation at supper was very gay. The king and the priest emptied the six bottles, and acknowledged there was not such good wine in Egypt. The chambermaid was attentive to make the servants in waiting drink. As for the princess, she took great care not to drink any herself, saying that she was ordered by her physician a particular regimen. They were all presently asleep.

The king of Egypt's almoner had one of the finest beards that a man of his rank could wear. Formosanta lopped it off very skillfully; then sewing it to a ribbon, she put it on her own chin. She then dressed herself in the priest's robes, and decked herself in all the marks of his dignity, and her waiting maid clad herself like the sacristan of the goddess Isis. At length, having furnished herself with his urn and jewels, she set out from the inn amidst the sentinels, who were asleep like their master. Her attendant had taken care to have two horses ready at the door. The princess could not take with her any of the officers of her train. They would have been stopped by the great guard.

Formosanta and Irla passed through several ranks of soldiers, who, taking the princess for the high priest, called her, "My most Reverend Father in God," and asked his blessing. The two fugitives arrived in twenty-four hours at Bassora, before the king awoke. They then threw off their disguise, which might have created some suspicion. They fitted out with all possible expedition a ship, which carried them, by the Straits of Ormus, to the beautiful banks of Eden in Arabia Felix. This was that Eden, whose gardens were so famous, that they have since been the residence of the best of mankind. They were the model of the Elysian fields, the gardens of the Hesperides, and also those of the Fortunate Islands. In those warm climates men imagined there could be no greater felicity than shades and murmuring brooks. To live eternally in heaven with the Supreme Being, or to walk in the garden of paradise, was the same thing to those who incessantly spoke without understanding one another, and who could scarce have any distinct ideas or just expressions.

As soon as the princess found herself in this land, her first care was to pay her dear bird the funeral obsequies he had required of her. Her beautiful hands prepared a small quantity of cloves and cinnamon. What was her surprise, when, having spread the ashes of the bird upon this funeral pyre, she saw it blaze of itself! All was presently consumed. In the place of the ashes there appeared nothing but a large egg, from whence she saw her bird issue more brilliant than ever. This was one of the most happy moments the princess had ever experienced in her whole life. There was but another that could ever be dearer to her; it was the object of her wishes, but almost beyond her hopes.

"I plainly see," said she, to the bird, "you are the phœnix which I have heard so much spoken of. I am almost ready to expire with joy and astonishment. I did not believe in your resurrection; but it is my good fortune to be convinced of it."

"Resurrection, in fact," said the phœnix to her, "is one of the most simple things in the world. There is nothing more in being born twice than once. Every thing in this world is the effect of resurrection. Caterpillars are regenerated into butterflies; a kernel put into the earth is regenerated into a tree. All animals buried in the earth regenerate into vegetation, herbs, and plants, and nourish other animals, of which they speedily compose part of the substance. All particles which compose bodies are transformed into different beings. It is true, that I am the only one to whom Oromasdes has granted the favor of regenerating in my own form."

Formosanta, who from the moment she first saw Amazan and the phœnix, had passed all her time in a round of astonishment, said to him:

"I can easily conceive that the Supreme Being may form out of your ashes a phœnix nearly resembling yourself but that you should be precisely the same person—that you should have the same soul, is a thing, I acknowledge, I cannot very clearly comprehend. What became of your soul when I carried you in my pocket after your death?"

"Reflect one moment! Is it not as easy for the great Oromasdes to continue action upon a single atom of my being, as to begin afresh this action? He had before granted me sensation, memory, and thought. He grants them to me again. Whether he united this favor to an atom of elementary fire, latent within me, or to the assemblage of my organs, is, in reality, of no consequence. Men, as well as phœnixes are entirely ignorant how things come to pass; but the greatest favor the Supreme Being has bestowed upon me is to regenerate me for you. Oh! that I may pass the twenty-eight thousand years which I have still to live before my next resurrection, with you and my dear Amazan."

"My dear phœnix, remember what you first told me at Babylon, which I shall never forget, and which flattered me with the hope of again seeing my dear shepherd, whom I idolize; 'we must absolutely pay the Gangarids a visit together,' and I must carry Amazan back with me to Babylon."

"This is precisely my design," said the phœnix. "There is not a moment to lose. We must go in search of Amazan by the shortest road, that is, through the air. There are in Arabia Felix two griffins who are my particular friends, and who live only a hundred and fifty thousand leagues from here. I am going to write to them by the pigeon post, and they will be here before night. We shall have time to make you a convenient palankeen, with drawers, in which you may place your provisions. You will be quite at your ease in this vehicle, with your maid. These two griffins are the most vigorous of their kind. Each of them will support one of the poles of the canopy between their claws. But, once for all, time is very precious."

He instantly went with Formosanta to order the carriage at an upholsterer's of his acquaintance. It was made complete in four hours. In the drawers were placed small fine loaves, biscuits superior to those of Babylon, large lemons, pine-apples, cocoa, and pistachio nuts, Eden wine, which is as superior to that of Chiras as Chiras is to that of Surinam.

The two griffins arrived at Eden at the appointed time. The vehicle was as light as it was commodious and solid, and Formosanta and Irla placed themselves in it. The two griffins carried it off like a feather. The phœnix sometimes flew after it, and sometimes perched upon its roof. The two griffins winged their way toward the Ganges with the velocity of an arrow which rends the air. They never stopped but a moment at night for the travelers to take some refreshment, and the carriers to take a draught of water.

They at length reached the country of the Gangarids. The princess's heart palpitated with hope, love, and joy. The phœnix stopped the vehicle before Amazan's house; but Amazan had been absent from home three hours, without any one knowing whither he had gone.

There are no words, even in the Gangaridian language, that could express Formosanta's extreme despair.

"Alas! this is what I dreaded," said the phœnix; "the three hours which you passed at the inn, upon the road to Bassora, with that wretched king of Egypt, have perhaps been at the price of the happiness of your whole life. I very much fear we have lost Amazan, without the possibility of recovering him."

He then asked the servants if he could salute the mother of Amazan. They answered, that her husband had died only two days before, and she could speak to no one. The phœnix, who was not without influence in the house, introduced the princess of Babylon into a saloon, the walls of which were covered with orange-tree wood inlaid with ivory. The inferior shepherds and shepherdesses, who were dressed in long white garments, with gold colored trimmings, served up, in a hundred plain porcelain baskets, a hundred various delicacies, amongst which no disguised carcasses were to be seen. They consisted of rice, sago, vermicelli, macaroni, omelets, milk, eggs, cream, cheese, pastry of every kind, vegetables, fruits, peculiarly fragrant and grateful to the taste, of which no idea can be formed in other climates; and they were accompanied with a profusion of refreshing liquors superior to the finest wine.

Whilst the princess regaled herself, seated upon a bed of roses, four peacocks, who were luckily mute, fanned her with their brilliant wings; two hundred birds, one hundred shepherds and shepherdesses, warbled a concert in two different choirs; the nightingales, thistlefinches, linnets, chaffinches, sung the higher notes with the shepherdesses, and the shepherds sung the tenor and bass. The princess acknowledged that if there was more magnificence at Babylon, nature was infinitely more agreeable among the Gangarids; but whilst this consolatory and voluptuous music was playing tears flowed from her eyes, whilst she said to the damsel Irla:

"These shepherds and shepherdesses, these nightingales, these linnets, are making love; and for my part, I am deprived of the company of the Gangaridian hero, the worthy object of my most tender thoughts."

Whilst she was taking this collation, her tears and admiration kept pace with each other, and the phœnix addressed himself to Amazan's mother, saying:

"Madam, you cannot avoid seeing the princess of Babylon; you know——"

"I know every thing," said she, "even her adventure at the inn, upon the road to Bassora. A blackbird related the whole to me this morning; and this cruel blackbird is the cause of my son's going mad, and leaving his paternal abode."

"You have not been informed, then, that the princess regenerated me?"

"No, my dear child, the blackbird told me you were dead and this made me inconsolable. I was so afflicted at this loss, the death of my husband, and the precipitate flight of my son, that I ordered my door to be shut to every one. But since the princess of Babylon has done me the honor of paying me a visit, I beg she may be immediately introduced. I have matters of great importance to acquaint her with, and I choose you should be present."

She then went to meet the princess in another saloon. She could not walk very well. This lady was about three hundred years old; but she had still some agreeable vestiges of beauty. It might be conjectured, that about her two hundred and fortieth, or two hundred and fiftieth year, she must have been a most charming woman. She received Formosanta with a respectful nobleness, blended with an air of interest and sorrow, which made a very lively impression upon the princess.

Formosanta immediately paid her the compliments of condolence upon her husband's death.

"Alas!" said the widow, "you have more reason to lament his death than you imagine."

"I am, doubtless, greatly afflicted," said Formosanta; "he was father to——." Here a flood of tears prevented her from going on. "For his sake only I undertook this journey, and which I have so narrowly escaped many dangers. For him I left my father, and the most splendid court in the universe. I was detained by a king of Egypt, whom I detest. Having escaped from this tyrant, I have traversed the air in search of the only man I love. When I arrive, he flies from me!" Here sighs and tears stopped her impassioned harangue.

His mother then said to her:

"When the king of Egypt made you his prisoner—when you supped with him at an inn upon the road to Bassora, when your beautiful hands filled him bumpers of Chiras wine, did you observe a blackbird that flew about the room?"

"Yes, really," said the princess, "I now recollect there was such a bird, though at that time I did not pay it the least attention. But in collecting my ideas, I now remember well, that at the instant when the king of Egypt rose from the table to give me a kiss, the blackbird flew out at the window giving a loud cry, and never appeared after."

"Alas! madam," resumed Amazan's mother, "this is precisely the cause of all our misfortunes; my son had dispatched this blackbird to gain intelligence of your health, and all that passed at Babylon. He proposed speedily to return, throw himself at your feet, and consecrate to you the remainder of his life. You know not to what a pitch he adores you. All the Gangarids are both loving and faithful; but my son is the most passionate and constant of them all. The blackbird found you at an inn, drinking very cheerfully with the king of Egypt and a vile priest; he afterward saw you give this monarch who had killed the phœnix—the man my son holds in utter detestation—a fond embrace. The blackbird, at the sight of this, was seized with a just indignation. He flew away imprecating your fatal error. He returned this day, and has related every thing. But, just heaven, at what a juncture! At the very time that my son was deploring with me the loss of his father and that of the wise phœnix, the very instant I had informed him that he was your cousin-german——"

"Oh heavens! my cousin, madam, is it possible? How can this be? And am I so happy as to be thus allied to him, and yet so miserable as to have offended him?"

"My son is, I tell you," said the Gangaridian lady, "your cousin, and I shall presently convince you of it; but in becoming my relation, you rob me of my son. He cannot survive the grief that the embrace you gave to the king of Egypt has occasioned him."

"Ah! my dear aunt," cried the beautiful Formosanta, "I swear by him and the all-powerful Oromasdes, that this embrace, so far from being criminal, was the strongest proof of love your son could receive from me. I disobeyed my father for his sake. For him I went from the Euphrates to the Ganges. Having fallen into the hands of the worthless Pharaoh of Egypt, I could not escape his clutches but by artifice. I call the ashes and soul of the phœnix, which were then in my pocket, to witness. He can do me justice. But how can your son, born upon the banks of the Ganges, be my cousin? I, whose family have reigned upon the banks of the Euphrates for so many centuries?"

"You know," said the venerable Gangaridian lady to her, "that your grand uncle, Aldea, was king of Babylon, and that he was dethroned by Belus's father?"

"Yes, madam."

"You know that this Aldea had in marriage a daughter named Aldea, brought up in your court? It was this prince, who, being persecuted by your father, took refuge under another name in our happy country. He married me, and is the father of the young prince Aldea Amazan, the most beautiful, the most courageous, the strongest, and most virtuous of mortals; and at this hour the most unhappy. He went to the Babylonian festival upon the credit of your beauty; since that time he idolizes you, and now grieves because he believes that you have proved unfaithful to him. Perhaps I shall never again set eyes upon my dear son."

She then displayed to the princess all the titles of the house of Aldea. Formosanta scarce deigned to look at them.

"Ah! madam, do we examine what is the object of our desire? My heart sufficiently believes you. But where is Aldea Amazan? Where is my kinsman, my lover, my king? Where is my life? What road has he taken? I will seek for him in every sphere the Eternal Being hath framed, and of which he is the greatest ornament. I will go into the star Canope, into Sheath, into Aldebaran; I will go and tell him of my love and convince him of my innocence."

The phœnix justified the princess with regard to the crime that was imputed to her by the blackbird, of fondly embracing the king of Egypt; but it was necessary to undeceive Amazan and recall him. Birds were dispatched on every side. Unicorns sent forward in every direction. News at length arrived that Amazan had taken the road toward China.

"Well, then," said the princess, "let us set out for China. I will seek him in defiance of both difficulty and danger. The journey is not long, and I hope I shall bring you back your son in a fortnight at farthest."

At these words tears of affection streamed from his mother's eyes and also from those of the princess. They most tenderly embraced, in the great sensibility of their hearts.

The phœnix immediately ordered a coach with six unicorns. Amazan's mother furnished two thousand horsemen, and made the princess, her niece, a present of some thousands of the finest diamonds of her country. The phœnix, afflicted at the evil occasioned by the blackbird's indiscretion, ordered all the blackbirds to quit the country; and from that time none have been met with upon the banks of the Ganges.

V

*Formosanta Visits China and Scythia in Search of Amazan*

The unicorns, in less than eight days, carried Formosanta, Irla, and the phœnix, to Cambalu, the capital of China. This city was larger than that of Babylon, and in appearance quite different. These fresh objects, these strange manners, would have amused Formosanta could any thing but Amazan have engaged her attention.

As soon as the emperor of China learned that the princess of Babylon was at the city gates, he dispatched four thousand Mandarins in ceremonial robes to receive her. They all prostrated themselves before her, and presented her with an address written in golden letters upon a sheet of purple silk. Formosanta told them, that if she were possessed of four thousand tongues, she would not omit replying immediately to every Mandarin; but that having only one, she hoped they would be satisfied with her general thanks. They conducted her, in a respectful manner, to the emperor.

He was the wisest, most just and benevolent monarch upon earth. It was he who first tilled a small field with his own imperial hands, to make agriculture respectable to his people. Laws in all other countries were shamefully confined to the punishment of crimes: he first allotted premiums to virtue. This emperor had just banished from his dominions a gang of foreign Bonzes, who had come from the extremities of the West, with the frantic hope of compelling all China *to think like themselves*; and who, under pretence of teaching truths, had already acquired honors and riches. In expelling them, he delivered himself in these words, which are recorded in the annals of the empire:

*"You may here do as much harm as you have elsewhere. You have come to preach dogmas of intolerance, to the most tolerant nation upon earth. I send you back, that I may never be compelled to punish you. You will be honorably conducted to my frontiers. You will be furnished with every thing necessary to return to the confines of the hemisphere from whence you came. Depart in peace, if you can be at peace, and never return."*

The princess of Babylon heard with pleasure of this speech and determination. She was the more certain of being well received at court, as she was very far from entertaining any dogmas of intolerance. The emperor of China, in dining with her *tête-à-tête*, had the politeness to banish all disagreeable *etiquette*. She presented the phœnix to him, who was gently caressed by the emperor, and who perched upon his chair. Formosanta, toward the end of the repast, ingenuously acquainted him with the cause of her journey, and entreated him to search for the beautiful Amazan in the city of Cambalu; and in the meanwhile she acquainted the emperor with her adventures, without concealing the fatal passion with which her heart burned for this youthful hero.

"He did me the honor of coming to my court," said the emperor of China. "I was enchanted with this amiable Amazan. It is true that he is deeply afflicted; but his graces are thereby the more affecting. Not one of my favorites has more wit. There is not a gown Mandarin who has more knowledge—not a military one who has a more martial or heroic air. His extreme youth adds an additional value to all his talents. If I were so unfortunate, so abandoned by the Tien and Changti, as to desire to be a conqueror, I would wish Amazan to put himself at the head of my armies, and I should be sure of conquering the whole universe. It is a great pity that his melancholy sometimes disconcerts him."

"Ah! sir," said Formosanta, with much agitation and grief, blended with an air of reproach, "why did you not request me to dine with him? This is a cruel stroke you have given me. Send for him immediately, I entreat you."

"He set out this very morning," replied the emperor, "without acquainting me with his destination."

Formosanta, turning toward the phœnix, said to him:

"Did you ever know so unfortunate a damsel as myself?" Then resuming the conversation, she said:

"Sir, how came he to quit in so abrupt a manner, so polite a court, in which, methinks, one might pass one's life?"

"The case was as follows," said he. "One of the most amiable of the princesses of the blood, falling desperately in love with him, desired to meet him at noon. He set out at day-break, leaving this billet for my kinswoman, whom it hath cost a deluge of tears:

> Beautiful princess of the mongolian race. You are deserving of a heart that was never offered up at any other altar. I have sworn to the immortal gods never to love any other than Formosanta, princess of Babylon, and to teach her how to conquer one's desires in traveling. She has had the misfortune to yield to a worthless king of Egypt. I am sure the most unfortunate of men; having lost my father, the phœnix, and the hope of being loved by Formosanta. I left my mother in affliction, forsook my home and country, being unable to live a moment in the place where I learned that Formosanta loved another than me. I swore to traverse the earth, and be faithful. You would despise me, and the gods punish me, if I violated my oath. Choose another lover, madam, and be as faithful as I am.

"Ah! give me that miraculous letter," said the beautiful Formosanta; "it will afford me some consolation. I am happy in the midst of my misfortunes. Amazan loves me! Amazan, for me, renounces the society of the princesses of China. There is no one upon earth but himself endowed with so much fortitude. He sets me a most brilliant example. The phœnix knows I did not stand in need of it. How cruel it is to be deprived of one's lover for the most innocent embrace given through pure fidelity. But, tell me, whither has he gone? What road has he taken? Deign to inform me, and I will immediately set out."

The emperor of China told her, that, according to the reports he had received, her lover had taken the road toward Scythia. The unicorns were immediately harnessed, and the princess, after the most tender compliments, took leave of the emperor, and resumed her journey with the phœnix, her chambermaid Irla, and all her train.

As soon as she arrived in Scythia, she was more convinced than ever how much men and governments differed, and would continue to differ, until noble and enlightened minds should by degrees remove that cloud of darkness which has covered the earth for so many ages; and until there should be found in barbarous climes, heroic souls, who would have strength and perseverance enough to transform brutes into men. There are no cities in Scythia, consequently no agreeable arts. Nothing was to be seen but extensive fields, and whole tribes whose sole habitations were tents and chars. Such an appearance struck her with terror. Formosanta enquired in what tent or char the king was lodged? She was informed that he had set out eight days before with three hundred thousand cavalry to attack the king of Babylon, whose niece, the beautiful princess Aldea, he had carried off.

"What! did he run away with my cousin?" cried Formosanta. "I could not have imagined such an incident. What! has my cousin, who was too happy in paying her court to me, become a queen, and I am not yet married?" She was immediately conducted, by her desire, to the queen's tent.

Their unexpected meeting in such distant climes—the uncommon occurrences they mutually had to impart to each other, gave such charms to this interview, as made them forget they never loved one another. They saw each other with transport; and a soft illusion supplied the place of real tenderness. They embraced with tears, and there was a cordiality and frankness on each side that could not have taken place in a palace.

Aldea remembered the phœnix and the waiting maid Irla. She presented her cousin with zibelin skins, who in return gave her diamonds. The war between the two kings was spoken of. They deplored the fate of soldiers who were forced into battle, the victims of the caprice of princes, when two honest men might, perhaps, settle the dispute in less than an hour, without a single throat being cut. But the principal topic was the handsome stranger, who had conquered lions, given the largest diamonds in the universe, written madrigals, and had now become the most miserable of men from believing the statements of a blackbird.

"He is my dear brother," said Aldea. "He is my lover," cried Formosanta. "You have, doubtless, seen him. Is he still here? for, cousin, as he knows he is your brother, he cannot have left you so abruptly as he did the king of China."

"Have I seen him? good heavens! yes. He passed four whole days with me. Ah! cousin, how much my brother is to blame. A false report has absolutely turned his brain. He roams about the world, without knowing whither he is destined. Imagine to yourself his distraction of mind, which is so great, that he has refused to meet the handsomest lady in all Scythia. He set out yesterday, after writing her a letter which has thrown her into despair. As for him, he has gone to visit the Cimmerians."

"God be thanked!" cried Formosanta; "another refusal in my favor. My good fortune is beyond my hopes, as my misfortunes surpass my greatest apprehensions. Procure me this charming letter, that I may set out and follow him, loaded with his sacrifices. Farewell, cousin. Amazan is among the Cimmerians, and I fly to meet him."

Aldea judged that the princess, her cousin, was still more frantic than her brother Amazan. But as she had herself been sensible of the effects of this epidemic contagion, having given up the delights and magnificence of Babylon for a king of Scythia; and as the women always excuse those follies that are the effects of love, she felt for Formosanta's affliction, wished her a happy journey, and promised to be her advocate with her brother, if ever she was so fortunate as to see him again.

## VI
## *The Princess Continues Her Journey*

From Scythia the princess of Babylon, with her phœnix, soon arrived at the empire of the Cimmerians, now called Russia; a country indeed much less populous than Scythia, but of far greater extent.

After a few days' journey, she entered a very large city, which has of late been greatly improved by the reigning sovereign. The empress, however, was not there at that time, but making a journey through her dominions, on the frontiers of Europe and Asia, in order to judge of their state and condition with her own eyes—to enquire into their grievances, and to provide the proper remedies for them.

The principal magistrate of that ancient capital, as soon as he was informed of the arrival of the Babylonian lady and the phœnix, lost no time in paying her all the honors of his country; being certain that his mistress, the most polite and generous empress in the world, would be extremely well pleased to find that he had received so illustrious a lady with all that respect which she herself, if on the spot, would have shown her.

The princess was lodged in the palace, and entertained with great splendor and elegance. The Cimmerian lord, who was an excellent natural philosopher, diverted himself in conversing with the phœnix, at such times as the princess chose to retire to her own apartment. The phœnix told him that he had formerly traveled among the Cimmerians, but that he should not have known the country again.

"How comes it," said he, "that such prodigious changes have been brought about in so short a time? Formerly, when I was here, about three hundred years ago, I saw nothing but savage nature in all her horrors. At present, I perceive industry, arts, splendor, and politeness."

"This mighty revolution," replied the Cimmerian, "was begun by one man, and is now carried to perfection by one woman—a woman who is a greater legislator than the Isis of the Egyptians, or the Ceres of the Greeks. Most lawgivers have been, unhappily, of a narrow genius and an arbitrary disposition, which confined their views to the countries they governed. Each of them looked upon his own race as the only people existing upon the earth, or as if they ought to be an enmity with all the rest. They formed institutions, introduced customs, and established religions exclusively for themselves. Thus the Egyptians, so famous for those heaps of stones called pyramids, have dishonored themselves with their barbarous superstitions. They despise all other nations as profane; refuse all manner of intercourse with them; and, excepting those conversant in the court, who now and then rise above the prejudices of the vulgar, there is not an Egyptian who will eat off a plate that has ever been used by a stranger. Their priests are equally cruel and absurd. It were better to have no laws at all, and to follow those notions of right and wrong engraven on our hearts by nature, than to subject society to institutions so inhospitable.

"Our empress has adopted quite a different system. She considers her vast dominions, under which all the meridians on the globe are united, as under an obligation of correspondence with all the nations dwelling under those meridians. The first and most fundamental of her laws, is an universal toleration of all religions, and an unbounded compassion for every error. Her penetrating genius perceives, that though the modes of religious worship differ, yet morality is every where the same. By this principle, she has united her people to all the nations on earth, and the Cimmerians will soon consider the Scandinavians and the Chinese as their brethren. Not satisfied with this, she has resolved to establish this invaluable toleration, the strongest link of society, among her neighbors. By these means, she obtained the title of the parent of her country; and, if she persevere, will acquire that of the benefactress of mankind.

"Before her time, the men, who were unhappily possessed of power, sent out legions of murderers to ravage unknown countries, and to water with the blood of the children the inheritance of their fathers. Those assassins were called heroes, and their robberies accounted glorious achievements. But our sovereign courts another sort of glory. She has sent forth her armies to be the messengers of peace; not only to prevent men from being the destroyers, but to oblige them to be the benefactors of one another. Her standards are the ensigns of public tranquillity."

The phœnix was quite charmed with what he heard from this nobleman. He told him, that though he had lived twenty-seven thousand nine hundred years and seven months in this world, he had never seen any thing like it. He then enquired after his friend Amazan. The Cimmerian gave the same account of him that the princess had already heard from the Chinese and the Scythians. It was Amazan's constant practice to run away from all the courts he visited, the instant any lady noticed him in particular and seemed anxious to make his acquaintance. The phœnix soon acquainted Formosanta with this fresh instance of Amazan's fidelity—a fidelity so much the more surprising, since he could not imagine his princess would ever hear of it.

Amazan had set out for Scandinavia, where he was entertained with sights still more surprising. In this

## THE PRINCESS OF BABYLON

place, he beheld monarchy and liberty subsisting together in a manner thought incompatible in other states; the laborers of the ground shared in the legislature with the grandees of the realm. In another place he saw what was still more extraordinary; a prince equally remarkable for his extreme youth and uprightness, who possessed a sovereign authority over his country, acquired by a solemn contract with his people.

Amazan beheld a philosopher on the throne of Sarmatia, who might be called a king of anarchy; for he was the chief of a hundred thousand petty kings, one of whom with his single voice could render ineffectual the resolution of all the rest. Eolus had not more difficulty to keep the warring winds within their proper bounds, than this monarch to reconcile the tumultuous discordant spirits of his subjects. He was the master of a ship surrounded with eternal storms. But the vessel did not founder, for he was an excellent pilot.

In traversing those various countries, so different from his own, Amazan persevered in rejecting all the advances made to him by the ladies, though incessantly distracted with the embrace given by Formosanta to the king of Egypt, being resolved to set Formosanta an amazing example of an unshaken and unparalleled fidelity.

The princess of Babylon was constantly close at his heels, and scarcely ever missed of him but by a day or two; without the one being tired of roaming or the other losing a moment in pursuing him.

Thus he traversed the immense continent of Germany, where he beheld with wonder the progress which reason and philosophy had made in the north. Even their princes were enlightened, and had become the patrons of freedom of thought. Their education had not been trusted to men who had an interest in deceiving them, or who were themselves deceived. They were brought up in the knowledge of universal morality, and in the contempt of superstition.

They had banished from all their estates a senseless custom which had enervated and depopulated the southern countries. This was to bury alive in immense dungeons, infinite numbers of both sexes who were eternally separated from one another, and sworn to have no communication together. This madness had contributed more than the most cruel wars to lay waste and depopulate the earth.

In opposing these barbarous institutions, so inimical to the laws of nature and the best interests of society, the princes of the north had become the benefactors of their race. They had likewise exploded other errors equally absurd and pernicious. In short, men had at last ventured to make use of their reason in those immense regions; whereas it was still believed almost every where else, that they could not be governed but in proportion to their ignorance.

## VII

### Amazan Visits Albion

From Germany, Amazan arrived at Batavia; where his perpetual chagrin was in a good measure alleviated, by perceiving among the inhabitants a faint resemblance to his happy countrymen, the Gangarids. There he saw liberty, security, and equality—with toleration in religion; but the ladies were so indifferent, that none made him any advances; an experience he had not met with before. It is true, however, that had he been inclined to address them, they would not have been offended; though, at the same time, not one would have been the least in love; but he was far from any thoughts of making conquests.

Formosanta had nearly caught him in this insipid nation. He had set out but a moment before her arrival.

Amazan had heard so much among the Batavians in praise of a certain island called Albion, that he was led by curiosity to embark with his unicorns on board a ship, which, with a favorable easterly wind, carried him in a few hours to that celebrated country, more famous than Tyre, or Atlantis.

The beautiful Formosanta, who had followed him, as

it were on the scent, to the banks of the Volga, the Vistula, the Elbe, and the Weser, and had never been above a day or two behind him, arrived soon after at the mouth of the Rhine, where it disembogues its waters into the German Ocean.

Here she learned that her beloved Amazan had just set sail for Albion. She thought she saw the vessel on board of which he was, and could not help crying out for joy; at which the Batavian ladies were greatly surprised, not imagining that a young man could possibly occasion so violent a transport. They took, indeed, but little notice of the phœnix, as they reckoned his feathers would not fetch near so good a price as those of their own ducks, and other water fowl. The princess of Babylon hired two vessels to carry herself and her retinue to that happy island, which was soon to possess the only object of her desires, the soul of her life, and the god of her idolatry.

An unpropitious wind from the west suddenly arose, just as the faithful and unhappy Amazan landed on Albion's sea-girt shore, and detained the ships of the Babylonian princess just as they were on the point of sailing. Seized with a deep melancholy, she went to her room, determined to remain there till the wind should change; but it blew for the space of eight days, with an unremitting violence. The princess, during this tedious period, employed her maid of honor, Irla, in reading romances; which were not indeed written by the Batavians; but as they are the factors of the universe, they traffic in the wit as well as commodities of other nations. The princess purchased of Mark Michael Rey, the bookseller, all the novels which had been written by the Ausonians and the Welch, the sale of which had been wisely prohibited among those nations to enrich their neighbors, the Batavians. She expected to find in those histories some adventure similar to her own, which might alleviate her grief. The maid of honor read, the phœnix made comments, and the princess, finding nothing in the *Fortunate Country Maid,* in *Tansai,* or in the *Sopha,* that had the least resemblance to her own affairs, interrupted the reader every moment, by asking how the wind stood.

## VIII
## Amazan Leaves Albion

In the meantime Amazan was on the road to the capital of Albion, in his coach and six unicorns, all his thoughts employed on his dear princess. At a small distance he perceived a carriage overturned in a ditch. The servants had gone in different directions in quest of assistance, but the owner kept his seat, smoking his pipe with great tranquillity, without manifesting the smallest impatience. His name was my lord What-then, in the language from which I translate these memoirs.

Amazan made all the haste possible to help him, and without assistance set the carriage to rights, so much was his strength superior to that of other men. My lord What-then took no other notice of him, than saying, "a stout fellow, by Jove!" In the meantime the neighboring people, having arrived, flew into a great passion at being called out to no purpose, and fell upon the stranger. They abused him, called him an outlandish dog, and challenged him to strip and box.

Amazan seized a brace of them in each hand, and threw them twenty paces from him; the rest, seeing this, pulled off their hats, and bowing with great respect, asked his honor for something to drink. His honor gave them more money than they had ever seen in their lives before. My lord What-then now expressed great esteem for him, and asked him to dinner at his country house, about three miles off. His invitation being accepted, he went into Amazan's coach, his own being out of order from the accident.

After a quarter of an hour's silence, my lord Whatthen, looking upon Amazan for a moment, said: "How d'ye do?" which, by the way, is a phrase without any meaning; adding, "You have got six fine unicorns there." After which he continued smoking as usual.

## THE PRINCESS OF BABYLON

The traveler told him his unicorns were at his service, and that he had brought them from the country of the Gangarids. From thence he took occasion to inform him of his affair with the princess of Babylon, and the unlucky kiss she had given the king of Egypt; to which the other made no reply, being very indifferent whether there were any such people in the world, as a king of Egypt, or a princess of Babylon.

He remained dumb for another quarter of an hour; after which he asked his companion a second time how he did, and whether they had any good roast beef among the Gangarids.

Amazan answered with his wonted politeness, "that they did not eat their brethren on the banks of the Ganges." He then explained to him that system which many ages afterward was surnamed the Pythagorean philosophy. But my lord fell asleep in the meantime, and made but one nap of it till he came to his own house.

He was married to a young and charming woman, on whom nature had bestowed a soul as lively and sensible as that of her husband was dull and stupid. A few gentlemen of Albion had that day come to dine with her; among whom there were characters of all sorts; for that country having been almost always under the government of foreigners, the families that had come over with these princes had imported their different manners. There were in this company some persons of an amiable disposition, others of superior genius, and a few of profound learning.

The mistress of the house had none of that awkward stiffness, that false modesty, with which the young ladies of Albion were then reproached. She did not conceal by a scornful look and an affected taciturnity her deficiency of ideas and the embarrassing humility of having nothing to say. Never was a woman more engaging. She received Amazan with a grace and politeness that were quite natural to her. The extreme beauty of this young stranger, and the involuntary comparison she could not help making between him and her prosaic husband, did not increase her happiness or content.

Dinner being served, she placed Amazan at her side, and helped him to a variety of puddings, he having informed her that the Gangarids never dined upon any thing which had received from the gods the celestial gift of life. The events of his early life, the manners of the Gangarids, the progress of arts, religion, and government, were the subjects of a conversation equally agreeable and instructive all the time of the entertainment, which lasted till night: during which my lord What-then did nothing but push the bottle about, and call for the toast.

After dinner, while my lady was pouring out the tea, still feeding her eyes on the young stranger, he entered into a long conversation with a member of parliament; for every one knows that there was, even then, a parliament called Wittenagenot, or the assembly of wise men. Amazan enquired into the constitution, laws, manners, customs, forces, and arts, which made this country so respectable; and the member answered him in the following manner.

"For a long time we went stark naked, though our climate is none of the hottest. We were likewise for a long time enslaved by a people who came from the ancient country of Saturn, watered by the Tiber. But the mischief we have done one another has greatly exceeded all that we ever suffered from our first conquerors.

"To those times of infamy and debasement, succeeded the ages of barbarity and confusion. Our country, more tempestuous than the surrounding ocean, has been ravaged and drenched in blood by our civil discords. Many of our crowned heads have perished by a violent death. Above a hundred princes of the royal blood have ended their days on the scaffold, whilst the hearts of their adherents have been torn from their breasts, and thrown in their faces. In short, it is the province of the hangman to write the history of our island, seeing that this personage has finally determined all our affairs of moment.

"But to crown these horrors, it is not very long since some fellows wearing black mantles, and others who cast white shirts over their jackets, having become aggressive and intolerant, succeeded in communicating their madness to the whole nation. Our country was then divided into two parties, the murderers and the murdered, the executioners and the sufferers, plunderers and slaves; and all in the name of God, and whilst they were seeking the Lord.

"Who would have imagined, that from this horrible abyss, this chaos of dissension, cruelty, ignorance, and fanaticism, a government should at last spring up, the most perfect, it may be said, now in the world; yet such has been the event. A prince, honored and wealthy, all-powerful to do good, but without power to do evil, is at the head of a free, warlike, commercial, and enlightened nation. The nobles on one hand, and the representatives of the people on the other, share the legislature with the monarch.

"We have seen, by a singular fatality of events, disorder, civil wars, anarchy and wretchedness, lay waste the country, when our kings aimed at arbitrary power: whereas tranquillity, riches, and universal happiness, have only reigned among us, when the prince has remained satisfied with a limited authority. All order had been subverted whilst we were disputing about mysteries, but was reestablished the moment we grew wise enough to despise them. Our victorious fleets carry our flag on every ocean; our laws place our lives and fortunes in security; no judge can explain them in an arbitrary manner, and no decision is ever given without the reasons assigned for it. We should punish a judge as an assassin, who should condemn a citizen to death without declaring the evidence which accused him, and the law upon which he was convicted.

"It is true, there are always two parties among us, who are continually writing and intriguing against each other; but they constantly re-unite, whenever it is needful to arm in defence of liberty and our country. These two parties watch over one another, and mutually prevent the violation of the sacred *deposit* of the laws. They hate one another, but they love the state. They are like those jealous lovers, who pay court to the same mistress, with a spirit of emulation.

"From the same fund of genius by which we discovered and supported the natural rights of mankind, we have carried the sciences to the highest pitch to which they can attain among men. Your Egyptians, who pass for such great mechanics—your Indians, who are believed to be such great philosophers—your Babylonians, who boast of having observed the stars for the course of four hundred and thirty thousand years—the Greeks, who have written so much, and said so little, know in reality nothing in comparison to our inferior scholars, who have studied the discoveries of our great masters. We have ravished more secrets from nature in the space of an hundred years, than the human species had been able to discover in as many ages.

"This is a true account of our present state. I have concealed from you neither the good nor the bad; neither our shame nor our glory; and I have exaggerated nothing."

At this discourse Amazan felt a strong desire to be instructed in those sublime sciences his friend had spoken of; and if his passion for the princess of Babylon, his filial duty to his mother whom he had quitted, and his love for his native country had not made strong remonstrances to his distempered heart, he would willingly have spent the remainder of his life in Albion. But that unfortunate kiss his princess had given the king of Egypt, did not leave his mind at sufficient ease to study the abstruse sciences.

"I confess," said he, "having made a solemn vow to roam about the world, and to escape from myself."

Amazan had spoken in so agreeable a manner; his voice was so charming; his whole behavior so noble and engaging, that the mistress of the house could not resist the pleasure of having a little private chat with him in her turn. She accordingly sent him a little billet-doux intimating her wishes in the most agreeable language. Amazan had once more the courage to resist the fascination of female society, and, according to custom, wrote the lady an answer full of respect—representing to her the sacredness of his oath, and the strict obligation he was under to teach the princess of Babylon to conquer her passions by his example; after which he harnessed his unicorns and departed for Batavia, leaving all the company in deep admiration of him, and the lady in profound astonishment. In her confusion she dropped Amazan's letter. My lord What-then read it next morning:

"D—n it," said he, shrugging up his shoulders, "what stuff and nonsense have we got here?" and then rode out a fox hunting with some of his drunken neighbors.

Amazan was already sailing upon the sea, possessed of a geographical chart, with which he had been presented by the learned Albion he had conversed with at lord What-then's. He was extremely astonished to find the greatest part of the earth upon a single sheet of paper.

His eyes and imagination wandered over this little space; he observed the Rhine, the Danube, the Alps of Tyrol, there specified under their different names, and all the countries through which he was to pass. But he more particularly fixed his eyes upon the country of the Gangarids, upon Babylon, where he had seen his dear princess, and upon the country of Bassora, where she had given a fatal kiss to the king of Egypt. He sighed, and tears streamed from his eyes at the unhappy remembrance. He agreed with the Albion who had presented him with the universe in epitome, when he averred that the inhabitants of the banks of the Thames were a thousand times better instructed than those upon the banks of the Nile, the Euphrates, and the Ganges.

As he returned into Batavia, Formosanta proceeded toward Albion with her two ships at full sail. Amazan's ship and the princess's crossed one another and almost touched; the two lovers were close to each other, without being conscious of the fact. Ah! had they but known it! But this great consolation tyrannic destiny would not allow.

## IX
## *An Unfortunate Adventure in Gaul*

In all the provinces through which Amazan passed, he remained ever faithful to the princess of Babylon, though incessantly enraged at the king of Egypt. This model of constancy at length arrived at the new capital of the Gauls. This city, like many others, had alternately submitted to barbarity, ignorance, folly, and misery. The first name it bore was Dirt and Mire; it then took that of Isis from the worship of Isis, which had reached even here. Its first senate consisted of a company of watermen. It had long been in bondage, and submitted to the ravages of the heroes of the Seven Mountains; and some ages after, some other heroic thieves who came from the farther banks of the Rhine had seized upon its little lands.

Time, which changes all things, had formed it into a city, half of which was very noble and very agreeable, the other half somewhat barbarous and ridiculous: this was the emblem of its inhabitants. There were within its walls at least a hundred thousand people, who had no other employment than play and diversion. These idlers were the judges of those arts which the others cultivated. They were ignorant of all that passed at court; though they were only four short miles distant from it: but it seemed to them at least six hundred thousand miles off. Agreeableness in company, gaiety and frivolity, formed the important and sole considerations of their lives. They were governed like children, who are extravagantly supplied with gewgaws, to prevent their crying. If the horrors were discussed, which two centuries before had laid waste their country, or if those dreadful periods were recalled, when one half of the nation massacred the other for sophisms, they, indeed, said, "this was not well done," then, presently, they fell to laughing again, or singing of catches.

In proportion as the idlers were polished, agreeable, and amiable, it was observed that there was a greater and more shocking contrast between them and those who were engaged in business.

Among the latter, or such as pretended so to be, there was a gang of melancholy fanatics, whose absurdity and knavery divided their character—whose appearance alone diffused misery—and who would have overturned the world, had they been able to gain a little credit. But the nation of idlers, by dancing and singing, forced them into obscurity in their caverns, as the warbling birds drive the croaking bats back to their holes and ruins.

A smaller number of those who were occupied, were the preservers of ancient barbarous customs, against which nature, terrified, loudly exclaimed. They consulted nothing but their worm-eaten registers. If they there discovered a foolish or horrid custom, they considered it as a sacred law. It was from this vile practice of not daring to think for themselves, but extracting their ideas from the ruins of those times when no one thought at all, that in the metropolis of pleasure there still remained some shocking manners. Hence it was that there was no proportion between crimes and punishments. A thousand deaths were sometimes inflicted upon an innocent victim, to make him acknowledge a crime he had not committed.

The extravagancies of youth were punished with the same severity as murder or parricide. The idlers screamed loudly at these exhibitions, and the next day thought no more about them, but were buried in the contemplation of some new fashion.

This people saw a whole age elapse, in which the fine arts attained a degree of perfection that far surpassed the most sanguine hopes. Foreigners then repaired thither, as they did to Babylon, to admire the great monuments of architecture, the wonders of gardening, the sublime efforts of sculpture and painting. They were charmed with a species of music that reached the heart without astonishing the ears.

True poetry, that is to say, such as is natural and harmonious, that which addresses the heart as well as the mind, was unknown to this nation before this happy period. New kinds of eloquence displayed sublime beauties. The theatres in particular re-echoed with masterpieces that no other nation ever approached. In a word, good taste prevailed in every profession to that degree, that there were even good writers among the Druids.

So many laurels that had branched even to the skies soon withered in an exhausted soil. There remained but a very small number, whose leaves were of a pale dying verdure. This decay was occasioned by the facility of producing; laziness preventing good productions, and by a satiety of the brilliant, and a taste for the whimsical. Vanity protected arts that brought back times of barbarity; and this same vanity, in persecuting persons of real merit, forced them to quit their country. The hornets banished the bees.

There were scarce any real arts, scarce any real genius. Talent now consisted in reasoning right or wrong upon the merit of the last age. The dauber of a signpost criticised with an air of sagacity the works of the greatest painters; and the blotters of paper disfigured the works of the greatest writers. Ignorance and bad taste had other daubers in their pay. The same things were repeated in a hundred volumes under different titles. Every work was either a dictionary or a pamphlet. A Druid gazetteer wrote twice a week of obscure annals of an unknown people possessed with the devil, and of celestial prodigies operated in garrets by little beggars of both sexes. Other Ex-Druids, dressed in black, ready to die with rage and hunger, set forth their complaints in a hundred different writings, that they were no longer allowed to cheat mankind—this privilege being conferred on some goats clad in grey; and some Arch-Druids were employed in printing defamatory libels.

Amazan was quite ignorant of all this, and even if he had been acquainted with it, he would have given himself very little concern about it, having his head filled with nothing but the princess of Babylon, the king of Egypt, and the inviolable vow he had made to despise all female coquetry in whatever country his despair should drive him.

The gaping ignorant mob, whose curiosity exceeds all the bounds of nature and reason, for a long time thronged about his unicorns. The more sensible women forced open the doors of his *hôtel* to contemplate his person.

He at first testified some desire of visiting the court; but some of the idlers, who constituted good company and casually went thither, informed him that it was quite out of fashion, that times were greatly changed, and that all amusements were confined to the city. He was invited that very night to sup with a lady whose sense and talents had reached foreign climes, and who had traveled in some countries through which Amazan had passed. This lady gave him great pleasure, as well as the society he met at her house. Here reigned a decent liberty, gaiety without tumult, silence without pedantry, and wit without asperity. He found that *good company* was not quite ideal, though the title was frequently usurped by pretenders. The next day he dined in a society far less amiable, but much more voluptuous. The more he was satisfied with the guests, the more they were pleased with him. He found his soul soften and dissolve, like the aromatics of his country, which gradually melt in a moderate heat, and exhale in delicious perfumes.

After dinner he was conducted to a place of public entertainment which was enchanting; but condemned, however, by the Druids, because it deprived them of their auditors, which, therefore, excited their jealousy. The representation here consisted of agreeable verses, delightful songs, dances which expressed the movements of the soul, and perspectives that charmed the eye in deceiving it. This kind of pastime, which included so many kinds, was known only under a foreign name. It was called an *Opera,* which formerly signified, in the language of work, care, occupation, industry, enterprise, business. This exhibition enchanted him. A female singer, in particular, charmed him by her melodious voice, and the graces that accompanied her. This child of genius, after the performance, was introduced to him by his new friends. He presented her with a handful of diamonds; for which she was so grateful, that she could not leave him all the rest of the day. He supped with her and her companions, and during the delightful repast he forgot his sobriety and became heated and oblivious with wine. * * * What an instance of human frailty!

The beautiful princess of Babylon arrived at this juncture, with her phœnix, her chambermaid Irla, and her two hundred Gangaridian cavaliers mounted on their unicorns. It was a long while before the gates were opened. She immediately asked, if the handsomest, the most courageous, the most sensible, and the most faithful of men was still in that city. The magistrates readily concluded that she meant Amazan. She was conducted to his *hôtel.* How great was the palpitation of her heart! —the powerful operation of the tender passion. Her whole soul was penetrated with inexpressible joy, to see once more in her lover the model of constancy. Nothing could prevent her entering his chamber; the curtains were open; and she saw the beautiful Amazan asleep and stupefied with drink.

Formosanta expressed her grief with such screams as made the house echo. She swooned into the arms of Irla. As soon as she had recovered her senses, she retired from this fatal chamber with grief blended with rage.

"Oh! just heaven; oh, powerful Oromasdes!" cried the beautiful princess of Babylon, bathed in tears. "By whom, and for whom am I thus betrayed? He that could reject for my sake so many princesses, to abandon me for the company of a strolling Gaul! No! I can never survive this affront."

"This is the disposition of all young people," said Irla to her, "from one end of the world to the other. Were they enamoured with a beauty descended from heaven, they would at certain moments forget her entirely."

"It is done," said the princess, "I will never see him again whilst I live. Let us depart this instant, and let the unicorns be harnessed."

The phœnix conjured her to stay at least till Amazan awoke, that he might speak with him.

"He does not deserve it," said the princess. "You would cruelly offend me. He would think that I had desired you to reproach him, and that I am willing to be reconciled to him. If you love me, do not add this injury to the insult he has offered me."

The phœnix, who after all owed his life to the daughter of the king of Babylon, could not disobey her. She set out with all her attendants.

"Whither are you going?" said Irla to her.

"I do not know," replied the princess; "we will take the first road we find. Provided I fly from Amazan for ever, I am satisfied."

The phœnix, who was wiser than Formosanta, because he was divested of passion, consoled her upon the road. He gently insinuated to her that it was shocking to punish one's self for the faults of another; that Amazan had given her proofs sufficiently striking and numerous of his fidelity, so that she should forgive him for having forgotten himself for one moment in social company; that this was the only time in which he had been wanting of the grace of Oromasdes; that it would render him only the more constant in love and virtue for the future; that the desire of expiating his fault would raise him beyond himself; that it would be the means of increasing her happiness; that many great princesses before her had forgiven such slips, and had had no reason to be sorry afterward; and he was so thoroughly possessed of the art of persuasion, that Formosanta's mind grew more calm and peaceable. She was now sorry she had set out so soon. She thought her unicorns went too fast, but she did not dare return. Great was the conflict between her desire of forgiving and that of showing her rage—between her love and vanity. However, her unicorns pursued their pace; and she traversed the world, according to the prediction of her father's oracle.

When Amazan awoke, he was informed of the arrival and departure of Formosanta and the phœnix. He was also told of the rage and distraction of the princess, and that she had sworn never to forgive him.

"Then," said he, "there is nothing left for me to do, but follow her, and kill myself at her feet."

The report of this adventure drew together his festive companions, who all remonstrated with him. They said that he had much better stay with them; that nothing could equal the pleasant life they led in the centre of arts and refined delicate pleasures; that many strangers, and even kings, preferred such an agreeable enchanting repose to their country and their thrones. Moreover, his vehicle was broken, and another was being made for him according to the newest fashion; that the best tailor of the whole city had already cut out for him a dozen suits in the latest style; that the most vivacious, amiable, and fashionable ladies, at whose houses dramatic performances were represented, had each appointed a day to give him a regale. The girl from the opera was in the meanwhile drinking her chocolate, laughing, singing, and ogling the beautiful Amazan—who by this time clearly perceived she had no more sense than a goose.

A sincerity, cordiality, and frankness, as well as magnanimity and courage, constituted the character of this great prince; he related his travels and misfortunes to his friends. They knew that he was cousin-german to the princess. They were informed of the fatal kiss she had given the king of Egypt. "Such little tricks," said they, "are often forgiven between relatives, otherwise one's whole life would pass in perpetual uneasiness."

Nothing could shake his design of pursuing Formosanta; but his carriage not being ready, he was compelled to remain three days longer among the idlers, who were still feasting and merry-making. He at length took his leave of them, by embracing them and making them accept some of his diamonds that were the best mounted, and recommending to them a constant pursuit of frivolity and pleasure, since they were thereby made more agreeable and happy.

"The Germans," said he, "are the greyheads of Europe; the people of Albion are men formed; the inhabitants of Gaul are the children—and I love to play with children."

## X
## *Amazan and Formosanta Become Reconciled*

The guides had no difficulty in following the route the princess had taken. There was nothing else talked of but her and her large bird. All the inhabitants were still in a state of fascination. The banks of the Loire, of the Dordogue—the Garonne, and the Gironde, still echoed with acclamation.

When Amazan reached the foot of the Pyrenees, the magistrates and Druids of the country made him dance, whether he would or not, a *Tambourin;* but as soon as he cleared the Pyrenees, nothing presented itself that was either gay or joyous. If he here and there heard a peasant sing, it was a doleful ditty. The inhabitants stalked with much gravity, having a few strung beads and a girted poniard. The nation dressed in black, and appeared to be in mourning.

If Amazan's servants asked passengers any questions, they were answered by signs; if they went into an inn, the host acquainted his guests in three words, that there was nothing in the house, but that the things they so pressingly wanted might be found a few miles off.

When these votaries to taciturnity were asked if they

had seen the beautiful princess of Babylon pass, they answered with less brevity than usual: "We have seen her —she is not so handsome—there are no beauties that are not tawny—she displays a bosom of alabaster, which is the most disgusting thing in the world, and which is scarce known in our climate."

Amazan advanced toward the province watered by the Betis. The Tyrians discovered this country about twelve thousand years ago, about the time they discovered the great Atlantic Isle, inundated so many centuries after. The Tyrians cultivated Betica, which the natives of the country had never done, being of opinion that it was not their place to meddle with anything, and that their neighbors, the Gauls, should come and reap their harvests. The Tyrians had brought with them some Palestines, or Jews, who, from that time, have wandered through every clime where money was to be gained. The Palestines, by extraordinary usury, at fifty per cent., had possessed themselves of almost all the riches of the country. This made the people of Betica imagine the Palestines were sorcerers; and all those who were accused of witchcraft were burnt, without mercy.

The princess of Babylon alighted in that city which has since been called Sevilla. Her design was to embark upon the Betis to return by Tyre to Babylon, and see again king Belus, her father; and forget, if possible, her perfidious lover—or, at least, to ask him in marriage. She sent for two Palestines, who transacted all the business of the court. They were to furnish her with three ships. The phœnix made all the necessary contracts with them, and settled the price after some little dispute.

The hostess was a great devotee, and her husband, who was no less religious, was a Familiar: that is to say, a spy of the Inquisitors or *Anthropokaies*.

He failed not to inform them, that in his house was a sorceress and two Palestines, who were entering into a compact with the devil, disguised like a large gilt bird.

The Inquisitors having learned that the lady possessed a large quantity of diamonds, swore point blank that she was a sorceress. They waited till night to imprison the two hundred cavaliers and the unicorns (which slept in very extensive stables), for the Inquisitors are cowards.

Having strongly barricaded the gates, they seized the princess and Irla; but they could not catch the phœnix, who flew away with great swiftness. He did not doubt of meeting with Amazan upon the road from Gaul to Sevilla.

He met him upon the frontiers of Betica, and acquainted him with the disaster that had befallen the princess.

Amazan was struck speechless with rage. He armed himself with a steel cuirass damasquined with gold, a lance twelve feet long, two javelins, and an edged sword called the Thunderer, which at one single stroke would rend trees, rocks, and Druids. He covered his beautiful head with a golden casque, shaded with heron and ostrich feathers. This was the ancient armor of Magog, which his sister Aldea gave him when upon his journey in Scythia. The few attendants he had with him all mounted their unicorns.

Amazan, in embracing his dear phœnix, uttered only these melancholy expressions: "I am guilty! Had I not dined with the child of genius from the opera, in the city of the idlers, the princess of Babylon would not have been in this alarming situation. Let us fly to the *Anthropokaies.*" He presently entered Sevilla. Fifteen hundred Alguazils guarded the gates of the inclosure in which the two hundred Gangarids and their unicorns were shut up, without being allowed anything to eat. Preparations were already made for sacrificing the princess of Babylon, her chambermaid Irla, and the two rich Palestines.

The high *Anthropokaie,* surrounded by his subaltern *Anthropokaies,* was already seated upon his sacred tribunal. A crowd of Sevillians joined their two hands, without uttering a syllable, when the beautiful princess, the maid Irla, and the two Palestines were brought forth, with their hands tied behind their backs and dressed in masquerade habits.

The phœnix entered the prison by a dormer window, whilst the Gangarids began to break open the doors. The invincible Amazan shattered them without. They all sallied forth armed, upon their unicorns, and Amazan put himself at their head. He had no difficulty in overthrowing the Alguazils, the Familiars, or *Anthropokaies*. Each unicorn pierced dozens at a time. The thundering Amazan cut to pieces all he met.

Amazan collared the high Inquisitor upon his tribunal, and threw him upon the pile, which was prepared about forty paces distant; and he also cast upon it the other Inquisitors, one after the other. He then prostrated himself at Formosanta's feet. "Ah! how amiable you are," said she; "and how I should adore you, if you had not forsaken me for the company of an opera singer."

Whilst Amazan was making his peace with the princess, whilst his Gangarids cast upon the pile the bodies of all the *Anthropokaies,* and the flames ascended to the clouds, Amazan saw an army that approached him at a distance. An aged monarch, with a crown upon his head, advanced upon a car drawn by eight mules harnessed with ropes. An hundred other cars followed. They were accompanied by grave looking men mounted upon very fine horses. A multitude of people, with greasy hair, followed silently on foot.

Amazan immediately drew up his Gangarids about him, and advanced with his lance couched. As soon as the king perceived him, he took off his crown, alighted from his car, and embraced Amazan's stirrup, saying to him: "Man sent by the gods, you are the avenger of human kind, the deliverer of my country. These monsters, of which you have purged the earth, were my masters. I was forced to submit to their criminal power. My people would have deserted me, if I had only been inclined to moderate their abominable crimes. From this moment I breathe, I reign, and am indebted to you for it."

He afterward respectfully kissed Formosanta's hand, and entreated her to get into his coach (drawn by eight mules) with Amazan, Irla, and the phœnix.

The two Palestine bankers, who still remained prostrate on the ground through fear and terror, now raised their heads. The troops of unicorns followed the king of Betica into his palace.

As the dignity of a king who reigned over a people of characteristic brevity required that his mules should go at a very slow pace, Amazan and Formosanta had time to relate to him their adventures. He also conversed with the phœnix, admiring and frequently embracing him. He easily comprehended how brutal and barbarous the people of the West should be considered, who ate animals, and did not understand their language; that the Gangarids alone had preserved the nature and dignity of primitive man; but he particularly agreed, that the most barbarous of mortals were the *Anthropokaies*, of whom Amazan had just purged the earth. He incessantly blessed and thanked him. The beautiful Formosanta had already forgotten the affair in Gaul, and had her soul filled with nothing but the valor of the hero who had preserved her life. Amazan being made acquainted with the innocence of the embrace she had given to the king of Egypt, and being told of the resurrection of the phœnix, tasted the purest joy, and was intoxicated with the most violent love.

They dined at the palace, but had a very indifferent repast. The cooks of Betica were the worst in Europe. Amazan advised the king to send for some from Gaul. The king's musicians performed, during the repast, that celebrated air which has since been called the *Follies of Spain*. After dinner, matters of business came upon the carpet.

The king enquired of the handsome Amazan, the beautiful Formosanta, and the charming phœnix what they proposed doing. "For my part," said Amazan, "my intention is to return to Babylon, of which I am the presumptive heir, and to ask of my uncle Belus the hand of my cousin-german, the incomparable Formosanta."

"My design certainly is," said the princess, "never to separate from my cousin-german. But I imagine he will agree with me, that I should return first to my father, because he only gave me leave to go upon a pilgrimage to Bassora, and I have wandered all over the world."

"For my part," said the phœnix, "I will follow every where these two tender, generous lovers."

"You are in the right," said the king of Betica; "but your return to Babylon is not so easy as you imagine. I receive daily intelligence from that country by Tyrian ships, and my Palestine bankers, who correspond with all the nations of the earth. The people are all in arms toward the Euphrates and the Nile. The king of Scythia claims the inheritance of his wife, at the head of three hundred thousand warriors on horseback. The kings of Egypt and India are also laying waste the banks of the Tigris and the Euphrates, each at the head of three hundred thousand men, to revenge themselves for being laughed at. The king of Ethiopia is ravaging Egypt with three hundred thousand men, whilst the king of Egypt is absent from his country. And the king of Babylon has as yet only six hundred thousand men to defend himself.

"I acknowledge to you," continued the king, "when I hear of those prodigious armies which are disembogued from the East, and their astonishing magnificence—when I compare them to my trifling bodies of twenty or thirty thousand soldiers, which it is so difficult to clothe and feed; I am inclined to think the Eastern subsisted long before the Western hemisphere. It seems as if we sprung only yesterday from chaos and barbarity."

"Sire," said Amazan, "the last comers frequently outstrip those who first began the career. It is thought in my country that man was first created in India; but this I am not certain of."

"And," said the king of Betica to the phœnix, "what do you think?"

"Sire," replied the phœnix, "I am as yet too young to

have any knowledge concerning antiquity. I have lived only about twenty-seven thousand years; but my father, who had lived five times that age, told me he had learned from his father, that the Eastern country had always been more populous and rich than the others. It had been transmitted to him from his ancestors, that the generation of all animals had begun upon the banks of the Ganges. For my part, said he, I have not the vanity to be of this opinion. I cannot believe that the foxes of Albion, the marmots of the Alps, and the wolves of Gaul are descended from my country. In the like manner, I do not believe that the firs and oaks of your country descended from the palm and cocoa trees of India."

"But from whence are we descended, then?" said the king.

"I do not know," said the phœnix; "all I want to know is, whither the beautiful princess of Babylon and my dear Amazan may repair."

"I very much question," said the king, "whether with his two hundred unicorns he will be able to destroy so many armies of three hundred thousand men each."

"Why not?" said Amazan. The king of Betica left the force of this sublime question, "Why not?" but he imagined sublimity alone was not sufficient against innumerable armies.

"I advise you," said he, "to seek the king of Ethiopia. I am related to that black prince through my Palestines. I will give you recommendatory letters to him. As he is at enmity with the king of Egypt, he will be but too happy to be strengthened by your alliance. I can assist you with two thousand sober, brave men; and it will depend upon yourself to engage as many more of the people who reside, or rather skip, about the foot of the Pyrenees, and who are called Vasques or Vascons. Send one of your warriors upon an unicorn, with a few diamonds. There is not a Vascon that will not quit the castle, that is, the thatched cottage of his father, to serve you. They are indefatigable, courageous, and agreeable; and whilst you wait their arrival, we will give you festivals, and prepare your ships. I cannot too much acknowledge the service you have done me."

Amazan realized the happiness of having recovered Formosanta, and enjoyed in tranquillity her conversation, and all the charms of reconciled love—which are almost equal to a growing passion.

A troop of proud, joyous Vascons soon arrived, dancing a *Tambourin.* The haughty and grave Betician troops were now ready. The old sun-burnt king tenderly embraced the two lovers. He sent great quantities of arms, beds, chests, boards, black clothes, onions, sheep, fowls, flour, and particularly garlic, on board the ships, and wished them a happy voyage, invariable love, and many victories.

Proud Carthage was not then a seaport. There were at that time only a few Numidians there, who dried fish in the sun. They coasted along Bizacenes, the Syrthes, the fertile banks where since arose Cyrene and the great Chersonese.

They at length arrived toward the first mouth of the sacred Nile. It was at the extremity of this fertile land that the ships of all commercial nations were already received in the port of Canope, without knowing whether the god Canope had founded this port, or whether the inhabitants had manufactured the god—whether the star Canope had given its name to the city, or whether the city had bestowed it upon the star. All that was known of this matter was, that the city and the star were both very ancient; and this is all that can be known of the origin of things, of what nature soever they may be.

It was here that the king of Ethiopia, having ravaged all Egypt, saw the invincible Amazan and the adorable Formosanta come on shore. He took one for the god of war, and the other for the goddess of beauty. Amazan presented to him the letter of recommendation from the king of Spain. The king of Ethiopia immediately entertained them with some admirable festivals, according to the indispensable custom of heroic times. They then conferred about their expedition to exterminate the three hundred thousand men of the king of Egypt, the three hundred thousand of the emperor of the Indies, and the three hundred thousand of the great Khan of the Scythians, who laid siege to the immense, proud, voluptuous city of Babylon.

The two hundred Spaniards, whom Amazan had brought with him, said that they had nothing to do with the king of Ethiopia's succoring Babylon; that it was sufficient their king had ordered them to go and deliver it; and that they were formidable enough for this expedition.

The Vascons said they had performed many other exploits; that they would alone defeat the Egyptians, the Indians, and the Scythians; and that they would not march unless the Spaniards were placed in the rear-guard.

The two hundred Gangarids could not refrain from laughing at the pretensions of their allies, and they maintained that with only one hundred unicorns, they could put to flight all the kings of the earth. The beautiful Formosanta appeased them by her prudence, and by her enchanting discourse. Amazan introduced to the black monarch his Gangarids, his unicorns, his Spaniards, his Vascons, and his beautiful bird.

Every thing was soon ready to march by Memphis, Heliopolis, Arsinoe, Petra, Artemitis, Sora, and Apamens, to attack the three kings and to prosecute this memorable war, before which all the wars ever waged by man sink into insignificance.

Fame with her hundred tongues has proclaimed the victories Amazan gained over the three kings, with his Spaniards, his Vascons, and his unicorns. He restored the beautiful Formosanta to her father. He set at liberty all his mistress's train, whom the king of Egypt had reduced to slavery. The great Khan of the Scythians declared himself his vassal; and his marriage was confirmed with princess Aldea. The invincible and generous Amazan was acknowledged the heir to the kingdom of Babylon, and entered the city in triumph with the phœnix, in the presence of a hundred tributary kings.

The festival of his marriage far surpassed that which king Belus had given. The bull Apis was served up roasted at table. The kings of Egypt and India were cup-bearers to the married pair; and these nuptials were celebrated by five hundred illustrious poets of Babylon.

# The Horns Of Elfland

## Alfred Lord Tennyson

SHAKESPEARE, Spenser and Kipling are very far from being the only English poets to turn their quill to dealing with the Matter of Faerie. In fact, I could fill half of another book this size with poems about Elves, Fairies, Goblins, and with "kobolds, divergers, nisses, cluricaunes, succubas, djinns, deevs, pigwidgeons, boggarts, and loup-garous."

But I shall let one last example suffice. It is a very lovely poem, a haunting little lyric, almost perfect of its kind . . .

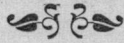

The splendour falls on castle walls
    And snowy summits old in story:
The long light shakes across the lakes
    And the wild cataract leaps in glory.
Blow, bugle, blow, set the wild echoes flying,
Blow, bugle; answer, echoes, dying, dying, dying.

O hark, O hear! how thin and clear
    And thinner, clearer, farther going,
O sweet and far from cliff and scar

The horns of Elfland faintly blowing!
Blow, let us hear the purple glens replying:
Blow, bugle; answer, echoes, dying, dying, dying.

O love, they die in yon rich sky
   They faint on hill or field or river:
Our echoes roll from soul to soul
   And grow for ever and for ever.
Blow, bugle, blow, set the wild echoes flying,
And answer, echoes, answer, dying, dying, dying.

Thus far we have explored the ancient authors of epic and saga, myth, tale, legend and romance.

We have sampled the fantasy literature of Britain, Iceland, Persia, Finland, Denmark, Wales, Russia, Italy, Scotland and France.

The companion volume to this anthology is called *The Young Magicians*. It has been published simultaneously with this book. In it you will discover how the same themes of magic and adventure in imaginary worlds have been used by fourteen modern writers, from William Morris and Lord Dunsany to C. S. Lewis and Jack Vance.

Again, I wish you a pleasant voyage!

LIN CARTER

# GREAT MASTERPIECES OF ADULT FANTASY

*Available in Ballantine Books Editions*

| | |
|---|---|
| A VOYAGE TO ARCTURUS | David Lindsay |
| TITUS GROAN—Volume I | Mervyn Peake |
| GORMENGHAST—Volume II | Mervyn Peake |
| TITUS ALONE—Volume III | Mervyn Peake |
| THE WORM OUROBORUS | E. R. Eddison |
| MISTRESS OF MISTRESSES | E. R. Eddison |
| A FISH DINNER IN MEMISON | E. R. Eddison |
| THE MEZENTIAN GATE | E. R. Eddison |
| TOLKIEN: A LOOK BEHIND THE LORD OF THE RINGS | Lin Carter |
| A FINE AND PRIVATE PLACE | Peter S. Beagle |
| THE LAST UNICORN | Peter S. Beagle |
| THE BLUE STAR | Fletcher Pratt |
| THE KING OF ELFLAND'S DAUGHTER | Lord Dunsany |
| LAND OF UNREASON | L. Sprague de Camp & Fletcher Pratt |
| THE WOOD BEYOND THE WORLD | William Morris |
| LILITH | George Macdonald |
| THE SILVER STALLION | James Branch Cabell |
| FIGURES OF EARTH | James Branch Cabell |

Uniformly priced at 95¢ each
(Plus 5¢ per book mailing charge)

---

To order by mail, send for our complete catalog, add your address with zip code and enclose $1.00 per title. Send to: Dept. CS, Ballantine Books, 36 West 20th Street, New York, New York 10003.

The great masterpieces of fantasy by
J. R. R. TOLKIEN

# The Hobbit

*and*

# *The Lord of the Rings*

Part I—THE FELLOWSHIP OF THE RING

Part II—THE TWO TOWERS

Part III—THE RETURN OF THE KING

*plus*
# The Tolkien Reader

# Smith of Wootton Major and Farmer Giles of Ham

# The Road Goes Ever On: A Song Cycle
(music by Donald Swann)

Note: These are the complete and authorized paperbound editions, published only by Ballantine Books.

To order by mail, send $1.00 for each book (except for *The Road Goes Ever On* which requires $3.00) to Dept. CS, Ballantine Books, 36 W. 20th St., New York, N.Y. 10003.

# EXCITING SCIENCE FICTION FROM THE BALLANTINE LIST

|  |  |  |
|---|---|---|
| SEEDS OF DESTRUCTION | Dan Thomas | 75¢ |
| DRAGONFLIGHT | Anne McCaffrey | 75¢ |
| THE MASKS OF TIME | Robert Silverberg | 75¢ |
| NEUTRON STAR | Larry Niven | 75¢ |
| THE SEVEN SEXES | William Tenn | 75¢ |
| THE WOODEN STAR | William Tenn | 75¢ |
| THE SQUARE ROOT OF MAN | William Tenn | 75¢ |
| OF MEN AND MONSTERS | William Tenn | 75¢ |
| DAUGHTERS OF THE DOLPHIN | Roy Meyers | 75¢ |
| MORE THAN HUMAN | Theodore Sturgeon | 75¢ |
| OMNIVORE | Piers Anthony | 75¢ |
| PRIEST-KINGS OF GOR | John Norman | 75¢ |
| DOUBLE, DOUBLE | John Brunner | 75¢ |
| BROTHER ASSASSIN | Fred Saberhagen | 75¢ |
| THE CAVES OF KARST | Lee Hoffman | 75¢ |
| THE ALIENS AMONG US | James White | 75¢ |
| XENOGENESIS | Miriam Allen deFord | 75¢ |

Uniformly priced at 75¢ each
(Plus 5¢ per book mailing charge)

---

To order by mail, list the titles you want, add your address with zip code, and enclose 80¢ per title. Send to: Dept. CS, Ballantine Books, 36 West 20th Street, New York, New York 10003.